# THE LOVE GAP

# THE LOVE GAP

## A RADICAL PLAN
## TO WIN IN LIFE *AND* LOVE

## JENNA BIRCH

GRAND CENTRAL
Life & Style
NEW YORK • BOSTON

Grand Central Life & Style
Hachette Book Group
1290 Avenue of the Americas, New York, NY 10104
grandcentrallifeandstyle.com
twitter.com/grandcentralpub

First Edition: January 2018

Grand Central Life & Style is an imprint of Grand Central Publishing. The Grand Central Life & Style name and logo are trademarks of Hachette Book Group, Inc.

The publisher is not responsible for websites (or their content) that are not owned by the publisher.

The Hachette Speakers Bureau provides a wide range of authors for speaking events. To find out more, go to www.hachettespeakersbureau.com or call (866) 376-6591.

Library of Congress Cataloging-in-Publication Data

Names: Birch, Jenna, author.
Title: The love gap : a radical plan to win in life and love / Jenna Birch.
Description: First edition. | New York : Grand Central Life & Style, [2018] | Includes bibliographical references.
Identifiers: LCCN 2017034276 | ISBN 9781478920045 (hardcover) | ISBN 9781478923695 (audio downloadable) | ISBN 9781478920038 (ebook open)
Subjects: LCSH: Single women—Psychology. | Man-woman relationships. | Success.
Classification: LCC HQ800.2 .B54 2018 | DDC 306.7—dc23
LC record available at https://lccn.loc.gov/2017034276

ISBNs: 978-1-4789-2004-5 (hardcover), 978-1-4789-2003-8 (ebook)

Printed in the United States of America

LSC-C

10  9  8  7  6  5  4  3  2  1

*For my mom and dad, who taught me never to settle*

# contents

· · · · · · · · · · · ·

## PART FOUR
## a radical plan

# hey girl, I understand you

The year: 1998. The film: *You've Got Mail*. So began my personal journey toward understanding what it means to find love as a modern woman.

It was almost Christmas, and I was still in grade school. My aunt was in town for the day, and my mom decided the three of us girls would go to the local theater and check out the newest rom-com—my very first rom-com. I was less than enthused. Maybe it was the title, and I just didn't get it, but I distinctly remember tears were shed. "I don't want to see a stupid movie about a stupid mailbox," I said. (I'd seen the movie poster; there was a mailbox—that I was sure of.) My mom told me to suck it up.

I did indeed watch Meg Ryan and Tom Hanks fall in love on-screen that day, and thus skyrocketed into the ranks of die-hard romantics everywhere. Falling in love looked utterly magical—set against the backdrop of New York City, with someone who was so wrong yet so right—and I decided then and there that relationships represented an ideal worth pursuing.

At the time, I had this adorably naive idea of what my trajectory toward love would look like. I would "grow up" and meet my first and only boyfriend at age 16. In my dreamy, vivid inner world, he was going to be a modern-day Prince Charming type. He would be my safe place, the person to dry all my tears, someone with whom I'd "do life." (I also imagined he would be incredibly witty, much like Tom

Hanks's Joe Fox in *Mail*, a coveted quality that refuses to die in my mind to this day.)

But then something really interesting happened. When I finally tallied 16 candles on my birthday cake, I had never had an intriguing dating prospect. Instead, I had gained an ambitious set of goals for my life that didn't include a hero sweeping me off my feet. Friends, college, career, and my future felt far more pressing and real than any teenage relationship I might muster. I'd begun planning a path forward on my own terms, one where a magical prom date was secondary to finding a mentor or scoring a journalism internship.

I didn't go to my prom, actually. But that same year, I did land my first freelance writing assignments, completely bypassing my internship plans.

See, somewhere around age 10, I'd brought home my first straight-A report card. When I surveyed those perfect scores, and my parents proceeded to sing my praises at home, that sucker was like a dopamine hit. I wanted more. Instead of ambling through life following whatever new whim was on my radar, I was suddenly serious. I studied, learned the meaning of delayed gratification, and made real goals for myself every few months—just in time for each new report card. I never got a B again.

Throughout school, I was like a Teenage Life Ninja, setting benchmarks for myself and reaching them with elite-level precision. I thrived on overachievement—something characteristic of many women in my generation, where every door seemed open to us. When I finally looked up at the end of high school, I was studious and well-respected by my peers and teachers...but not exactly "hot stuff." I hadn't forgotten Tom and Meg and love and witty romance. It had just fallen off the radar for a while. I'd built key life skills. I had great friends and a great résumé. But I hadn't let myself get lost in a crush, stumbled through an awkward date, or even had my heart broken yet. As some of my friends flirted with guys and I remained completely inept, I was alarmed by the possibility that I was missing something formative—something our parents went through, and their parents before them—like dating, relationships, love. But that alarm was, like, tiny, because I had college plans. I just needed a romance plan, too.

I started editing my academic and athletic goals to include silent relationship ones—goals I'd figured out on my own, of course, because it was very *uncool* to admit you were clueless in the boy department. I spent months trying different approaches, yet my "plan" (pay attention; oscillate between receptive and aloof) wasn't working. *The Rules* had lied. I was checking off personal goals left and right—a 4.0+ GPA, the National Honor Society, editor in chief of the school newspaper, all-state softball player and captain of the team, about to earn my acceptance to the University of Michigan (the only school I'd ever wanted to attend)—but I couldn't seem to make any headway in the relationship department.

On the cusp of college, I finally just decided to make like Elizabeth Bennet and be as badass as possible until Mr. Darcy showed up. I had to admit: Lifelong, I could count my crushes on one hand. And most of them turned out to be lackluster, the more I got to know them. But I kept love as a goal. I did want to meet someone, someday. Maybe I was just too mature, I thought, and it would all even out *eventually*. Little did I know, my journey toward the book you hold was about to get a key flourish.

In 2009, I was leafing through an issue of *Harper's Bazaar* when I started to read a profile about a Hollywood producer. SUSAN DOWNEY: IRON WOMAN was the headline of the story, written by journalist Kimberly Cutter.[1] I had never heard of Susan Downey but was vaguely familiar with her husband, Robert Downey Jr., who was rising to success (again) as superhero Iron Man and legendary detective Sherlock Holmes.

Susan, Cutter writes, was known around Hollywood circles as the "miracle" that saved her husband's career. She was a young producer, an overachiever, a "straight arrow." He was a talented but struggling actor who had bounced from substance abuse to jail to rehab in a series of bizarre incidents that left his reputation in question. They met on the set of the film *Gothika*, which she produced and he starred in.

Several things stood out to me. Susan was smart, and had been incredibly successful on her own before ever meeting her now-husband. Robert was a risk, so far from the Prince Charming prototype that was the stuff of *my* early imagination. And yet there was something about him that just clicked for her. "More than anything, I never doubted it," she told Cutter. "There was something in my gut that knew really quickly. I knew three months in that this was it."

The director of *Sherlock Holmes*, Guy Ritchie, told *Bazaar* that the pair represented "the greatest illustration of a symbiotic marriage that I've ever seen." Susan tried to explain the connection, too. "There was something magical there, something we couldn't put our finger on," she said. "He always says that we became this third thing when we got together—something that neither of us could have become by ourselves—and I think that's true."

Susan was sure of herself, and thus, sure of her connection with Robert. "I don't have a history of making bad choices," she said. "And if my parents had any reservations—whether they were scared about [his being] an actor or an addict or that he'd gone to prison or had a kid and an ex-wife, the whole shebang of things I claimed I would never want in a guy, and add some new things to it—they never shared them with me. They saw how happy I was."

Reading that profile was probably the first moment I became aware that there was another type of relationship—one that surpassed simple support, love, and admiration of each other. It was whatever Robert and Susan had—"this third thing," a relationship that makes you better and encompasses both your personal goals and professional aspirations. A relationship that helps you grow.

I came away with two realizations: (1) If I didn't combine with someone to become a greater "third thing," in my own mind I would be settling; (2) I wanted to feel my romantic decisions deep down in my core.

Perhaps that's why no relationships had ever panned out for me early in life. I was sure, at that point, that no one had ever ignited such feelings in me—and I was sure that I wasn't the only one with this frustration.

By college, I'd catapulted out of my small hometown and entered a city alive with ambitious, bright young men and women. I felt at home, with my life and with love. I discovered more people who were chasing the sort of relationship ideal I was now seeking—one that felt truly worth it and bettering—yet I felt romantic angst around every corner.

In just a few short years, I'd gotten a full education in "modern dating"—and it was completely removed from what I'd ever imagined it would be. Apps were starting to become pervasive, online dating was a legitimate way to meet a significant other, and the age of marriage was inching toward 30 for college-educated career men and women. Suddenly, I seemed to have plenty of time to figure it out and tons of new ways to tiptoe into the game.

I was sort of an outsider in college: I lived off-campus and was free-lancing full-time hours in addition to my full course load. I had my eye on a career in journalism, and my drive to achieve hadn't let up once I entered higher education. And my closest friend was six years my senior, and I hung out with her circle frequently. But I also had a slew of friends my own age and was engaging in a lot of girl talk. I was learning more than ever from everyone's collective dating trials. I approached the scene like a good reporter—listening, taking notes, investigating, drawing conclusions—all in the name of finally getting a handle on this love thing for myself. I chewed on some newly formed theories:

- A great connection was no guarantee of a lasting relationship—or any relationship at all for that matter.
- Men behaved kind of erratically. They were hot and cold, off and on, in and out.
- Singles were picking up dating apps in this new-age wave, but most felt frustrated by them.
- No one knew exactly what it meant to "settle," but everyone knew the concept was abhorrent.
- Lasting relationships were sort of scarce or took *forever* to solidify.
- Couples who got together in college usually did so accidentally. Label-less hooking up was common, and usually led to dicey

waters colored with an array of feelings, ranging from indifference to confusion, love to obsession. The remnants of that confusion seemed to be bleeding off-campus, too.

- Hooking up, dating, and serious relationships seemed to occupy three separate spheres; there was some overlap, but not nearly as much as you'd think.

- Men held the reins to relationships but, for whatever reason, the guys I knew seemed really high-strung about it all. "Boys will be boys" or "He needs to sow his wild oats" did not encompass their attitude—it was almost as if they wanted something greater in love (and in life) but weren't allowed to admit it. Sometimes, they couldn't even acknowledge it to themselves.

- Apps and postgrad career shuffling encouraged an extended adolescence; lots of well-educated men and women seemed to step off campus unable to really date, build relationships, or even communicate feelings.

The media seemed to echo that brains over beauty was the new, highest relationship ideal—but it didn't feel that way in real life. Most of the brainy ladies I knew were always single, or mired in drama with guys who didn't treat them like this prototypical "ideal."

There were gaps. Lots of gaps.

So I processed all of this in my subconscious, for years, learning and filing away information. I was also dating here and there, and noticed a fascinating trend: Guys were either endeavoring to wife me up or did not seem interested at all—at least not in the way I'd hoped. The middle ground was completely lacking, or befuddling. Yet in my early 20s, this middle "building" ground was exactly where I wanted to be. I'd found yet another gap.

So, again, like the journalist I was training to be, I turned to research. I started to notice studies and experts who spoke to some of the baffling dating phenomena surrounding me. I needed help closing the gaps. Then, finally, in 2015, a couple of illuminating studies hit my radar—research that helped me begin to connect the dots of our culture's underlying relationship crisis: In a world where we have every possible option in life and love, why is it still insanely hard to *land just one that lasts*—the right one at the right time?

* * *

Dating isn't dead but, rather, evolving in weird, unexpected ways.

Beginning in my 20s, I went on a lot of first dates with guys—actual honest-to-goodness dinner dates, where we sat in a restaurant and attempted to make small talk for two hours—but I felt next to nothing. I thanked them for taking me out and told them I had an early morning. Then I went home and ate ice cream, watching *Real Housewives* until my brain had melted, like the remnants of Moose Tracks at the bottom of my bowl.

Sometimes, guys were just not that into me (crazy, I know). I met guys who had totally different interests and guys whose personalities or life philosophies were awkwardly at odds with my own. All in all, there wasn't much chemistry for me with a large subset of men—but my problem wasn't that I didn't connect with guys. Like most women, I did connect with a *smaller* subset of men.

I didn't have a type, per se. Some were entrepreneurs; others, doctors. Still others were academics, and a few were business types. The one thing they all had in common was passion. Whatever it was they were pursuing, whether a PhD or a seedling of a business idea, they were *committed*—to change, self-improvement, growth, goals. These guys were almost always getting their lives in order—doing a residency; working insane hours; contemplating a move; choosing a grad school; building businesses—to the point where I never blamed them for being a little scattered. (My mom always told me that "men don't multitask well.") However, they weren't just scattered. They seemed to defy all that old relationship wisdom proclaiming a man always knows what woman he wants—and will go after her.

They regularly ghosted and came back (hey, zombie!), which annoyed me to no end. They also often applied the brakes on even nonrelationships really quickly—sometimes before things had even approached lift-off, sometimes after one date—which seemed awfully premature. I began to label them as "skittish," something women began to applaud me for. "OMG, yes! That's the word!" my friends would say.

I wasn't always going on real dates with these guys either. Romance was suddenly this charged, nebulous entity, which didn't always include explicit declarations of interest. It was *felt*. It was *frustrating*. It was *noticed* by others.

One guy in my circle is a prime example. I had been tangoing around actually dating him for months. Since he wasn't making a legit move, I had resorted to only acknowledging him in passing and simply letting it go. I was kind and interested in his life, but the buck stopped there. If he didn't text, he wasn't interested . . . right? If he didn't ask me out, he didn't like me . . . right? I'd given him lots of chances. So when a friend expressed interest in the same guy, I gave her the okay to go for him. Then, one fine day after a party where Tango Guy and I had inadvertently talked for most of the night, my friend called me up to apologize for ever making a move. "There's obviously a connection between you two," she said. "I realized the other night he doesn't look at me the way he looks at you." *Huh.*

I'd always assumed that when you felt a connection, you put yourself out there and you went for it. When you got a phone number, you used it. Those digits were pure gold! But the modern relationship equation is more complicated and layered; amid the sea of endless options, sometimes connection isn't acted upon right away. Or at all.

Today, we often can't define why a guy is a prospect, but we usually know if he is. I'd coined the term "The Look" for when it would hit me—that starry-eyed stare that would wash across his face at some spontaneous moment in the getting-to-know-you phase. If this moved out of nebulous-romantic-thing territory and into a relationship, you already knew there was an established connection and mutual regard for each other. It would probably take a leap of *real* commitment in the relationship wasteland among college-educated career folks—stepping up, knowing the stakes—more serious than a campus hookup.

However, to men, especially, it seemed, serious was scary.

I attempted to be superchill as I began dating my first real boyfriend; he wasn't my type, per se, but his brain absolutely fascinated me and I had fun going on dates with him. He is still one of the smartest people I've ever met, and at the time we started dating, he was also rising professionally. He'd founded two burgeoning start-ups, and he was constantly busy, but he also walked me through the paces of early dating; he knew all the right moves and had high EQ (the product of two psychologist parents). But roughly six weeks into dating, after spending the vast majority of his birthday weekend together, we *both* felt the whoa-this-is-serious shift. Except while *I* was finally easing into a relationship based on real connection for the first time, he just panicked. He broke up with me, then reconciled just one day later. "I think I'm falling in love with you, and it's scary," he told me. We were up and down, on and off, for the rest of our short relationship, which never felt truly safe again.

When that relationship had run its course, the parade of skittish guys continued.

I went on three dates in five days with a guy who then suddenly disappeared. I awkwardly ran into him at a coffee shop when I'd assumed he was ghosting me, which led to a two-hour heart-to-heart about whether or not he could "do commitment" at that moment. He'd apparently promised himself he'd stay single after his most recent breakup. He hadn't expected to meet me, he said; I hadn't expected him to commit to me after one week of dating.

I connected with another guy on a dating app. We liked offbeat discussion topics and enjoyed a similar strand of quirky banter; communication was nonstop before and after a spontaneous 90-minute coffee date, where I'd showed up low-key (in workout clothes). I could tell he was excited to spend time with me, or even talk to me; his nerves gave him away. I thought it was sweet...before I got this text: *Sincerely, I like you. I liked hanging out with you. You're funny and interesting and exquisite. I like talking to you most importantly, but I'm not convinced I'm very good for you.*

My girlfriends all *died*. "What?! What does that mean?" they said.

I then recounted the story to one of my best guy friends—perhaps to ease my developing complex. He laughed and said, "So basically, he thinks you're amazing but just wants to sleep with other girls right now." While I thought that was an appropriate surface-level reasoning, those endearing first-date nerves spoke to a more complicated internal framework.

I have endless examples of this skittish guy behavior on file in my brain—and in my journal, because I started to write them all down. A pattern was emerging in the group of guys with whom I felt the greatest connection: When the feelings hit, it was time to flee.

And it didn't help that I'd grown up on *He's Just Not That Into You* and *The Rules*, which taught me to make men work for it. They *weren't* working for it—and I didn't even get a say in the matter. The men I connected with were not the casual, free-flowing let's-take-it-one-day-at-a-time creatures I'd been promised. Just because they were dating did *not* mean they were actually open to a relationship of substance, a relationship with potential for real heartbreak and hurt (and capital *L* Love). So if the men in the dating pool aren't even open to Love, how do I find it?

If you've ever wondered that very same thing, don't worry. I've got some ideas.

* * *

It's been a lifelong process, an emotional roller coaster to bring this book to fruition. I've lived and breathed this journey—literally, metaphorically. I've woken up in the middle of the night on multiple occasions with ideas so major that I wanted to start working at 3:00 a.m. I've analyzed the research. I've talked to some of the best experts and major relationship influencers working today. I've had the pleasure of talking to more than 100 career-focused men and women of all backgrounds and ages, in depth, about their love lives—people from New York to LA; Chicago to Charlotte; DC to San Fran; expats from Indonesia to the UK. The ideas, echoes, and stories I heard were a dash of everything: chaotic, frustrating, brilliant, lovely, dramatic, sweet, sure, epic, thrilling, steady, erratic, very wrong—and, yes, sometimes, *oh so right*. The revelations were thoroughly modern and, I think, hopeful.

Researching and writing this book was life-changing for me; I learned more about love in one year than I had in the previous two decades. I hope that from reading it you get a sliver of the satisfaction and understanding that I've gotten from writing it. I want you to know: It's out there. The *exact love* that you want *is* out there. But it takes patience, growth, tenacity, investment, discernment, a dash of timing, and just the right chemistry.

I know you want that lasting love—"it," capital *L* Love, The One, your soul mate. But don't rush; enjoy the ride. The ups and downs of this journey will only make the final destination that much more meaningful. Your love story is already in the making, set to intertwine with someone else's.

It's not easy. But it's worth it. *All of it.* I promise. And it starts now.

part one

\* \* \*

# IDENTIFYING THE GAP

## CHAPTER 1

# meet the full-package woman: you

Each year, Match.com releases data on American singles (not just those on Match), which the media gobbles up immediately. With nearly half of the American population over age 18 identifying as single,[1] dating and marriage trends make for great headlines. But the 2015 Singles in America study[2] came with particularly heavy fanfare from women's magazines. I still remember when this piece of research hit my desk, and I leaned forward a little bit in my chair to read its seemingly feminist ink.

After looking into the mating preferences of more than 5,000 men and women by way of survey, researcher and biological anthropologist Helen Fisher, PhD, writes that we are seeing a "Clooney Effect" in this country—a nod to the recent marriage of America's favorite bachelor, actor George Clooney, to human rights lawyer Amal Alamuddin. According to Fisher's numbers, men desire smart, strong, successful women; 87 percent of men said they would date a woman who was more intellectual than they were, who was better educated, and who made considerably more money than they did, while 86 percent said they were in search of a woman who was confident and self-assured.

Plenty of articles around the web followed,[3] saying this was a win for women (and men, too)—but there I was in early 2015, reading those headlines with an eyebrow raised and an air of skepticism.

I am lucky to be surrounded by some brilliant women—verifiable "catches." Gorgeous women my guy friends *always* ask me about. I have also watched these same smart, independent women struggle in bad relationships or fly solo for extended periods of time, despite their best efforts to land a good guy. So, what did this mean? If 87 percent of men were actively looking to couple with them, why were they still single?

Plus, the ladies of my friend circle who were actually in healthy relationships did not exactly fit the description laid out by Fisher. Although they were supersmart and attractive in their own right, the perpetually matched in my sphere did not fit a clear-cut profile, and I would not automatically group them into the same category as very career-oriented, put-together Amal. Clearly they had some secret sauce of attraction, but what? I wasn't sure.

I began floating casual questions by the guys in my life to try to gain a better understanding: "So, like, what's your type?" (I was breezy about it, I swear.) As one of my male friends put it, the general consensus was: "The smarter and more successful, the better! There are no limits." I'd then hear about a doctor, nearing thirty, who was about to give up on dating because she didn't feel like men valued her brains.

Huh.

So now I was confused by the research, the real-life relationships around me, and the response from men—gaps, gaps, gaps between all these pieces that seemingly did not fit together.

## The Science of a Changing Landscape

I finally did what any skeptical journalist would do: I kept my eyes open for more research. In late 2015, an intriguing new study emerged in the *Personality and Social Psychology Bulletin*,[4] which had further clues into all the holes I was seeing firsthand in this new theory of dating. The study proposes this: Men like more-intelligent women in theory—when they *imagine* them as romantic partners, or when they have psychological distance from them. However, when they actually have to interact with such a woman, something interesting happens.

In the study of 105 men, researchers laid out several scenarios. In the first, they told men that "a woman down the hall," whom they never saw, either outperformed or underperformed them on an intelligence test. Then they were told to imagine this woman as a romantic partner. Unsurprisingly, the guys more frequently desired the woman who *out-performed* them (#feminists).

However, in the second round, men were given an intelligence test and then told that they were about to *meet* a woman who had bested them on the same exam. Ah, yes. The mythic smart, successful, beautiful woman every guy supposedly wanted.

In the study, the men didn't go after this awesome woman, according to lead researcher Lora Park, PhD, a professor in psychology at University at Buffalo. "When the woman was psychologically near—a real-life face-to-face interaction—men moved their chair further away from the woman, as an indicator of less interest in her, and reported less romantic attraction toward the woman when she outperformed versus underperformed him on a test," she tells me.

The way Park explains it, men only *think* they know what they want—or they know what they want in theory, not what they'd choose when put to the test IRL. "Men seem to be influenced less by their ideal partner preferences and more by their emotions or feelings at the moment," she says. "Specifically, when men were outperformed by a woman in a domain that they cared about—intelligence—they felt threatened, assessed by diminished self-ratings of masculinity, which then led them to act in a way counter to what their expressed ideal preferences were." In other words, these guys felt way inferior in the smarter woman's presence, and so they went rogue; they ditched their self-described dream gal for someone who didn't best their intelligence.

*Wow,* I thought. *Eureka!* This study actually helped explain Fisher's Singles in America numbers from a psychological perspective—and then explained what I'd been seeing anecdotally. I was a contributing writer for Yahoo Health at the time, and I immediately pitched an idea to my editor—which she cleared me to write. I began researching a story with this question at the center: *Are men intimidated by a woman who is the full package?*

I talked to many men. And when all was said and done, I was forced to acknowledge that I was onto something bigger—a paradigm shift that I couldn't explain in one simple article. My research complicated the wisdom we were being fed about what men are looking for in a partner, who they date, and why they date them. Saying that men like smart women encompassed about 1 percent of the nuanced reality.

As a writer, I'm constantly chewing on questions. People ask me about my job, and I usually say, "When I don't have answers, I see if someone will employ me to find them." Well, this question became the center of my work life. (And, eventually, my real life as a dater.) Modern-day dating dynamics, in a world where women can *do* and *be* anything, are so layered and fascinating you're likely not even *aware* of some of the phenomena in play. I began finding connections in every new data set I encountered, and on every date I ventured out on.

When I began my research, almost all the guys I interviewed or chatted up insisted that when it came to the women they wanted, "the more, the better." They also said that while they were not *personally* intimidated by smart, successful, attractive women, they felt most other men were. But as I got guys talking—*really* talking—they started to say some more revelatory things.

I talked to my good friend Jack, a witty and self-aware 27-year-old consultant. When I asked him what he was looking for in a lifelong partner, he said that, of course, he wanted a smart, independent, successful, beautiful woman (yada yada). However, later in our conversation, he also said that if he didn't feel like he could win over a girl who fit the bill, he'd "start looking for reasons to discount her." And he told me, "You can pretty easily convince yourself that you never really wanted her to begin with."

I went on a date with a handsome real estate broker a few years my senior, someone with the fearless facade of a man hardened to rejection and immune to the effects of deflected attention. He acted entirely secure in himself—but off the cuff, when I casually brought up the question of whether he would be intimidated to date the quintessential accomplished woman, he was quite candid. "I want her to be smart and successful," he said, "but not as smart and successful as I am."

One of my girlfriends (a lovely, brilliant-yet-soft-spoken entrepreneur) once went on a first date with a guy who runs in our social sphere. He made her a sushi dinner, in fact, and they had five hours of great conversation before calling it a night. Interestingly, though, he seemed to push her away very quickly afterward—right into "friend" territory. He wasn't going to date her, yet he'd drop *everything* to meet her for a last-minute happy hour after work, or hand over his football tickets to her friends, as a show of respect.

When I asked him to explain his reluctance to pursue her (one night over 1:00 a.m. beers, where I clearly do fine research), he gave me some of his reasons. "She's as close to perfect as I've ever found," he said. "But I think I'd drive her crazy. I think she'd tire of my energy."

Relationship expert Susan Walsh, founder of popular dating site Hooking Up Smart, once told me, "When a man tries to convince you not to date him, listen."

Still, if men know a great thing when they find it, why don't they pull the trigger?

## The Love Gap

You've probably been discussing this dating gray area with your friends for eons, but allow me to finally define and label it for you:

**The Love Gap,** *n.*—the reason men don't always pursue the women they claim to want; frequently, women like you.

The Love Gap is a thoroughly modern phenomenon, which now exists *between* the sexes—which is why we're focusing on heterosexual pairings here. The dynamics are unique to 21st-century men and women with evolved desires for a relationship, who also have to get around generations and generations of the ingrained male provider/female nurturer framework.

What lies in the Love Gap? Oh, I don't know…Let's start with a few things. Psychological distance. Timelines. Past heartbreaks. Ancient gender roles. Socialized differences in the sexes' view of love, emotions, and vulnerability. A lack of genuine "relationship nurturing" qualities today. Games, because everybody wants "the upper hand." How the sexes respond to their partner's "reflected glory."

I could extrapolate for days—and I will, because we need to identify the Love Gap in our daily lives, so that we can understand and navigate it. If we want to finally build fulfilling relationships with compatible partners, we need to grasp why we believe what we believe—and parse out why those beliefs are not always accurate. This entire modern landscape starts with you in all your awesomeness.

I want to introduce you to the "End Goal" woman, a.k.a. you—EG for short.

> **End Goal,** *n.*—(1) a smart, successful "full-package" woman who men admire, date, and deem aspirational; she contains the sort of substance and carries the type of connection they want to lock down—someday; (2) a modern woman who knows what she wants in love and in life; she has an ultimate objective in mind for her future, and she is unwilling to settle in getting there.

Before this book was even a sparkle in my eye, I was consistently baffled by the dating stories I'd hear from career women. Women who had their lives together—for the most part. It's not like they didn't ever make questionable decisions; we all spend unreasonable amounts of cash on six new lipsticks at Sephora or forget to call our mom sometimes. But these women had substance, charm, and goals that they were actively reaching for. In fact, many of these girls were my favorite people in the whole world! Women who always filled my life with fun and positive energy.

And yet, I was still fielding sob-filled phone calls about men who were breaking their hearts. I listened to a lot of their stories—and then, to help me understand, I started talking to a lot of guys. Eventually, I mapped out an explanation, a conclusion I'd felt for the entirety of my adult life but never identified before in black and white: Men don't always date the women they claim to want at any given time in their lives. And it's not because they're "just not that into you."

Let's dig deeper.

## CHAPTER 2

# why you're still single

"Why are you *still* single?" "I can't believe you're still single." "You should *not* be single!" EGs have heard every form of that quip. You probably don't know how to reply either; you're single a whole lot. Since everyone else seems to think you're "a catch," I'm sure you've tried to figure out the root of the problem—or thought *you* were the root of the problem. Your singleness is not for lack of desire.

In true EG fashion, most of the awesome single women who did interviews with me (and the *formerly* single ones) were good students. They'd read *The Rules* and adopted some of these tactics to try to snare men; it didn't work. They'd read *He's Just Not That Into You* and written off guys who kept coming back into their lives; they weren't any less single, but at least they had less trouble?

They'd even been considering the concept of "settling," because… maybe everyone does it? Or *should* do it? Aziz Ansari's book, *Modern Romance*, introduced them to Barry Schwartz's "paradox of choice," and now they were concerned that today's practically endless pool of dating "options" might be the root of their problems. So maybe they needed to just pick one? Or maybe *they* were the problem? Women often try to shoulder the blame. (In reality, I want us to stop pointing fingers.)

As we go further into the many whys behind the Love Gap, I have to report that, yes, it *appears* EG women are modern-day dream girls. Experts will attest to the many theoretical benefits of marrying a woman who is not a dependent, but a partner with potential earning power. In a competitive world, having a dual-income household means more security if someone loses a job, more opportunities to travel and have experiences, and even a greater ability to afford children.

But let's be clear: Not every guy wants a full-blown EG, and individual preferences vary. Maybe he's got enough earning power on his own, and would rather find a woman who's more willing to manage affairs at home and raise kids. Cool. Let's not demonize traditional setups, including women who want to stay home with children, or the men who will seek them out. Many of our households were ruled by similar strong, benevolent women.

However, there are more women completing higher education and saturating the job market than ever before. And research shows that many men are in fact into the idea of locking down an EG. For a 2013 study published in the journal *PLOS One*, for example, 288 men and women were asked to rank six traits of an "ideal" partner (wealth, dominance, intelligence, height, kindness, and attractiveness) within the context of four hypothetical living conditions (status quo/nowadays; violence/postnuclear; poverty/resource exhaustion; prosperity/global well-being).[1] Both sexes ranked intelligence as the trait they desired most in a partner in each living condition. Although attractiveness was more important to guys than to women, smarts still won out in every scenario.

This is not supershocking. Peter Buston and Stephen Emlen's 2003 "likes attract" hypothesis indicates that men who are educated and successful will also value similar traits in a partner.[2] Recently, Marisa T. Cohen, psychology professor and cofounder of the Self-Awareness and Bonding Lab, riffed off this research with a colleague, presenting their findings in March 2015 at the annual conference of the Eastern Psychological Association.[3]

Their study set out to test how the "likes attract" hypothesis related to academic motivation—so, would more driven men seek out intelligent, educated women? "As intrinsic motivation increased, the importance of education and intelligence in a mate also increased," Cohen says (unsurprisingly). "However, it is important to realize that participants were rating *hypothetical* traits, which, like Helen Fisher's Singles in America work, is pretty abstract. As we didn't explore actual mate selection behaviors experimentally, how these beliefs would translate into actual real-life mate selection is still unclear."

But it's becoming clearer. Research points to the fact that men's answers about what they *want* in a woman are often influenced by their psychological distance and by survey or study setups. When you start to close that gap, however, and men start to engage with the living, breathing full-package women they desire, they often push back against these girls as "threats"—just like in the 2015 *Personality and Social Psychology Bulletin* study where men distanced themselves from the women who outperformed them on exams, showing less interest in them as romantic partners.

## The Threat of the "Full Package"

We can think of a full-package woman as an attractive prospect who has her life set up (a.k.a., *so* many EGs). This girl is self-sustaining, financially independent, and doesn't "need" a man to keep her afloat like past generations of women.

In a man's subconscious, though, this woman might provoke both awe and fear.

A 2006 study out of Columbia University published in the *Quarterly Journal of Economics* is another example of the "threat" factor.[4] The study looked at the qualities speed daters said they preferred in prospective dates. Before the study began, all participants were asked to rate their own level of intelligence on a scale of 1 to 10. They were also asked to rank the intelligence of the daters they encountered during each round of matching.

The result? Men were interested in women who they perceived to be intelligent and ambitious—but that interest had limits. Guys were *less* into the ladies they perceived to be smarter or more driven than themselves. This sentiment continued to bear out in 2016, when economists from Warsaw, Poland, analyzed this same speed-dating data in new ways.[5] In the research, women liked smarter men absolutely—a guy's attractiveness increased as his intelligence increased. The same did not hold for men; no matter a woman's level of physical attractiveness, the researchers found men rated optimal intelligence level to be right around 7 out of 10.

Intelligence doesn't exist in a vacuum. A smarter woman might find more ways to fend for herself, have more career prospects, earn more money, and maintain financial independence. But intelligence, career success, and earning power have long been traditionally masculine spheres. When a full-package woman bests her male counterpart, sparks may fly—partly from allure, partly from friction, as she asserts a new role or dominates a formerly male foothold.

Some studies assert that smart women who earn more money and hold more power than their male partners threaten a man's deeply rooted sense of masculinity, the effects of which researchers are just beginning to test. A fascinating 2016 political survey from Fairleigh Dickinson University sought to examine how a woman's income would affect a man's vote in the upcoming presidential election. The questionnaire was, for the most part, standard political fare—except for the most important question on the list, which asked men whether they earned more, less, or the same as their spouse.

"Now, this question wasn't there because we cared about the actual answers," study author Dan Cassino writes in *Harvard Business Review*.[6] "The reason we asked the question was to push men to think about potential threats to their gender roles. Being the breadwinner has been a linchpin of U.S. men's masculinity for decades, so even the potential of making less than one's spouse threatens accepted gender roles." The results bore this assumption out.

Men who were asked about their wives' income late in the survey preferred Hillary Clinton to Donald Trump by a whopping 16-point margin; they hadn't been primed to think about their wives' financial prospects as they answered questions. Men who were asked about their wives' paycheck just before their voting preference, and were subsequently forced to consider her potential earning power, preferred Trump by an 8-point margin.

That's a 24-point difference, based on the position of one question about their wife's income. "In this case, men were responding to a threat to their masculinity by saying they would prefer a man, rather than a woman, in a presidential race," Cassino explains in *HBR*. Intimidation is a powerful force. The very threat of female intelligence and success—their own partner's, no less—was enough to change a man's political opinion.

## The "Full-Package Threat" in Action

So we've established the basics: When we ask men what kind of woman they want in an abstract way, they tell us the most fabulous one possible, of course. But when these same guys encounter Ms. Fabulous in real life ways, many have very mixed emotions.

Here's what's going on. A lot of what we feel—and how we act—is influenced by our latent psychology and current socialization as men and women. So while men *want* the smartest, most successful, most attractive woman in the bunch, they also have a deeply ingrained *need* to feel useful and valuable to her—as *some* sort of a provider. The more advantages a woman has, the lower the chance a man will feel he can add to her life. If she seems too self-sufficient, if she's entirely kick-ass on her own and thus no longer needs the masculine breadwinner, the modern man may see his role as seemingly usurped.

Some of the brightest, most confident women I interviewed told me the same thing—over and over. They'd had at least one ex-boyfriend, if not more, tell them, "You just don't need me." Abby, a 27-year-old mechanical engineer from New York, has heard that line so many times that she's starting to lose count. "Once they get an inkling that I'm a boss girl, I just can't avoid it," she tells me. "They have literally said, 'You don't need me at all.' I'm like, 'That's a compliment! I *want* you!'"

Abby's greatest love was with a fellow engineer; she met her now-ex at a Chicago music festival. Their initial chemistry was "so organically awesome" that she couldn't help but fall hard. "He made me laugh, the sex was great, *and* he was intellectually stimulating," she says. However, those initial sparks eventually gave way to some of her guy's hidden insecurities. When Abby suggested a few dinner locations he claimed were "too lavish" or "too uptight," he started to get curious; he poked around the subject, trying to get Abby to disclose her salary. When she didn't, he eventually asked point-blank and she revealed the number. "He could not look past the fact that I made more money than he did," she says. "He even told me that I was *overpaid.*"

That key moment was the beginning of the end in their relationship. "He eventually confided in me that he'd told his mentor at work he felt emasculated by my career, and didn't know what he should do about it," Abby says. "He ultimately cheated on me while I was on a work trip in India." His parting line? "You didn't deserve this." Eek.

A man may go MIA on the full-package woman whenever she (unconsciously) exposes weaknesses in his protector/provider armor. Let's go back to Lora Park's study, the one with the awesome woman down the hall competing against subjects on an IQ test. In addition to the base finding, Park also collected data on the guys in her study who'd been bested by a female counterpart. "Men who were outperformed by a 'real-life' woman in a physically close or near context felt less masculine than when the woman performed worse than him or was psychologically distant," she says of her preliminary tests.

The bright, ambitious, financially independent woman's "role take-over" is shaking up the dating game. "If the gender role stereotypes tell us that he is required to be the provider, and her intelligence threatens his ability to be firmly seated in that role, a threat exists," says Karla Ivankovich, PhD, a clinical counselor and adjunct psychology instructor. "Throughout history, it has been an adaptation of the fittest to eliminate the threat—and this includes the smartest." Or the most attractive. Or the most successful. Or the cleverest.

In past generations, a man and woman would often serve complementary purposes in a marriage: breadwinner and homemaker. That's not a given anymore. It's more common that, to marry your equal in education and income, you'll be marrying a theoretical competitor. What are the new roles? What if a man and woman both have long-term career plans? If she has a more high-potential position, what's a man to do? It's anyone's guess.

For a column in Edge, renowned evolutionary psychologist David Buss was enlisted to answer the website's annual question for "complex and sophisticated minds." The 2016 query: "What do you consider the most interesting recent scientific news? What makes it important?" His answer: "The mating crisis among educated women."[7]

Buss is a professor at the University of Texas at Austin, where the gender ratio is skewed—54 percent of the student population is women, compared with 46 percent men. "This imbalance may not seem large at first blush," he writes. "But when you do the math it translates into a hefty 17 percent more women than men in the local mating pool."

This rush of women on campus has caused a shift toward short-term mating, says Buss. When men aren't necessarily looking to settle down early and they outnumber their female counterparts, they control the market. "The modern environment is activating a subset of our psychology in an unprecedented way," he tells me.

Not everyone agrees with this evolutionary angle, but it is true that the landscape's realities are new. Buss thinks men, at least those close to the campus subset, are grappling with a loss of power as women gain more options. "I think it's cliché, but true," he explains. "We often say men are intimidated by women who are smarter, but it's because…a financially independent woman is more likely to leave if she's not happy. Men can't rely on the fact that they're pulling in the paycheck anymore."

So, therein lies another threat. It's possible that men are finally coming to terms with an anxiety women have dealt with for endless generations: They have no dependent, and their partner is free to leave for any reason. We are true equals.

Men enjoy pairing off with their equals. Buss says the research continually shows that marriages among those with similar academic and intellectual profiles are the happiest and most secure. But how do we get those couples together for the long haul? And how do we account for individualized differences in mate preferences among our 21st-century daters? Not everyone cares about, or even wants, a traditional setup with typical gender roles—but for those who want to couple for longevity, our ingrained biology and psychology make for a slightly trickier puzzle. And our *socialization* may make relationships trickier still.

## Can Both Men and Women Have It All?

"The biggest mistake of feminism is the attack on good feminine qualities," 27-year-old resident physician James tells me, pointing to a possible reason for career women's singleness. While the word "mistake" might draw ire, he's right in the sense that modern feminism has permanently altered the roles and attitudes of women in the dating game—although it is much more nuanced than he likely realizes. Let me explain.

In the 2017 book *American Hookup*, which describes the trials and perils of hookup culture, sociologist Lisa Wade, PhD, writes that feminism has two key aims. "Feminists wanted women to be able to do the things in life that were valued, things associated with men, but they also wanted everyone to sit up and notice that the things women had been doing all along were valuable, too."

Wade argues that feminists got the former but not the latter. "The first thing is sexism," she explains to me. "The world centers around masculinity as ideal, and femininity as 'less than.' Everyone is trying to be masculine." She points to a shift in our upbringings. All of a sudden, little girls began to garner applause for mastering what's been traditionally considered masculine. In our minds, baking cupcakes and playing dress-up now pales in comparison to excelling at math, learning to code, and beating the boys at soccer.

Wade says that the new purported ideal for women is typically a blend of masculine *and* feminine qualities—and that most young girls are still exposed to caretaking role models and skill sets from a young age, in some fashion. All that said, society largely ignores boys' emotions in the process of opening masculine doors for girls.

From the time they're kids, men are *not* encouraged to develop interpersonal and emotional skills that might lend to the development of strong romantic relationships. And why would they be? As long as traditional masculinity is ideal and femininity is "lesser than," men will simply cling harder to the ground they've occupied for centuries. As women have started to enter, and excel in, typically masculine spheres, says Wade, a whole lot of men have simply become *more* masculine to keep up.

It does appear that men may experience a lot of anxiety holding on to those longtime male ideals. A 2016 meta-analysis of 78 studies (and close to 20,000 men) found that conforming to masculine norms, like "power over women," "self-reliance," and a "playboy" lifestyle, increased men's mental health issues.[8] The research identified one male-centered ideal that did *not* negatively impact the men in the studies—"primacy of work," or the importance of one's career. In fact, men have told me over and over again that they derive much of their self-esteem from their work lives. According to the study authors, "work and career can also be an important source of meaning in life." It is not a bad thing to derive satisfaction from your work, but many men have told me they cling to career milestones as markers of their own personal value—creating a pretty specific timeline for their lives as a result.

Consciously or unconsciously, men may focus much of their energy on living up to a masculine ideal—a fact that modern women aren't always attuned to in their own quest for establishing equal footing at work and at home. As women continue to ask "Can I have it all?" men are struggling with their own set of deep-seated psychological needs. They are more prone to ask, "When will I feel comfortable taking my eyes off the prize?" with their career goals and personal development.

At the same time, feminine nurturing qualities have been going by the wayside. The skills women have honed to compete and succeed at work don't always translate to relationship-building with their male peers. Harper, a 34-year-old creative director, explains that many of her single thirtysomething friends in New York were "perfect" modern women—yet they didn't know how to find real relationships. They were looking for "perfect" modern men, perhaps, perusing the dating field like they'd glance over a résumé. "We'd analyze," she says, lumping herself into the group. "We'd see if he was successful, had a good career, was living in a nice home. But then I moved to LA, and learned relationships are really about connection." Connection. *Feeling.* Often abandoned in favor of analytical dating, checklists, and résumés.

Harper admits that it took a major shift to find and settle down with her now-husband. "At my core, nothing about me had changed," she says of opening up to a less analytical approach. "But that lack of vulnerability is probably the number one thing that took me so long...Women don't realize how much power and responsibility they have in building relationships." Or *could* have. *Maybe.* Because at one time, we did.

With high-stakes career goals taking center stage for both men and women, there appears to be less time for development in other, emotionally safer, spaces. Even as men typically do the stuff that feels big on the surface—asking for the first date, putting a ring on it—women have *always* done the lion's share of emotional work, creating an atmosphere of positive vibes and ego safeguarding, where vulnerability can be encouraged. As women push to compete, and move further away from nurturing as a primary role, who is left to fill the gap? How much energy can a woman today focus on building "soft skills" like caretaking and emotional openness when she's working on her dissertation or putting in extra hours for that job promotion? Women are tired, too. It becomes harder to come home and be warm, fuzzy, and accommodating when you're competing in tough academic and career realms for eight or ten hours each day. Realms that often train and reward you for the exact opposite skills you're supposed to use at home. And how much, *really*, are men encouraged to pick up this emotional slack?

Unfortunately for us ladies, biology has given guys the upper hand in the timing of relationships. Women are primed to look for a supportive partner quicker, thanks to that good ol' biological clock. But today's career men are more inclined to simply delay deep and vulnerable relationships that take energy to maintain—and emotional maturity to lay your ego on the line. Relationships play a supporting role to building empires. Men don't want anything, or anyone, to distract them from their overall work goals—or add to that fear of falling behind.

I'm sure you've met these men in the wild. They are the ones who wade into the relationship pond slowly, with women who don't seem to take up too much psychological energy; they leave girls who they imagine will be higher-maintenance or, possibly scarier, a flight risk. They're looking for something *a little less taxing* in a culture that's taught them they have "options." For them, relationships don't stick. Sometimes, they ghost nearly everyone, because there always seems to be *a little better fit* out there on the horizon…maybe. Sometimes, they adopt an overall-negative playboy lifestyle, devoid of emotional attachments altogether.

While there are clearly exceptions (see: that amazing guy your friend married at 25), on the whole, men have more work to do emotionally before they're going to be stellar relationship partners. Renowned marriage researcher John Gottman points out the differences between the sexes when he describes little girls and little boys at play in his book *The Seven Principles for Making Marriage Work.*[9] When boys play together, the focus is often on competition and winning—and there's no emotional work involved. If feelings are hurt, they're never discussed. The game simply goes on. While some little girls play to win, they also frequently just play together. They often focus on talk, or interpersonal themes—playing a made-up game on the jungle gym, perhaps, or pretending Barbies are sword-wielding sidekicks! (Something like that.) If a little girl is offended, the show stops until the friendship is repaired. Gottman points out this "basic truth" about men and women: "Women are more oriented toward discussing and understanding feelings than are men."

If little girls are told, "You can do anything," young men are still told, "Boys don't cry," and "Grow a pair." Recent research from Emory University shows that even fathers interact differently with their children based on sex.[10] In the study, dads were more "attentively engaged with their daughters, sang more to their daughters, used more analytical language and language related to sadness and the body with their daughters." In contrast, when fathers interacted with their sons, they used "rough and tumble play," and more "achievement language" like "top," "win" and "proud." As a result, young girls are often more well-rounded than their male peers, which may be one big reason they're outachieving them.

Sooo…what we're seeing today is shown in "The Path to Relationship Chaos" flow chart.

## The Path to Relationship Chaos

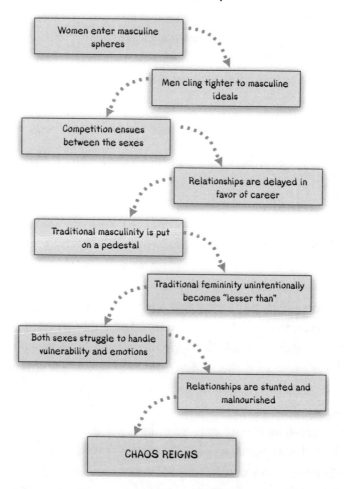

Gottman says that, of course, there are plenty of men who are more emotionally intelligent than women, and plenty of women who don't exactly get an A+ in relationship building—everyone falls along a spectrum for any sex-associated trait. But women are exposed to the building blocks of successful romantic partnerships at a younger age and more frequently. "The plain truth is that 'girlish' games offer far better preparation for marriage and family life because they focus on relationships," he writes.

We can debate the source of these relationship skills forever. Gottman believes much is innate in the sexes. "Because it occurs in virtually every culture, I suspect that biology rather than socialization is the cause," he writes. Whether socialized, biological, or a mix of the two, it doesn't really matter—emotionality is a deep part of our female psyche. It is where you, as a woman, have the upper hand over most men. Society just isn't encouraging you to flex your nurturing muscle enough.

## Why Men Miss Their Grandmothers

For 40 years, researchers have had high school seniors take the same survey on gender roles at work, at home, and beyond. While you'd think each new generation would become more hip and egalitarian than the last, sociologist David Cotter, PhD, a professor at Union College, and Joanna Pepin, a doctoral candidate at the University of Maryland, found a strange twist in the latest set of data, analyzed in early 2017.[11]

While the latest batch of high school seniors support more equal employment opportunities for men and women, their views of the best family setup have gotten a little retro. The study authors write: "In 1976, when they were asked whether 'it is usually better for everyone involved if the man is the achiever outside the home and the woman takes care of the home and family,' fewer than 30 percent of high school seniors disagreed. By 1994, disagreement with the claim that the male breadwinner–female homemaker family is the best household arrangement had almost doubled, rising to 58 percent. By 2014, however, it had *fallen back* to 42 percent—a decline of 16 percentage points since its peak in 1994. In 1976, a majority of high school seniors (59 percent) disagreed with the statement that 'the husband should make all the important decisions in the family.' This rose to 71 percent by 1994 but fell back to 63 percent by 2014." Hmm, right?

Cotter and Pepin explain the importance of focusing on a set of 17- and 18-year-olds; "their values are important for predicting future trends," the researchers write. "Youths' attitudes capture changing cultural ideals that are less likely to have been reconciled with adulthood realities, such as unpaid maternity leave and the expenses of childcare, making their opinions of gender unique views from below." When the duo analyzed the trends, they concluded that "young men have consistently been less egalitarian than young women."

In another recent paper, researchers reported that in 1994, 83 percent of young men disagreed that a male breadwinner–female homemaker setup was superior to other family dynamics, whereas in 2014, only 55 percent of guys disagreed.[12] According to analysis in the *New York Times* by historian Stephanie Coontz, when the 2016 data was released, millennials were still trending traditional.[13] This, she writes, possibly stems from "young people witnessing the difficulties experienced by parents in two-earner families." She hypothesizes that millennial men's conservative attitudes in particular *might* "reflect an attempt to compensate for men's loss of dominance in the work world."

It's not my goal to proclaim you are the ultimate fix for better relationships; that burden falls on both sexes. But, after conducting hundreds of interviews, I have gained some insight into how men are feeling from the other side. It seems that they need some help dealing with these new dynamics; they're not as secure or as sure of themselves as they often pretend to be.

Samuel, a well-educated 26-year-old banker from North Carolina, says he is not at all picky when it comes to the women he dates. "I have never been the person to say 'I need X,'" he explains. "I'm just looking for a nice girl who treats me right, someone driven and ambitious, who makes me better. Someone who is perceptive and thoughtful, who looks out for herself and me, too."

Samuel is a supersolid guy, extremely articulate and emotionally intelligent—a catch, by any definition. He's not asking for anything more than he's prepared to offer. He wants someone smart and kind, who builds him up and is a team player. However, he's noticed something among women he's dated. "A lot of girls seem desensitized to what their mothers and grandmothers understood: Men have fragile egos," he says.

In fact, I was shocked how many men mentioned their parents' and grandparents' marriages as something to which they aspired, while still insisting they'd love a wife who was independent, ambitious, and bright. Perhaps this is because those bonds had lasted 30, 40, or

50+ years, or perhaps men were feeling a little nostalgic for some old-fashioned nurturing.

Either way, these men want their marriages to last—and that means more sensitivity. Samuel remembers that he wasn't fond of a college girlfriend's criticism of her unemployed father's efforts around the house. She was keeping score on her mother's behalf, he says, instead of having a "free-flowing, open partnership." And she didn't stop to think about the potential toll of job loss on her father's psyche as she ganged up against him about his behavior—over and over again. "I tell my little sisters this all the time," Samuel explains. " 'I'm not sexist. I'm as feminist as you are. Men and women should be equal, but men and women *are* different.' "

Guys are willing to support your career—but they're also looking for that soft place to fall, which they've seen modeled in generations before them, according to 39-year-old entrepreneur Brody, who is married to Harper (and has a background in psychology, no less). "We can't get past our millions of years of evolution, and some elements of gender roles are undeniable," he explains. There is definitely some flexibility; Brody's wife cooks and handles finances, for instance. "The problem is that women are set up for failure. The intellectual and primal parts of the brain are at odds, and society sends mixed messages."

## "Never Underestimate the Male Ego"

Max, a 33-year-old tech entrepreneur, has big dreams—and does not think a career-minded woman (his professed type!) currently lines up with obtaining them. "This is a terrible thing to say," he says. Let me stop here for a moment and tell you how many men have prefaced their deepest desires or true feelings with such a statement. A lot of men hate that they can't be 100 percent politically correct—because they want to be. They do not want to be misunderstood. They *love* smart, successful women. But they're not *just* looking for "smart," and successful is more of a bonus.

First and foremost, they are looking for something in a woman they can't get anywhere else: an emotional safe haven. "I consider myself a feminist," he says. "I repeatedly say I want a career type who challenges me and balances me. But I have this back-of-my-mind idea that my career will be more important." Max pauses, clearly hating himself at this point. "There is definitely ego involved, and I don't think I can be with a girl who obliterates that." You can think of "emotional safety" as a combination of trust, commitment, intimacy, kindness, *and* how someone feels with you; the more smarts, power, and prestige you hold, the scarier trying to hold on to you becomes.

Max acknowledges that not every single guy is like him; if you don't want a guy who defines himself by his success, three cheers. Other guys embrace other dynamics—like one of Max's best friends. "He is the smartest guy I know, and he's married to a cute doctor!" says Max. "He could literally be the president's chief of staff. He is the smartest guy of my entire friend group—but he will probably accomplish the least because *her* career comes first."

This friend of Max's seems quite evolved, and very content with his relationship dynamic. He literally said in his wedding vows that his wife was "settling" for *him*. But the interesting flip side is that Max sees his friend as settling for his *career*. "I look at him with this combination of envy and admiration, because his natural intelligence is at a level that I do not have," he explains. "My friend is both capable and happy. His career just won't reach the heights that I know it could have."

All his life, Max has wanted to be one of the best in his field—not just good at his job, but a serial innovator. He wants his "name on buildings," he declares. And until he is sure that the relationship he wants won't hinder name-on-buildings success, he won't be able to comfortably allow it to move forward. "Never underestimate the male ego," he says with a chuckle. "A whole book could be written on how ego affects our decision-making."

## We've All Got Needs

When a catch of a modern woman tells me her guy problems, they typically fall into one of two categories: distancing or disappearing. The guy in question either creates distance from her and tries to remain in her life while dealing with his personal development, or he goes "poof" with little warning, to make sure she's not a mental barrier to his success and growth.

I have a hard time giving advice without getting to the root of the issue first; it's the journalist in me. To further explain the high-achieving woman's singleness predicament, I turned to psychologist Karla Ivankovich. She sent me to dig up psychologist Abraham Maslow's "hierarchy of needs," a theory he unveiled way back in 1943.

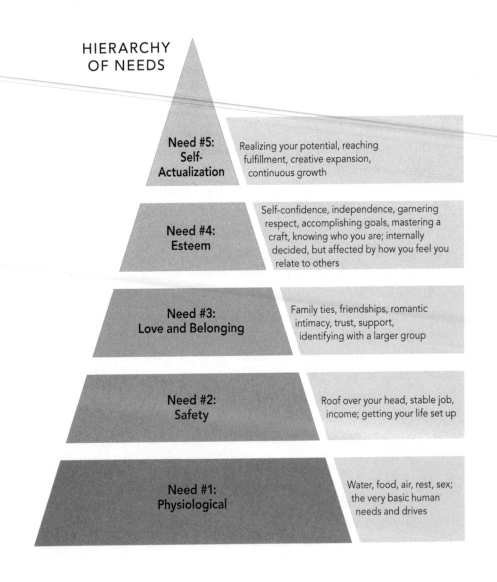

HIERARCHY OF NEEDS

**Need #5: Self-Actualization** — Realizing your potential, reaching fulfillment, creative expansion, continuous growth

**Need #4: Esteem** — Self-confidence, independence, garnering respect, accomplishing goals, mastering a craft, knowing who you are; internally decided, but affected by how you feel you relate to others

**Need #3: Love and Belonging** — Family ties, friendships, romantic intimacy, trust, support, identifying with a larger group

**Need #2: Safety** — Roof over your head, stable job, income; getting your life set up

**Need #1: Physiological** — Water, food, air, rest, sex; the very basic human needs and drives

I'm a visual person, so let's stack this hierarchy up and take a look. Need fulfillment begins with #1, the most critical:

We're all trying to reach our highest potential—the apex of the hierarchy, self-actualization (a.k.a. Maslow's need for continual "growth"). But before a man can move on to self-actualization, he'll need to check some of these other need boxes.

- ☑ He'll need the safety of a fairly stable job, income, and place to live.
- ☑ He'll need love and support from people who help him feel valued, respected, and happy—especially from a partner.
- ☑ He'll also need to know who he is, what he brings to the table, the sort of life he's looking for long-term, and the sort of mate he wants at his side.

Amazing women like you—with your stellar career, big paycheck, can-do-anything attitude, and oodles of passion—are dumped every day. Why? Because you're ahead of him in the hierarchy, or multitasking your way through it in a way he can't fathom doing himself. In other words, you've checked more boxes:

- ☑ You've got the safety of a fairly stable job, income, and place to live.
- ☑ You have love and support from people who help you feel valued, respected, and happy—and not just from a partner, but also from your friends, your mom and dad, your sibs, and everyone else who cheers you on every day. (Men don't usually have this same supportive structure.)
- ☑ You know who you are, what you bring to the table, the sort of life you're looking for long-term, and the sort of mate you want at your side.

"Girl power" culture (and, ya know, your biological clock) has taught you to set goals and look toward the future. Meanwhile, if I had a nickel for every guy who told me he "wasn't a great planner," I'd be rich. There's just less motivation for men to find themselves and settle down at a young age. The sexes' journeys through the hierarchy are just plain different.

Although the needs exist within a hierarchy, even Maslow himself explained that needs can overlap, kick in simultaneously, or ignite at various times over a life span. While need #1 is most vital, then #2, then #3, and so on, all five needs are basic. We are *constantly* trying to fulfill all of them. "They are motivated when a need goes unmet," Ivankovich tells me. "And most critically, the need will strengthen until it is met."

This is where relationship problems come into play. If a man perceives himself as focusing too much energy on a relationship he's not fully ready for—especially a growth-oriented one with an EG, which we'll get to—he's going to feel some angst. He might *want* you, but the guy has needs, too—and he's not always going to discuss 'em. He probably can't even identify the reasons he isn't settling into the relationship and maintaining those initial positive vibes. All the same, he's going to create a wedge. Maybe upon first glance, when he decides he is unlikely to win you over; perhaps after weeks or months of dating, when he decides that he is unlikely to keep you long-term; or when it's just *too* serious too soon and he's losing focus.

We are becoming an emotionally listless, tired generation. "Essentially, it's easier to accept rejection or supposed rejection than to continue on a path trying to meet his basic needs with someone he needs to prove himself to, or is intimidated by," Ivankovich explains. "It's why men are quick to hop from relationship to relationship until they find one that's emotionally comfortable for the place they're at in their lives."

With independent women slaying it professionally, and app dating taking over, the culture of relationship-hopping is worse than ever today. Ivankovich offers up the reality of the situation like a straight shot of tequila—smooth at first, then a slight burning, with a final zip to make your head swivel. "Imagine how the millennial population, with a strong desire for money, success, *and* relationship stability, can be thrown into a frenzy when they are not meeting these marks," she says. Whoa.

Granted, this isn't a millennial problem, or even a 21st-century problem.

Smart, successful women have been kicking butt for a good long while now. However, with all the opportunities out there for women today and all the opportunities to shuffle dating prospects until you feel comfortable, this dating wasteland is only primed to get worse if we can't understand what's happening and how to navigate it.

* * *

Before we go any further down the rabbit hole together, I want to put one harmful generalization to bed right now: Men are not out to screw you over (save for those few sociopaths out there). I honestly believe that *they believe* what they have all told me: They want the smartest, most successful, most badass woman on the face of the earth. The girl who commands the attention of a boardroom or an entire bar, loves sports and science, has a PhD and a six-figure paycheck, looks like a cross between Angelina Jolie and Grace Kelly—*and* fulfills all their dirtiest fantasies. (Or, ya know, some other version of fabulousness.)

These men are well-adjusted creatures. They are feminists, and see you as equals. They can appreciate the hard work it took you to climb to the top, and they admire how you stay there—all without a hair out of place, or a chip in that at-home mani. (Most of them think you're just as pretty without makeup anyway.)

What I'm trying to say is this: They worship the ground you walk on.

But I'm also here to tell you that men have pertinent needs that may overwrite the qualities they desire in a partner—and they don't always feel they can manage the pressures to succeed as a modern man while in an emotionally intense relationship with someone who requires them to bring their best self to the table every day.

It is why a man will tell you he wants you (or some girl who bears a *startling* resemblance to you) and then go off and couple up with some other girl with a much softer presence. Or why he darts from relationship to unfulfilling relationship until he's convinced himself love is dead and he doesn't want long-term commitment at all.

You, in your natural state, are a challenge and an end goal—like it or not.

When I ask a guy to describe what kind of woman he wants, from a journalist's perspective, I wish you could see him. Every single guy has the same reaction as the mental image materializes. He breaks eye contact, trying to put her into words. He pauses for a second, just to figure out where to start. And then he proceeds to gush in admiration of the EG.

He *knows*. If all things were equal, and he didn't have needs to be met before he could pursue such a woman, he *knows* exactly who he would choose—or will, someday, in his mind. She might vary slightly, depending on the guy—blonde or brunette, curvy or slender—but she is so often similar in all the ways we'd expect. Smart, pretty, successful, independent, assertive, strong-willed, educated, good. She motivates him to be a better—or really, the best—version of himself.

So he tells me he wants this amazing woman. He tells me he wants *you*. And then you know the frequent ending…He proceeds to push you away. The very sight of you makes him question if he's worthy, or "ready." He's swimming in discomfort—maybe he won't be able to keep you satisfied; maybe a better guy is going to swoop in and steal you away; maybe it's all too much to handle right now. He feels slightly emasculated by your independence, and oftentimes kinda useless, leaving him listless without an obvious purpose.

Psychologist Marisa T. Cohen tells me that a man doesn't usually realize any of this as he's fleeing the scene. A woman doesn't realize this either, as she's being emotionally locked out. She's just dumbfounded that every guy she likes seems to tell her that she is exactly what he wants, and then shuts down the relationship before she can figure out how it all went south.

A lot of dating books will tell you that men are not intimidated by you, that men know what they want—and if he's walking away or acting standoffish, what he wants is not you. Those books will tell you that your standards are too high, and perhaps you should "settle." That you're too independent, too strong, too self-assured.

I would never tell you to be less. But I am going to encourage you to date better for this modern age. And I am going to explain how to date better and smarter in a way that's entirely authentic to all that you are; if he doesn't like you for who you are, as you are, you are going to show him the door.

I will explain cultural trends and research in a way that makes sense in the real world, not just in a lab. I will tell you what men have told me about who they want, what they need, who they pursue, and why they end up with the women they do. And lastly, I will finally give you all the answers you want about why you're single, answers that you've never really gotten before.

You, my dear, are that End Goal prospect—a smart, successful, pulled-together woman who inspires awe and intrigue (and discomfort or fear) in the hearts of men.

Together, we will find your match. But you're going to need to do some emotional work, figure out what you're *really* looking for in a relationship, and have the courage to be vulnerable in finding it. If you're not up for that, put the book down. You could be doing better things with your time.

Still with me? All right. Let's go.

part two

\* \* \*

# IT TAKES
# TWO

CHAPTER 3

· · · · · · · · · ·

# don't look back in anger: the profiles

"I just don't get it." So many of my female interviewees repeated this line that it could have been the title of this book. Single women always expressed some level of confusion over promising dating prospects who ghosted, ended the relationship, or slowly faded back until the women were forced to deliver the final blow.

The great news is, deep down, you know yourself and what you want. You sense interest. You can feel potential. I don't have to tell you when there's no connection. That's the beauty of the modern "full-package" woman; you're just not hung up on guys who aren't giving you the time of day, who will never work out in a million years. We've all had plenty of those "meh" first dates, and quickie relationships that fizzled as fast as they started. Prospects aren't rare! You've got a life to live, and too many men with legitimate potential to discover.

Therefore, what you *really* want to know is what happened with those guys you felt a *real* connection with. Why did they keep distancing, disappear on you, or have this complete inability to have a functional relationship? Why didn't connection win out? Those are the guys who keep you up at night.

You are not delusional; the connection was there, and it will be again with new guys as you continue to date and form relationships. It took me years to "get it"—and now, I'm going to share everything with you.

First and foremost, I need you to be able to identify and understand different types of men in the dating pool. I also want you to identify, understand, and contextualize relationships (and significant nonrelationships) from your past. To do that, we need to set the second piece of our puzzle into place: the profiles.

I discovered a lot while interviewing, organizing, and writing this book. I found that those men with whom you feel the most "connection" tend to fall into four key groups—which I'm about to describe in detail. Once you've read the profiles, you're going to have this whole male backstory of modern dating crystallized in your mind. From that moment on, all sorts of men will pass through your life. You'll flirt, you'll go out, you'll hook up, you'll pair off, but in the back of your mind you're going to have this secret knowledge that will help you take the agency back in your relationships.

I ultimately want you to know *how to navigate* the dating scene—but first, I need you to know why some men behave the way they do, so that you know what kind of guy you're dealing with at any given moment. It is the foundation of the system.

I expect you to feel *all the emotions* while reading the profiles. This section might simultaneously bum you out and make you feel understood (finally!). I hope you'll get a little closure on some men you just could not figure out, and feel excited that great possibilities *do* exist out there. I want you to take careful notes the whole way. Life is a mystery, but there are predictive variables that can impact the outcome. We can see those coming. We can learn the signs and choose how to invest and proceed.

## My Process

I researched this book extensively. In addition to talking with researchers, analyzing recent studies and data, taking a look at classic social science (and projecting how new findings would impact it), I also interviewed over 100 men and women in depth.

The field was varied, but all my interviewees are career men and women who have dealt with new dynamics in this modern romantic landscape. Their ages fall across the 20s, 30s, and 40s, and are geographically diverse; areas all over the United States (and even some international locales) are represented. I talked to a mix of frustrated singles, confused daters, serial daters, serial monogamists, happy couples, and those stellar modern-day couples who met and married the loves of their lives.

The interview process was dynamic. I kept in contact with everyone over my months of research and writing. I wanted each chat to feel like a conversation; I asked tons of questions, shared a little about myself (and my dating life), and let the talk roll like we were old friends. I interviewed married and serious couples together and apart, so I was often able to identify the concepts that made them work so well (or not). I even held some roundtables, where I let men, or men and women, bat around theories and open up about their complicated feelings. I also gave daters a little relevant insight into their problems, and feedback on how it all worked together in today's grand view of relationships.

Beyond that, I also talked about relationships nonstop with interested friends, acquaintances, and strangers for two years. People were rapt. I had whole parties, tables, and rooms asking me questions, telling me stories, and ultimately propelling me closer to the puzzle pieces that fed the foundational principles of this book. This convinced me of one superamazing theory: Young men and women want to build healthy, lasting relationships.

As I identified some major problems and setbacks of daters, and the solutions found within the successful couples' stories, I hadn't realized exactly what I'd done in revealing just a little bit of info about my book and its modern concepts to my single-and-dating interviewees. The small bits of feedback I gave daters were actually vital. It wasn't by any means exhaustive. But most of them took what they learned, applied it to their lives, and ran with it. I was completely blown away by what they said in our follow-up conversations.

One guy told me that our talk helped him to actually deal with the emotions he hadn't yet processed from his first major breakup (almost a decade before!), and that he now feels less jaded and freaked-out about dating moving forward. One busy professional woman was inspired to take a more active role in her dating life, actually showing signs of interest to the men she encountered. An Ivy League student felt encouraged to take a leap of faith and try a long-distance relationship with the only guy in years she felt was worth her time. Another man broke up with his girlfriend of one year; after our talk, he realized something *was* really missing—and he believed "it" really *was* out there. Yet another man realized his flaws in communication, where his relationships were going awry, and that a little more feedback and chill could go a long way. Another couple, a pair I immediately pegged as healthy and stellar together, ended up getting engaged by the time I polished off the final draft of this book.

While results ranged, there was one common thread: positivity. Understanding had helped them feel better about their romantic lives, their past problems, and the promising results on the horizon for them.

## What I Want You to Take Away

I'm all for taking action, but not without "getting it" first.

Ultimately, I want to teach you a new skill set for navigating this modern relationship landscape; that is why we're here. But first and foremost, I want to highlight a simple lesson gleaned from my single interviewees—ultimately, the beta testers of this book's earliest insights and applications.

Understanding their personal relationship problems, in the context of new issues impacting the dating landscape today, *completely changed* their attitudes toward modern love. They were often able to put their past behind them and move forward, recognizing just what they were dealing with out there. Not one came back to me more jaded. If anything, they were reenergized—even months after our first conversation.

That's the magic of understanding. That's why I'm going to force you to revisit your past. That's why the profiles are so darn important, and we have to trudge through them before we can get to the meat. If you can finally understand your history, and "get" modern men, you can finally move on from those guys who hurt or disappointed you—and you'll recognize their biggest stumbling blocks to full-fledged commitment forever after.

Better yet, you can actually move forward armed with a brighter outlook on relationships, and the tools to create the love you want.

## CHAPTER 4

# meet the almost boyfriend

**Almost Boyfriend,** *n.*—a guy who looks like a boyfriend, acts like a boyfriend, and kinda treats you like a girlfriend, but, for some reason, is failing to fully commit to an exclusive relationship.

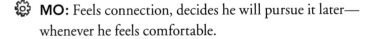

    **MO:** Feels connection, decides he will pursue it later— whenever he feels comfortable.

    **Category:** Not ready

    **Emotional Investment:** Minimal to moderate

✳ ✳ ✳

**The long game,** *n.*—going slow to ensure long-term success, instead of rushing the process and risking a poor outcome; in dating and relationships, men often "play the long game" with special women (a.k.a. End Goals) when they really don't want to screw it up.

✳ ✳ ✳

You know what they say: "If it looks like a duck, walks like a duck, and quacks like a duck, it's an Almost Boyfriend." Wait. They don't say that? Well, they should, because you know this boyfriend look-alike as "the man with whom I'm in some kind of nonrelationship."

It gets emotionally close but not physically close. Or physically close, but he puts the brakes on his emotional progress whenever you're poised to get deeper. He will act as a stand-in boyfriend for key parts of a relationship without ever progressing to full-blown relationship status. He tries to impress you—but it's like he's laying the groundwork for something when you'd rather he simply ask you out.

The most important piece of this puzzle is that he retains the license to be single, do some growing up, and—in his mind—still not disappoint you (much). He doesn't feel ready for the great potential of your connection, but he also doesn't want to let you go completely. So he invests in small doses, from a safe distance. He may or may not be telling you this, but you will see it in his distant-y behavior.

There are basically unlimited variations of this dude, and you may meet them almost every day and not know it—the guy who *almost* asked you out at the coffee shop, the guy who talked to you all night at a party and *almost* got your number. (*Eh*, they think. *Maybe someday!*) These are the guys most of your girlfriends would classically tell you are "intimidated" by you. Which isn't necessarily true. He's just playing a longer game with your type, until he readies himself to be the guy he would want you to have.

Most importantly, when an Almost Boyfriend sticks around in your life, there is some layer of real connection there—and I want to emphasize this, because there will be a whole peanut gallery of people telling you, "Let him go, sweetheart." That's a choice that may or may not be right for you.

He either lets you know how special you are, or treats you in ways he would never treat a casual hookup or a friend, which is why you hold out for him to get his sh*t together—or at least to get a clarification on what is happening. Because it feels SO CLOSE.

## The Orbiter

Jaime split with her longtime boyfriend when they both decided on different paths. She wanted to go to residency and follow her dreams;

he wanted to settle in the South and begin a career in politics. Her winding road took her to a city in the Midwest for the next leg of her training, and there she met Abe—a friend of a friend.

It was clear they were into each other from the get-go. Abe was also the breath of fresh air Jaime needed. Whereas her ex was a Southern-bred law school grad, desiring a traditional marriage and settled life-style, Abe was "a Midwestern, nerdy, hipster computer programmer" who, like Jaime, clung tight to egalitarian ideals. "I thought that would be a great fit, *long-term* long-term," she explains. "He was so supportive. He would never expect me to stay at home."

The pair quietly grew closer over the course of a couple months, and they seemed like a rare pair who might *easily* edge into more serious territory. But then one night as they were hanging out at Jaime's place, she decided to tell Abe how excited she was about him. They were *so* aligned, and *so* in sync (albeit undefined), she didn't see a reason to hold back—and thought an open, honest discussion about feelings might bring them even closer. Eek, no. "Everything was going great—but after that, he became so distant," she explains.

Eventually, Abe told Jaime that he "wasn't there yet." Jaime accepted this, based on his post-talk behavior, but she was also confused; she knew she wasn't imagining the strong connection. After all, they were spending *almost all their free time together*. They stopped seeing each other romantically, but, weirdly, Abe just never stopped coming around. "He still made an effort to be involved in my life," she says. "He started to shovel my driveway when it snowed. He would offer to do me favors. He even lent me his car when mine broke down."

Jaime started seeing other people—she describes a guy who was her plus-one to a couple weddings, some more insignificant encounters. Still, Abe was the most constant guy on the *periphery* of her life. She'd encounter him at group hangouts; he'd make kind gestures. He'd even start to hint sometimes that he "made a mistake" cooling things off with Jaime, while *also* repeating that "he needed to make more than one hundred thousand a year" to have the career he truly wanted. Hmm. "He doesn't know *what* he wants," she says. *Mhmm.*

A wise woman, Jamie is fully prepared to continue on her personal journey. Next stop? Her first real post-training job. (Yay!) Meanwhile, Abe is still in her orbit. "He's like this non-relationship relationship," the 30-year-old explains. She keeps taking his phone calls, too—but she's moving forward, letting him make any moves in her direction.

## The Shy Guy

Former DC dweller Zoe met her Almost Boyfriend at a popular gym among a sea of young singles in Oxford, England. "I always go around happy hour time, and so does he," the 25-year-old film school graduate says. "It's like a jungle."

Colt was cute and sweet, and he started acknowledging Zoe each day they'd cross paths. He'd always seem to hang around while she was lifting weights or running on the treadmill. For, like, months and months. Finally, in the summertime, Colt got up the gumption to (kind of) approach.

"I saw him as I was lifting, over in the corner checking his phone," Zoe says. "So eventually he comes over, and I'm thinking, 'This is it.'" The big ask-out?! "He says, 'Hey! Are you going to be doing cardio tomorrow like you usually do?' And I say, 'Yeah!' And he goes, 'Great. Uh, maybe I'll see you!' I literally facepalmed when he walked away."

Zoe was still 99 percent sure he had some sort of interest in her (duh), but she was 100 percent confused about his game plan.

Eventually, Colt did ask for Zoe's email, and they exchanged notes for two months. While Colt was vacationing with his family in the north of England, he finally asked her out. "It was buried in the fourth paragraph, but we did go out to this nice restaurant and bar," she says. "We had a great time...but there was no physical contact. He didn't offer to give me his arm while I was teetering around in heels, and he didn't kiss me."

*Okay, this isn't a problem, right? Clearly, the guy is shy,* she thought. *Maybe he just needs a signal?* Zoe's inner dialogue was throwing questions around like crazy. She was willing to roll with it—and everything would have been fine had Colt kissed her on any of the additional eight dates they went on over the next two months.

I had to ask Zoe how *sure* she was that they were romantically a thing. "My friend asked me that, too!" she exclaims, trying to make me see she is not delusional. "I'm totally sure. We have great conversations. We talk about the future. We dress up, we go out—he always pays."

Zoe insists she is not the type to make a first move. But after she'd spent months on Colt, she decided to put it out there after one of these probably-dates. "We exit the restaurant," she says, "and he asks me if I want to take a walk. I say yes—and since I'm in heels, I use this as the perfect excuse to ask for his arm, which he gladly gives me."

Zoe says Colt appeared pretty pleased at this turn of events. So they kept walking around a scenic park area, and finally, all the way back to her car. "We totally pause at the car, for a good long while," she insists. This is it, right? Clarity! "And after all that, he *still* doesn't kiss me," she says. "I get in the car, call my best friend, and I'm *freaking out*."

Her friend told her to chill out, maybe it was an English thing. But after one more attempt to force Colt's hand—a movie night, which ended in a kissless cuddle sesh at his place—Zoe was ready to throw in the towel. He also seemed to be distancing after she dropped hints that she'd really like to see him more than once a week; he acknowledged her request but didn't make good on it.

He did, however, accompany her to a formal dinner party when she invited him, charming all her friends at the party. We wish we could blame youthful inexperience here, too, but Colt is 40.

Just call it "The Curious Case of an EG and Her Shy Guy."

## The Guy Who Can't Grow Up

Kristine has known her Almost Boyfriend for 12 years. At first, I didn't think that number could possibly be real. "We met in college in Arizona," she says. "We were at our apartment complex pool, where it's like spring break all the time. My best friend, Laura, had met her now-husband, Tom, a couple weeks earlier, and Parker was his best friend."

At first, Parker wasted no time. "He came over, introduced himself, and asked me out," she says. "And he was *so* my type. We'd go on dates, and he was always kind of possessive. He'd always put his arm around me and keep me close. But he was not my boyfriend."

Parker never wanted to label it. "After a few months, he didn't want to commit," she says. "He 'wasn't ready.'" This pseudorelationship dance between Kristine and Parker went on for years. "I even had a boyfriend for a couple years, and he was not happy about it," she says. "But when we broke up and I gave him the chance to make a move, he still was not ready."

So, they entered a phase of friendship. Kristine moved back home out East, while Parker, now an entrepreneur, stayed in Arizona. When Kristine visited, she'd stay with Parker. They'd also talk on the phone frequently to keep up with each other's lives. Interestingly, Parker had just taken a new job in LA when Kristine decided to move back to Scottsdale. "He told me, 'Do you remember eight years ago when you wanted me to be your boyfriend? I'm ready now,'" she says. But they were living in different cities. Cruel world.

However, Parker didn't just drop it. He was finally in his early 30s and settling into life—and he wanted Kristine in it. "He said he didn't think we should give up on a relationship together," she explains. "He had always seen himself with me someday." This time, Kristine put her foot down. "My grandma had just died," she says. "I had just moved back to Arizona. I told him it just was not the time." Men aren't the only ones who get to claim bad timing.

The two did not talk to each other for around six months, Kristine guesses, but Parker eventually began to test the waters over text and phone. "We have this chemistry," she says. "Intellectual, emotional, and physical. We love the same things in life. We're both entrepreneurs. We're both very active. We're ideologically aligned."

But Parker has always had a wild side. It prevented them from getting together in college, and it's given Kristine, now also in her 30s, major pause. Case in point? She recently went out to LA for a bachelorette party, and Parker excitedly asked to plan dinner and drinks with her the next night. She agreed but warned him she was looking for a calm evening before her early flight the following morning.

Over the course of the night, Parker got wasted. Kristine slipped out the restaurant's back door near the bathrooms, called herself an Uber back to the hotel—no explanation. Kristine's mind immediately gravitated toward Luke, her *other* Almost Boyfriend back in Maryland. "We also have *seven* years of history," she explains. "He's the most amazing, respectful guy. He's smart, he comes from a good family."

The only problem? Kristine hesitates. "He spends more time on the couch watching football than any guy I've ever met," she says. "Our hobbies, lifestyles, and political affiliations differ. I like to travel, explore—and he's very vanilla. His motto is 'I'll do me, you do you.'" Kristine has always imagined doing life *with* her partner. For her, there's no sizzle-pop pursuing her passions solo instead of coupled.

## The Longtime Friend

Carli and Walker met when they were in kindergarten. At five years old! Adorably enough, Carli says, "Walker told his mom that he didn't mind going to school so much, because I was there." Aww.

The two had sporadic communication during middle school and high school, until they were thrown together in the same friend group. "He was very funny," says Carli. "He was always joking around. And we were friends; we would hang out from time to time, and were back in touch, but he had a girlfriend and I had a boyfriend."

The years passed, and both went their separate ways for college, but they'd always head back to their hometown for holidays and breaks and would sometimes see each other when they were around. The two even tried dating, although Carli says it ended in a matter of weeks. Walker did not have his life together, she recalls; he was still smoking cigarettes (of which she was not a fan), still trying to get through school, and was *not* in hot pursuit of this EG. Which was perfectly fine with her at the time. Both were headed back to classes at their respective schools anyway.

Walker settled down with a girlfriend at his college, while Carli continued to explore her options—even while Walker was hanging out in the back of her mind. Then, Walker and his girlfriend broke up, and he joined Facebook for the first time, where he added Carli. As it turned out, both were getting their own apartments in different areas of New York City. That's when subtle moves were made.

First came one happy hour. Then another. Walker came over to check out Carli's new apartment and "accidentally" grabbed her keys, which meant he had to come see her yet again. "Every time I was in Queens, I'd let him know," she says. "And he always wanted to see me. This happened over several months." But there was no movement on the relationship front. What on earth was going on?

Don't forget about Carli. We'll get back to her later.

## What You Can Learn from an Almost Boyfriend

Almost Boyfriends are an enigma—they often create distance with semireasonable excuses, but they're also selectively receptive to you. They stay in touch if you'll let them—but not *too* often. Or if you stay in touch, they'll respond positively—just not *too* positively or for *too* long. They'll want to keep tabs on you, because they maybe-sorta want to be your boyfriend down the road. You know. When they're "ready."

### Traits of an Almost Boyfriend

- You have a natural rapport with this person.
- He feels like your friend first—and any physical benefits that may or may not be happening are secondary, often innocent.
- He has unsettled business in his life—grad school to finish, a new job to settle into, a potential move on the horizon, wild oats to sow, a recent breakup, and so on.
- He's transient. Maybe his work requires him to travel a lot, or he's not sure where he's going to be in, like, six months.

- He is protective of you, both physically and emotionally. He has your back.
- He's not the most confident guy in the whole world *around you*. Either he's cocky (faux confidence) and constantly listing his résumé or positive qualities, or he's humble (building confidence) and seems oversensitive to signs of "rejection" from you.

## An Almost Boyfriend Will...

- Take you out on date-like activities, like out to dinner or to a play, but won't hint that these activities are in fact actual dates.
- Frequently pay for your tickets, dinners, drinks, etc.
- Do "couples things" with you, like going to Whole Foods or putting Ikea furniture together—or even, dare I say, cuddling.
- Drop everything—often, if not always—to spend time with you whenever you're in the same vicinity. It doesn't matter whether he's with a pack of girls or his buddies.
- Seem reluctant to make a physical move on you. Or if you once briefly shared that sort of connection, the physical side will die as you transition into a weird spot in the friend zone.
- Flirt with you only subtly, at best—as in, sometimes you ask yourself, *Was he flirting with me?*
- Seem nervous whenever you first meet up to hang out or if he notices you out at random.
- Distance himself whenever he feels too close to the cusp of a real relationship—he may ignore texts and phone calls, or blow off get-togethers.
- Indicate he's "not ready" if you discuss the nature of your relationship, or actively drop hints about how busy he is at work and how he has no time for a personal life.
- Act like your boyfriend, to the point that people mistake you for a couple or see this great connection. You have to tell a million people that no, you're not dating.

## How to Deal When He Seems Unsure

There are all kinds of Almost Boyfriends out there—from the former jock who thinks you're too smart for him, to the nerdy coworker who thinks you're too cool, to the up-and-comer who's panicked about settling down before he's "explored his options." The reason for his reluctance doesn't really matter, and if you don't know it already, you're not going to completely figure him out—no matter how much time you spend on it. But you can let this unsure guy approach you in a way that's comfortable to him, while you keep doing your thing in life.

You are an aspirational match for this man, and frankly, he doesn't want to screw it up—so he is waiting to fully *grow up* and *feel confident* before pursuing you. So when he says he's too busy to grab dinner (three weeks in a row) or turns down an offer to be your plus-one to that great show you have tickets to, citing [insert lame excuse here], I want you to be gracious. You're not going to act any more formidable than the woman he already imagines you to be.

Once this reluctant guy passes into the Almost Boyfriend bucket— you have solid evidence he has discounted himself enough to hang back, but still engages fairly thoughtfully—you're going to be friendly toward him if you still want him in your life.

Why just "be friendly"? Because this guy, in essence, has either friend-zoned himself, or allowed you to put him there. The friend zone is a respectable place—in fact, some guys put the *best* girls there. So spend roughly as much time on him as you might on a new friend or acquaintance, but not nearly as much energy as on a legit dating prospect. While you should never bank on unsure things, research does show us that the tides can eventually turn with this guy. But forcing the issue up front isn't going to get you there any quicker, because becoming your Almost Boyfriend is not only about liking you or being attracted to you. It's about respecting you, even if he isn't flawless in showing that. If he's going to pursue you, he will need to do so feeling like he can keep you around—which means developing a certain kind of comfort in himself, and in your connection.

As there are many mixed emotions with you, EG, he may or may not even be actively aware of how much he likes you romantically. There's a psychological phenomenon called "the mere exposure effect," where people tend to develop a preference for things as they become more familiar with them.[1] So if your Almost Boyfriend isn't as confident as you'd like him to be at first, he may feel better approaching a relationship with you over time. "In studies that deal with interpersonal attraction, the more often a person sees someone, the more pleasing and likeable they tend to rate them," dating expert Susan Walsh says, something she says has "enormous implications for dating."

In analyzing research on exposure and attraction, Walsh writes that familiarity breeds tons of positive effects: finding common ground to bond over; repeated responsiveness, including encouragement, support and humor; mutual self-disclosure, which brings you closer; feeling liked, and thus liking the person more in return; less critical views of any one interaction; and feelings of comfort and safety.[2] Men must feel this like you must feel this.

The more often you're around the guys in your Almost Boyfriend pool, the less intimidating you will seem—and, yes, the more you may like them and get to figure out if they could one day be your boyfriend. If you're unconvinced, look at this multipart 2015 University of Texas research from the journal *Psychological Science*.[3] These scientists rounded up 167 couples and determined how long they'd known each other before making it official. Roughly 40 percent of the couples included in the study were friends before dating.

That's a lot! So first lesson: Chill out, let him be friends with you, and don't get passive-aggressive if he goes slow. Just get to know him. Show him you're not scary—you're actually superfun, and you love hanging out with him as a person.

Some really decent guys need extra time to gear themselves up for a relationship with you. Case in point: The researchers in the 2015 Texas study had a bunch of strangers rank each half of the partner pairings on attractiveness to get the most objective measures possible. The results? Couples ranking close together on objective attractiveness tended to make it official much quicker—in under a month; those with a larger gap in objective attractiveness typically took longer to couple up, around nine months.

The researchers ultimately discovered that getting to know someone changed individuals' views of a given person. Perhaps some men know this on an innate level. In analyzing how the study might play out IRL, psychologist Dylan Selterman, PhD,[4] writes that one implication of this research "might be that the best strategy to date someone 'out of your league' is to become friends with them first and be patient. One of my childhood friends calls this 'playing the long game.'" Selterman notes that we don't really know how effective a strategy this is, but hey. You might not even know a guy is doing that. (Until now, of course.)

Here's *my* biggest takeaway for you: Everyone is aware of objective attractiveness. Visible markers like looks, intelligence, status, career, and popularity with the opposite sex might cause a guy to subconsciously grade you "out of his league." Objective measures might make an Almost Boyfriend wary, but they don't account for our individual preferences *at all*. You may think his nerdy side is extremely sexy or his awkwardness is adorable, or may not care that he's not totally figured out his life, but it may take him a while to convince *himself* that you're totally into him regardless.

If your objective rank is a little higher—hey, whatever. Get to know him at a steady pace. Be friendly. Be present. Be enthusiastic about spending time together. You may convince him you're not just passing time hanging out with him, waiting around for a guy who "looks the part" to show up. As shown by the UT study, *time* allows for real connection and individual attraction to grow.

## Meet the Back-Burner Prospect, a.k.a. YOU

You might not need much of an explanation for this phenomenon here if you've ever chased (or been towed along by) an Almost Boyfriend. To illustrate the Back-Burner Prospect, let me point to a 2014 study from Hope College.[5] The research was actually devised by a guy who admitted he kept women as "back burners" himself back in grad school.[6] I know that sounds bad, but stay with me here.

The study defines such a back burner as "a person to whom one is not presently committed, and with whom one maintains some degree of communication, in order to keep or establish the possibility of future romantic and/or sexual involvement." Single people have them. Coupled-up people have them. *You* probably have them, if you're totally honest with yourself. The point is, people keep the door open for something romantic or sexual *later*.

Just because you're on the back burner does not mean a guy doesn't value you. Later, I am going to show you an Almost Boyfriend who feels a stronger connection to you, his Back-Burner Prospect, than to his actual dates. Sometimes, he's not sure he's ready for the full-blown commitment that is you, or that he's evolved far enough from his baser instincts to "settle down." Sometimes, a guy knows a relationship with you is the absolute best dish on his menu—but it'll take the longest to cook, and he's whisking and tasting other pots of stew in the meantime.

However, I want you to be real with yourself when confronting whether "he's just not that into you." Most of this centers around three questions:

1. Is there a nonphysical connection and chemistry (mental and emotional)?
2. Do you feel like he respects you?
3. Is the pace *slow*, and is it building?

An Almost Boyfriend is not a hookup buddy. He resides in that weird corner of the friend zone where the electrical current runs high and sparks keep flying. Which is why I want you to pay attention and ask yourself:

"Is he basically friend-zoning himself, or allowing me to friend-zone him? Does he want to hang out with me doing nonphysical activities, while *occasionally* showing signs he feels more?"

If the answer is yes, then relax for a while; he wants to know you as a person. The friend zone is a perfectly respectable place for a guy to be—as long as it's not driving you nuts.

New York City–based entrepreneur Nathan, 30, is one such example of a man who keeps high-quality back burners around—and one of my more insightful male interviewees. He has been in all kinds of relationships, and in his mind, the women who pass through his life have different levels of meaning—some he's just getting to know, others he knows on a deeper level and there's some spark, and some he'd consider long-term relationships with (maybe). Each relationship is different and has fluctuating levels of significance.

While technically single, Nathan has an "ecosystem" of relationships at different stages—he's getting to know women. Nathan is in no rush to settle down, or even find one specific relationship or person. He seeks to be transparent if something changes with one of the women he's seeing, but he's aware that the nature of our ever-in-flux lives means that dating today isn't really about dating.

It's about getting to know people, forming relationships that matter, and letting life unfold. You have to trust that when you meet a potential right person at a potential right time, you both are going to recognize that and be able to push play on a relationship that mutually suits your long-term goals. "If your goals are very clear, there's no reason to compromise on them," Nathan says, insightfully. "But there are hundreds of ways to get there."

I want you to learn to breathe in ambiguity and let men categorize themselves—but also to relax a little and learn that good things take time. "Successful women want the science to predict how things are going to play out, and the indicators of a potential good partner," Nathan observes. "But I think one of the most vital skills in life is flexing the muscle of development that is 'not knowing.'"

As hard as it may seem for a type A woman, if you can get used to not knowing, you're going to expand your pool of options. (I didn't say this was going to be easy.)

## CHAPTER 5

# meet the disappearing act

**Disappearing Act,** *n.*—a guy with whom you have an incredible been-waiting-forever-for-this connection, who suddenly exits stage left with little to no explanation or closure.

⚙ **MO:** Doesn't feel he can balance a strong connection with his goals, and breaks things off.

🗂 **Category:** Not ready

💰 **Emotional Investment:** None

\* \* \*

The woman who does not require validation from anyone is
the most feared individual on the planet.
—Mohadesa Najumi

\* \* \*

You're swiping on an app. Or maybe you're at a friend's party. Or perhaps you're hanging out at a bar downtown. In any case, you spot a handsome blond prospect. He's got hair with flow, a polished sense of style, and you could see yourself being kind of into him. After mutually matching, lingering by the guacamole in his vicinity, or grabbing a drink near the side of the bar where he's hanging out, you two start chatting.

You don't talk that long, but you think he seems okay. So, you trade numbers and schedule a date for the following week—because meeting for drinks with a cute guy who shares your weird, offbeat views of the political landscape cannot possibly be the worst Thursday of your life, right?

When Thursday rolls around, it's one of the best Thursdays of your life. You find you have eerily similar small-town upbringings, and wind up trading stories with an emphatic sense of understanding. He does the most spot-on impression of your celebrity crush you've ever heard in your life, and you almost spit your beer out at least three times. He's so well-read (real hardcovers!), and has a million suggestions for your next trip to the library. He can even discuss existentialism without falling asleep on you, unlike your last boyfriend.

This date is so good that it turns into a marathon: You go until four in the morning (work be damned). You meet up three more times the following week, then have an awesome Saturday night the following weekend. And did I mention the chemistry? It's as if your intellectual discussions combusted the moment you touched.

Sometimes, this magic lasts for days or weeks of awesome dates. Other times, it lasts for months, all the way into the Realm of Official Coupledom. But suddenly, out of nowhere, there is a silently seismic shift. It is almost imperceptible at first, but you begin to sense its impacts undermining the strength of your connection.

He takes a bit too long to reply to your texts. He doesn't call you after work one day, like he normally does on his commute home. He goes out of town, and he's out of contact the whole time. His mom comes to town for the weekend, and he doesn't tell you; you find out after the fact. You start to wonder...and then, when the behavior continues, you start to worry. But since he's reassuring in all the interactions you do have with him, you try to put it out of your mind.

Until he does one of two things: He ghosts you, or he abruptly breaks it off. This is the whiplash nature of a Disappearing Act, where everything is going well—until it's not.

## The Ghosting Guy

Claire is a 32-year-old talent agent in NYC. She's whip-smart, assertive, and articulate, in a bubbly sponge-for-information sort of way. She's the girl you grab lattes with once a month, because your schedules are so packed, and there never seems to be enough time to catch up.

Like any New York City girl, Claire has had her fair share of… experiences. There was the Tinder guy who invited her to the bar beneath his apartment, then said he was too tired to venture downstairs for drinks. Then there was the man she dated for four months—who eventually told her one night over chocolate and red wine that he'd been seeing another girl for six months and was "not giving her up." For real.

She has a befuddled, slightly resigned stance on the whole dating debacle. "You could drop me in a room of eight hundred guys and I'd be able to pick out the ones who are Jewish, emotionally unavailable, and would be into me," she laughs.

But all kidding aside, there's one type of guy that Claire can't get over, after the type of scarring experience a bunch of women have had in the age of apps and ADD. Claire's biggest struggle has nothing to do with looks, nothing to do with career, and everything to do with connection. "These men are so amazing, because they just *get* you," she says. "You're on the date and you think, 'This is perfect!' "

Claire recalls her most recent failed prospect, whom she met through friends of friends. He "got" her. They laughed and had an awesome time having drinks on their first date. He even said, "Wow, Claire. You're the full package!"

Although she was skeptical of her handsome, witty suitor at first, things continued to go well. She went out with him a few times and decided to just enjoy the ride. By the end of the third date, she was starting to feel like a believer. "The connection was so great," she says. "Deep down I was like, 'This could be the dude.'" Cue the parade! The streamers! The confetti! But also, maybe not.

When date number 4 came around, however, the vibe was off. Claire felt this guy was acting "weird" when she arrived five to ten minutes late, after fighting Midtown traffic during rush hour on a Friday. He was slightly passive-aggressive as they grabbed drinks, and, although they talked about a date the following Saturday, she never heard from him. Poof.

It's not hard to see why Claire and a slew of other women are ready to tear their hair out. "The ghosting is so bad here—men just suddenly bail," Claire says of New York dating. "It's to the point where, if I don't hear from a guy when I think I should, I assume that's what is happening." She estimates that 60 percent of guys simply ghost their way out of a developing relationship, often even when she really feels a genuine, immediate spark. "It's really confusing. You think they really get you and like you," she explains. "All of a sudden, they're gone, and it feels like none of that is good enough. It is so much worse when you think they really 'get you,' and then, peace out."

This is the nature of dating today, perhaps especially for EGs. It's also not new. I remember once talking to my dad about a woman he went out with three or four times back when he was a single guy. He was maybe, like, 24 years old (he met my mom at 25!). He said she was smart, she was pretty, she was kind, she had a career. She was, by all accounts, a full-package woman.

But when it came time to call her for that fourth or fifth date, his fingers were rendered inept. "And the crazy thing was, she had obviously agreed to go out with me a bunch of times before," he told me. "But for whatever reason, I just couldn't pick up the phone and ask her out." He describes the sensation as a lingering mix of anxiety and self-doubt—and my dad is a baby boomer, y'all.

Things have gotten increasingly worse with Gen Xers and millennials, and the "options" that fill each metropolitan oasis. (Don't even get me started on poor Gen Z.) Every early date goes so well, or so you think in your head, until it's suddenly *not*. The guy you had such a great connection with suddenly ghosts and goes MIA. Or he decides he's not ready for something serious. Or he starts pursuing someone else. Or [insert your favorite excuse here].

## The Shoe-Drop Dude

Caroline is a 30-year-old Boston woman who is hardworking and career-focused and has "a full life." She travels. She spends time with friends and does yoga. Her default setting is busy. "Some weeks, I don't even have time to go grocery shopping," she says. That said, she puts in the time for dating, even though it's been unfruitful.

Since breaking up with her boyfriend of three years, she's struggled to find something that sticks. She's tried all the apps and online dating websites, all of which resulted in guys who've "dissipated" after two months. "It is frustrating," she explains. "It's almost like if it's not immediately perfect, they bail. I've had first dates that I thought went really well, but the guy never called." Caroline has inoculated herself against the blows of modern dating, and she preaches, "It ain't personal" over and over again.

What women, and men, are looking for is the elusive, capital S Spark—and after years of dating online, Caroline finally found it. Some guy had messaged her online roughly three or four weeks before our first chat. "He wouldn't have initially caught my eye at all, but it was the best first date I'd had in years," she recalls. "It was such a great, natural back-and-forth. Things were going so well we ended up going back to his place to have a beer on the roof deck. But he was super-respectful about it!"

The next date? Caroline says it "was even better." This is the moment Caroline allowed herself to hope—somewhere in the middle of that second date. It's the moment you've waited your whole dating life for. Caroline (and women everywhere) think, in Claire's words, *This could be the dude.*

They were lying on the lawn in downtown Boston under the stars (I kid you not), having a great conversation, when Dream Guy leaned over and whispered, "It's just not a good time right now."

Wait. Whaaa?

Naturally, Caroline's emotional trajectory came to a screeching halt, and she spaced out for a hot second. Upon her asking for clarification, he said, "If we'd have met six months from now, things would be different." And along came an ambling explanation: He was still figuring out his life in Boston. He calmly explained the demands of his new job, and that he knew his time would be very limited.

Dream Guy said that he knew what this was, he knew what kind of connection they had, and he knew that his job would put a strain on their bond. "You will resent me and you will end up hating me," he said.

Caroline walked a mile back to the train. She then UberPooled the rest of the way home, crying the whole time. Allowing yourself to embrace something good, after multiple years of ho-hum dates and ghosting guys, and then having *this* happen? Yeah, that sucks.

So Caroline went home and slept on it. After thinking it over, she wanted a few more clarifications and perhaps a little more closure. She didn't want to leave any stone unturned. "I have my own life," she says. "I like my own space. I travel a lot for work, and I work late often. The older you get, I feel like you become less needy. You have less need to be a constant unit. I am put-together, but I really am low-maintenance."

So she emailed him the next day. Caroline said all the aforementioned things. She said she'd still like to get to know him, and that she didn't feel they needed to completely sever ties. And his reply was yet another disappointing blow. "He said he'd just moved here two weeks ago, and was really just looking to meet people while online dating," she says. (As in, not *fall for* someone with whom he felt real feels.) He said he did not wish to stay in touch.

Caroline still talks about this guy with a sense of defeat. After meeting enough guys with whom she's felt connections—that handful, those magic few—she is constantly insulating herself against disappointment. She, and *tonnnns* of other End Goal women.

Over time, Caroline has come to anticipate the wreckage. She is now conditioned to think that when sparks fly, disappointment follows. "I'm always waiting for the other shoe to drop," she says.

## The Whiplash Guy

Imagine you're dating. You're rolling through app guy after app guy, with a few friends of friends sprinkled in for good measure. You feel like you're doing everything you can, and it's stressful AF. So you take a walk through Central Park to clear your head.

Just as you're beginning to daydream about unrelated things (cupcakes! taking a run tomorrow morning!), you run into—yes, physically right into—this guy taking his dog for a walk. Your head slams directly into his chin and you start to see stars, but then you look up into the face of an angel. You blink a few times, and, no, you are not dreaming. He helps you sit down on a park bench, and you two get to talking while his corgi sits there obediently and waits.

You guys chat for hours, first on the bench and then as you walk around the park. You talk about everything, and he laughs, with his million-dollar smile and sexy five-o'clock shadow. You two have the same eclectic taste in old rock music; you both grew up in small Southern towns. He tells you he recently moved to Midtown, and you know all the best after-work spots there.

So you meet for a drink two days later. This date goes just as well. In fact, the next three or four weeks of dates go just as well. Your eventual conversation about exclusivity is a mere formality, and you're in full-blown couple status six weeks after you meet. Things go really well for the next twelve months—and you're sure, your friends are sure, this is The One. "How could he not be when you're both this happy!" your best friend says over coffee, and you can barely bite back your smile.

You think you're building a life together. And then one day, it all stops. You come home from work, and he's got all the stuff he's left at your place in a box. This is when your world comes crashing down in an instant. Deep down, you thought he was The One.

Maddy and Karl met one spring, when they were both attending college out West. They both happened to be at the same concert near campus, and they discovered that they lived in adjacent buildings. Their first date consisted of gummy bears, Snapple, and lots of talking.

"You have so much time and proximity to accelerate quickly," she says. So they started to see each other right away, just before everyone on campus disbanded for the summer.

Of course, summer sucks when you're starting to see someone you're really excited about, but Maddy knew she had a connection with Karl unlike any other guy. He wasn't like the other "artsier" guys she'd dated in the past—he was more athletic, a little more charming, just as brilliant.

She went to visit him twice near his home over summer break. "We didn't define the relationship, but we felt emotionally exclusive," she says. She didn't ask about other girls; she didn't care. She was truly in awe of this unique connection with Karl, which she was spot-on in gauging. The pair became official very soon after they returned to college in the fall. He was a senior; she was a sophomore.

Maddy remembers juggling her course load, but everything else fell by the wayside as her relationship with Karl continued to deepen. "It felt very serious, and it was great," Maddy explains of her 19-year-old mind-set. "You have this single bedroom. You sleep together every night. It was very intense. I did not do a good job balancing my friendships with the relationship. I didn't understand the reality."

Karl, however, was starting to understand. Graduation was looming, and he had job offers in hand. He was weighing the demands of his career against the demands of his relationship. There were two particularly appealing offers on the table: one out East that would put his career on the fast track, another back West, just 30 minutes from his girlfriend, who was still finishing school. Karl had suddenly stopped referencing what was to come in their relationship. "*I* was more comfortable talking about the future," Maddy recalls.

However, after Karl graduated and Maddy finished her sophomore year, the two took the Roller-Coaster Road Trip. They laughed, and they cried—or some version of that. In between fun times on the road, chatting incessantly about all their common interests, came talks of that impending future decision. "There were these periodically horrible conversations about staying together, his concerns," Maddy says. "In my mind, I'm not in college that much longer! It's two more years. If he takes the job nearby, we'll still get to see each other a fair bit. As far as I could understand it at the time, you can make it work when you want to."

They reached something of a compromise; Karl decided to take the job out East, but they agreed to stay together, which Maddy felt was "a win" for her, and the relationship was finally settled—but that was short-lived. "Karl moved me back into my apartment at school," she says. "One week later, he broke up with me over the phone." Just like that, the line snapped—and Karl was gone.

## What You Can Learn from a Disappearing Act

Whereas an Almost Boyfriend will remain in your life at a distance while working on himself and his goals, a Disappearing Act will decide he needs to completely cut off the relationship (or budding relationship), lest he be distracted and unable to achieve said goals.

After a Disappearing Act bounces, there are tons of signs you may look back on and think, *Yeah, my gut knew before my head processed it.*

### Signs You've Met a Disappearing Act

- He puts up walls—emotionally or physically. He's holding back or bottling up emotions. He's sometimes evasive.
- You sense he's stressed a lot of the time, almost contemplative, especially when you're alone together.
- You know he's about to make a major life change, like moving to a new place or starting a new career or building a business—or maybe he just made the change. He keeps discussing how it may affect your relationship.
- He struggles to be happy for your successes; you are outpacing him.
- He talks a lot about goals he wants to reach, or how he doesn't feel like he's moving toward them.

A Disappearing Act can reveal himself after the first date or deep into a relationship. Although you won't always get an explanation if the guy peaces out early on, some Disappearing Acts will explain why they're about to flee.

Bubbly, assertive 25-year-old PR gal Mila is a born-and-bred Southern belle who landed in Columbus, Ohio, for work. She went on a date with a guy who had recently moved there, too. They grabbed dinner at a sushi bar, and hopped to another bar afterward, since things were going so well. She remembers great conversation, discussing their college experiences—and she admits, yeah, she seemed slightly more established than this guy. But Mila is a modern woman; she didn't exactly care. And this guy *had a new job and was working toward his goals.* All is cool, right?

Wrong. This is where it gets dicey. "I told him I'd gotten an academic scholarship in college," she says, trying to replay the date in her mind. "And with his reaction at the time, I remember suddenly feeling like I had to play it down. Still, he seemed very interested. We had close, deep conversation—you know when a guy looks at you like you're the only one in the room?" Yes, girl. YES.

He promised to set up a date, which he never did. However, this guy did add her on Snapchat, where he proceeded to pepper her with random photos for about a week—something Mila thought was "totally annoying" in the absence of another date invite. She is also not the type of woman who sits back and waits for life to happen to her—she's a take-the-bull-by-the-horns girl, the kind who "breaks off from the group at a bar and chats up a group of guys," just to break the ice for her friends. She has been called "intimidating." She wanted answers.

So after one Snapchat too many without setting up a *real* date, she called out her nondate Snapchatter right then and there via his medium of choice. "I simply wrote, 'So when are we going on that second date?'" she says. After a *boong* pause, he replied. "He was like, 'You're successful, you're crazy-smart, and you're beautiful. And I'm just not looking for that right now.'" After Mila called him out, he was gone.

It's hard to fathom that a guy could think you're rather awesome and not want to date you. It can give you a lifelong complex and an inability to see your own value. But, in fact, the phenomenon is real. Mila is still single (and fabulous), but it's evident this moment was a bit of a *Wait, huh?!* in her book of man misfires. Mila's Disappearing Act had other needs (per Maslow) to work on.

There are endless examples of this, of guys who did not feel ready to pursue you—from the crazy-nice dude you met at your cousin's wedding who never dialed your number or responded to your friend request to the man who didn't call you back after a stellar first date. He's focused on Maslow's base needs—like putting a roof over his head, banking some savings, or getting on a stable career track—and can't move forward with any kind of relationship.

The alternate version of the Disappearing Act is a guy who suddenly realizes, well into a relationship, that he's not managing you and his life very well. So let's say a guy starts out enamored with you. He seems confident. He's pretty successful. He's charming. And he gladly begins dating you, EG.

At first, he's jazzed. He's nabbed a smart, independent, stunning, crazy-fun woman…and the chemistry is beyond his wildest expectations. What more could he want? Welp, esteem. He doesn't want esteem, either. He NEEDS to build it, if we listen to Maslow. And you, kicking butt and moving through life at 100 miles per hour, are totally blind to his lagging self-confidence. Why? Because while you are likely to adopt his victories as your own, men do not always tick this same way.

According to psychologist Marisa T. Cohen, most women experience a psychological phenomenon called "basking in reflected glory," in which you share in the achievements of others close to you, including your guy's. "As such, women show a boost in self-esteem when their male partner does well or succeeds," she explains, citing a 2013 study published in the *Journal of Personality and Social Psychology*.[1]

When he gets a promotion? You feel great, too. When he charms the room? You glow with pride. When your girlfriends gush about how awesome he is? You perk up and say, "I know, right?" Problem is, when you're the one slaying it, your guy might be evaluating *himself* against *you*, determining if he's where he needs to be in his life and career.

"Research shows that males report lower self-esteem when their girl-friends score high on tests—and the effect isn't always something that they are conscious of," Cohen says.

Brayden was one of the most awesome, secure guys I interviewed. Frankly, his good-natured honesty was a breath of fresh air. At age 30, this German-born guy with a law degree was currently traveling Europe living in hostels—and he was completely, 100-percent ready to explore the bond he was creating with a woman he'd met two days after arriving in Switzerland. He'd been single for a couple of years. "Now, the first week here, we're kind of dating!" he says excitedly.

What I want to emphasize here is this: Brayden is now secure in himself, but once upon a time in another relationship, things were not quite the same. Back in law school, he dated a classmate for four years, but toward the end of their studies, their bond had started to erode. Brayden cites many possible reasons, from hanging out with "different crowds" to desiring different lifestyles, but eventually the root of the issue came to the forefront.

Brayden's ex-girlfriend happens to be very bright. "We were two law students, who had to make decisions as our studies were drawing to a close," he says. "It's a competitive field, and you see how your partner is doing. On the surface, no one would ever say, 'I got better grades,' or 'I'm doing better than you.' You tell yourself that you're not compet-ing." You might not be competing, but you are comparing—perhaps men especially. "She was much better than I was," Brayden says. "When she finished, she also had better opportunities."

What happened, exactly? "I took a practical term," Brayden says, which meant leaving school to gain some real-life experience. "I decided without telling her." Even mature, laid-back Brayden, who today is as awesome and ready as they come, turned into a Disappearing Act. He broke up with his ex, and they drifted apart.

And it's not that men don't want smart girlfriends. They just *kinda* want to feel worthy of their smart girlfriends, and feel that they are on your same trajectory. Men want to be useful to you. It is their major goal: to make your life easier in some way. It is why, when you only want to vent about your day at the office, he instantly tries to trouble-shoot your problems. It is why he's usually going to have an easier time fighting your dragons (a.k.a. killing your roaches) than gushing about how much he loves you.

Men are still, inherently, providers—if not full breadwinners. He has to see himself adding real value to your life. Not just now, but in the future. He cannot find himself stagnating. He cannot rest on your laurels.

The typical single, driven career man wants to achieve some level of success, make his mark, have an impact, reach a goal—or he may start to feel like he'll never be the man he wants to be if he's your part-ner. Worse yet, if he gauges your successes alongside his own, he may start to imagine the day you leave him to run off with a Brad Pitt or Mark Zuckerberg type—someone infinitely more successful than he is. "In his mind, the best way to address this is to preempt the strike," psychologist Karla Ivankovich tells me. In other words, he dumps you before he invests even more, falls off his career trajectory, and/or you eventually dump him.

Researchers have focused on fear as a major motivating factor for preemptive strikes in relationships—but a 2017 study published in the *Journal of Personality and Social Psychology* shows that defensive moves like breakups have more to do with feeling a *lack of hope* in the midst of insecurities and uncertainties.[2] Forecasting into the future, with a cur-rent state of doubt, some men just don't see everything working out... at least, not as things stand.

Disappearing Acts have a real reason for leaving: They genuinely feel it won't work, and it isn't about you. Frequently, they aren't settled or secure enough to have a mind-blowing connection in their lives—and maintain it. So, the way to deal with them is essentially universal in nature:

- Don't chase him.
- Don't try to make a deal.

- Don't stay in touch, by email or text, even sporadically, even just to keep it "lighter."
- Delete him from all forms of social media.
- Move on with your life.

Your emotional investment in a Disappearing Act, after he leaves, must hit zero. He is conveying that he needs real space to handle *himself*, so give him that. Don't look back. Keep moving forward with your life and dating other people. If there's even a remote chance he'll come back around, and you want that, the best break is a clean break.

## CHAPTER 6

# meet mr. all that but the bag of chips

**Mr. All That But the Bag of Chips,** *n.*—A man who is absolutely everything you want in a partner, with that sparkling "it" factor of connection... but he's not ready to commit in full.

⚙️ **MO:** Recognizes the connection and lays parameters to keep you at a distance without losing you while he gets it together.

🗂️ **Category:** Not ready

💰 **Emotional Investment:** Varied

**\* \* \***

**RORY:** Are you ever going to ask me out? You flirt with me. You act like you like me a little. You show up here, with a friend, not a date. I mean, aren't you? Ever?...

**LOGAN:** I have thought about asking you out, several times. I just don't think it's such a good idea.

**RORY:** Why not?

**LOGAN:** Because you're special.

**RORY:** Special? Like "Stop eating the paste" special?

**LOGAN:** You are beautiful. You are intelligent. You are incredibly interesting. You're definitely girlfriend material. I, however, am definitely not boyfriend material. I can't do commitment, and I don't want to pretend to you that I can. If I were to date you, there would be no dating. It would be something, right away, and I'm not that guy.

—*Gilmore Girls*, season 5, episode 13,
"Wedding Bell Blues"

* * *

Have you ever met a guy, you started to get to know each other, or even date, and you suddenly thought, *This feels too perfect*? This guy will suddenly walk into your life and do everything just right.

What do you value? Drive? Ambition? An oddball sense of humor? Practical intelligence? Yep, this guy has it. So you meet—perhaps through friends, perhaps on a blind date, or in a perfect meet-cute. And all of a sudden, you fit together like Cinderella and Prince Charming, Ross and Rachel, Carrie and Big, or Seth and Summer (pick your perfect-couple poison).

You'll fall for him, and mentally take yourself off the market for Mr. All That But the Bag of Chips. And everything is going to go swimmingly for weeks, months, years, until one fine day, he will announce that he is "not ready" for the happily-ever-after. Maybe it's another woman (or women). Maybe he has family issues. Maybe it's some other major life problem, like his job is in jeopardy. Maybe it's drinking, partying, or generally not taking responsibility for his behavior.

Perhaps out of all the categories, women were more likely to describe Mr. All That But as their best friend—which is what makes this category so hard. What makes him different from the Disappearing Act? Mr. All That But isn't necessarily going to panic and fly the coop when something goes wrong. He's going to try to set parameters—his parameters.

I've heard many incarnations of Mr. All That But the Bag of Chips. Maybe he'll suggest you see others, much to your dismay. Maybe he'll suggest you stay best friends but see other people. Maybe he'll suggest you date, instead of this full-fledged spend-all-your-time-together deal you've got going. Maybe he's going to do the relationship thing, but he will refuse to call it that or put any sort of label on it at all. Maybe he'll start pulling away emotionally and hope you accept that until he straightens his head out.

Basically, he will maintain or create the space he requires to get himself "ready," and then throw the ball into your court. He's going to let you decide if you're cool with a pause or backstep, all the while hoping you accept the relationship in its dented state.

So, what's up with this guy? He has no idea what to do with you. While he wasn't actively thinking about his timeline when you met—he just allowed himself to fall for an amazing girl—the serious evolution of your connection suddenly makes him keenly aware of exactly how "not ready" he is for whatever it is that's happening. He's going to try to slow the train, get back on his timeline, refocus on himself or his milestones. He will propose an alternative arrangement in an attempt to multitask, in his way—but frankly, he may not do the best job at it.

The mindf*ck of this situation is that he's the living definition of "it." He's ALL THAT. He's everything you've been waiting to find— *but* he's not ready to offer you the long-term partnership that might seem inevitable out of a bond as close and connected as yours. There is a "but"—he's not ready, he can't give you the "bag of chips," he can't do a full-fledged relationship right now—and that "but" is effectively destroying his ability to hang in there.

In the end, he's going to lay boundaries before basically making you decide how to deal with him. Sounds fun, right? (Just kidding. It's torture.)


### You're basically already in a relationship, but he "can't have a girlfriend right now."

Jillian met Zeke five years ago, when she was working in New York City. At first, actually, he was her boss—and she was coming off a divorce at the age of 28 that had left her embarrassed and confused.

Zeke was always there to lend a sympathetic ear, make sure she kept her focus at work, and empower her to make decisions that would ultimately lead to her happiness—like not backsliding toward her ex-husband when she felt like a stigmatized young divorcee, for instance. "It was a start-up of thirty people, so we worked closely together every day," she says. "We're the same age. He became my shoulder during the divorce. He listened, without judgment, and didn't look down on me. He pushed me to grow, be better—but respected me for who I was, as well. We really did become best friends."

Soon, Jillian did grow and heal—and all of a sudden, she started to see Zeke completely differently.

Their relationship began to deepen into Best Friend You're Also Attracted To territory. Neither was consciously seeking a relationship, but one did develop. Their friendship started to not only feel like a relationship but also look like one. They started hooking up, in addition to spending *all* their time together.

But Zeke was adamant that he could not be in a relationship at that moment in his life. "He was a committed bachelor," Jillian insists. "He was working on his company, and thought he was in no position to be in a relationship." If you were to ask about Jillian and Zeke's developing relationship, it'd be this ambiguous committed-but-not, sometimes "frustrating" entity, as Jillian says.

Almost everyone in Jillian's life told her she needed to let him go. However, there's something about a best friend—you don't just let go. That's what makes this version of the "not ready" guy so confusing. It's built upon actual deep connection.

There's more to this story—but I'm going to save it. We'll get back to Jillian later.

**You're about to get married, but he doesn't know if he's played the field enough yet.**

It was a freezing winter night in DC, and Adeline was at a restaurant having dinner with a friend. Friend, mind you. She had utterly sworn off dating for the past six months, had gotten her acceptance to a top grad program, and was focusing solely on herself.

She'd done the ho-hum few-month trial relationships. She'd had a long-term boyfriend from ages 19 to 22; she loved him but felt there was something missing. "He didn't turn to me when he had a crisis," she says. "When I was sick with pneumonia, I found out he was really emotional and upset—from his mother. He couldn't open up [to me]."

Adeline didn't want *close*. She wanted to meet the great and magical "it" person, whom she'd always dreamed of finding. Little did she know, one had been seated next to her, just a table over, that night at the restaurant. Adeline actually knew his date, an acquaintance from school, so she casually exchanged a "Hello, how are you?" before reentering her own conversation. But she felt something—an energy—with the guy.

The next morning, a Facebook friend request popped up from *that guy*. His name was Nolan. He'd been on a second date with her acquaintance, but he wanted to take Adeline to dinner. Both Nolan and Adeline are very intuitive; both felt *something*. They settled on Wednesday, and the connection was instant.

They were both into philosophy and creative endeavors, despite pursuing more traditionally successful, stable careers. They'd actually grown up just miles apart out West before crossing paths in DC. Adeline had never met anyone with whom she felt she could talk for hours and hours and never be bored. "I immediately knew," she says. "I didn't know what would happen, but I knew he'd be an important person in my life."

They moved quickly—in two months, they were living together. However, big decisions were on the horizon. After a few years in the workforce, they'd *both* been planning to attend separate grad schools before they met.

Something had silently shifted within Adeline, too: Although school was in the back of her mind, she wanted to pursue this relationship more. "With all these other guys, I'd always felt alpha," she explains. "Here, with Nolan, I wanted him to put his career first. I wanted to be beta." Adeline offered to defer her acceptance, and stayed with Nolan as he pursued his education. Everything was amazing. For a while.

Nolan was immersed in his studies and carrying on a serious relationship at the age of 26. His buddies, however, were enjoying the party lifestyle, dating around, drinking, and having a generally carefree time. And right before their relationship hit the one-year mark, Adeline started to realize Nolan might be jealous of that freedom.

There were so many comparisons going on. "He was never jealous of my career or success," she says. "But I did start to sense he was jealous that I had lived and partied...the way it worked out, *I* had dated a lot of people before him, yet he hadn't dated at all. He was in school, watching everyone go wild and have fun and hook up. I knew that he wanted to marry me—but he also wanted to have friends, be single, go out."

Despite this growing sense of FOMO, Nolan was sure that Adeline was his future wife. After about 14 months together, he proposed and she accepted—but something was still off. Eventually, Nolan came clean. One day, he simply said, "I may need to have more of those single experiences."

At first, they didn't know what to do. They tried to figure out a scenario in which they could remain in each other's lives. But they couldn't. "He knew early on that I was the only one, but it was like single life and our relationship were separate," she explains. "He couldn't shake this feeling that he had more to experience on his own, and I couldn't make him feel settled."

Adeline wanted him to feel sure about her, and about their relationship; she didn't want to rush a process she wanted to last for the rest of her life. She felt sure about Nolan—but she knew she had to give him space. After multiple breakup-and-makeups, Adeline finally cut the cord. She found a job in New York City, left the engagement ring, packed up her bags, cleared him from social media, and blocked his phone number and email. A clean break.

Nolan had begged to remain best friends, but Adeline laid firm boundaries. She couldn't live with his uncertainty, and she knew that they would never solve Nolan's need to feel single and free while he kept persuading her not to leave him. "I was so sure he would be the love of my life," Adeline says. "I just didn't know if we'd end up together."

**You guys are in love, but he thinks he's too young to settle down forever—and you're "forever."**

Samantha remembers her first love very clearly: a boyfriend named Jim who entered her life during the latter part of high school and exited it in the early part of college. Some first loves can scar you. Samantha's did, but for atypical reasons. "It was this loving, open commitment," the free-spirited 25-year-old blonde nonprofit worker explains. "But I started to feel this sense of dread creep in—right when he was attempting to get a place closer to mine the next school year."

Samantha started to have doubts about her relationship with Jim when a cute RA entered the picture her sophomore year. "I remember staying up one night talking to him," she says. "We both wanted to travel. We both cared about social issues. Here, my boyfriend is traditional, going to business school—things I don't care about at all."

Samantha broke up with Jim, things with the RA did not work out, and this EG spent the better part of the next two years "torturing and blaming" herself for obliterating an otherwise healthy, caring relationship. But even with doubts about what else was out there, she decided to fully embrace her need to explore, grow, and journey.

She went to South America, went to Germany, made new friends, and basically put love on permanent hold. Except, you know, this *one* guy. She was growing closer to Jamal, another student she had met late in her senior year. "I remember distinctly telling my mom that I never felt 'that kind of happiness' with anyone—except him," she says. "If he had come to me and said he wanted to date, I'd do it. I remember telling her, 'I've never met anyone like him.'"

He was cerebral, cute, nerdy, shared her quirky sense of humor—and they could talk endlessly about absolutely everything. The only hitch was that Jamal was heading to med school, some four hours away in another state, while Samantha was shipping off to Spain, where she'd signed on to teach English for a year. Both events led to reluctance from each party, despite the fact that they were quickly developing the sort of friendship that's an obvious mix of romantic chemistry and intellectual bonding.

Samantha visited Jamal a couple of times at school, and the second time—right before she left—she decided to lay it on the line. "I told him that I wanted to try," she says. "I said that if he found someone else he liked more while I was away, it was okay, he didn't need to feel bad, and we could break up. But I said I wanted to try."

His response: "That's exactly how I feel!"

Samantha was thrilled. "I'd thought about Jim and then the relationship I had with Jamal, and I was like, 'Yes! That's why the breakup had to happen. This is exactly who I'm supposed to be with right now.'"

So a long-distance relationship was born—and immediately tested by a six-hour time difference and thousands of miles. They weren't communicatively in sync, and weren't always in tune with the other's emotional state. That said, they hung their hat on the fact that things would even out when Samantha finally moved back to the States; she'd lined up a job in the very town where Jamal was attending med school, and a house nearby. Suddenly, the physical gap was about to close.

However, while Samantha's first relationship, with Jim, had been a smooth, straight line, her relationship with Jamal was about as smooth as a roller coaster at Six Flags. They were either spending entire weekends together, discussing current events and wild theories—*or* Samantha was getting locked out emotionally by her best friend/boyfriend. "I remember this one time, we went to a tailgate—and he left me alone for like a half hour, when I didn't know anyone at all," she says. "I couldn't find him! We fought about it, and then we didn't talk for like a day. So I tried to get back in touch with him, but he wouldn't answer my calls."

So, living close by, Samantha finally marched down the street to knock on her boyfriend's door. Samantha, visibly upset, wanted to rectify things. "He was like, 'What? What do you want?' And it was in that moment that I realized he did not have the same need for unity in a relationship that I did," she explains.

From there, things only disintegrated further. Jamal was, in fact, stressing out about his life. When Samantha returned from Spain to reconnect, he started dealing with those oh-so-familiar doubts about his first real relationship. He felt he'd been missing out on the full med-school experience, partying and making new friends, because he had a girlfriend overseas. Resentment had built—but he'd never shared it with Samantha. So she'd held on, mostly in the dark about the extent of his feelings. Jamal was her best friend, an intellectual equal with the same random interests. She could not imagine a better partner if he would just *be that* for her.

Finally, Samantha couldn't stand the what-are-we-doing-here fiasco they'd fallen into. "I asked him, 'Do you think we're ever going to get back together?' and he said, 'I don't know...I wish I could just press pause on you.'"

Obviously, "pause" is not a thing when it comes to people. Jamal wanted to stay best friends while he sorted himself out, or something, not completely lose her. Samantha was not down with that scenario. This time, she pulled the plug and was devastated—for months.

On the positive side, she started to build her life as a single woman in a relatively unexplored city, enjoy summer living in an empty college town, and build closer friendships. This freedom was tainted with sadness, but manageable—until an emotional night when she ran into Jamal for the first time in months.

The two started talking on the street where they both lived. They then moved to Jamal's porch. He still "wasn't ready," but he was working on himself and growing up. He said she'd taught him the importance of maintaining strong friendships. He apologized for stonewalling her for long periods of time, and for blaming her for his problems. "He said, 'You were so sure of what you wanted, and so mature—you never lashed out at me,'" Samantha recalls. "'And I felt infantile, because I didn't know.'"

## What You Can Learn from Mr. All That But

Mr. All That But is the guy you can easily see a future with. He's your best friend, lover, and confidant, and the connection with him is so rare and different that *you know*: This is it. The crazy thing is? Whether he says it or not, you can usually tell he senses it, too. He is guided by his feelings and sense of connection. He is looking for a partnership, a merging of minds. He's reasonably confident in where he's headed in life. But.

Somewhere along the way, he realizes he's not *fully* there yet.

He hasn't lived enough life. He's still sorting out some personal problems. He wants to play the field (especially if you've had more experiences than he has). He doesn't feel ready for forever, because he's young or transitioning into another phase of his life. You seem more mature and grown-up than he does. And he needs to reach that place, where you're at—where he can see his life settling down with you. Hopefully. For good.

### Signs You've Got a Mr. All That But

- You're more likely to refer to each other as "best friends," making a breakup that much harder to pull off.
- There are frequent on-again, off-again cycles.
- He often feels in some way inadequate, because he doesn't have something and you do. Maybe that's success, money, life experiences, a stable job. It's the crack in his self-esteem.
- He may try to hide the problem for a while, resulting in a feeling of growing unease or threat of failure in the relationship.

### He Might...

- Test your boundaries to see how much he can get away with while still keeping you around.
- Suggest a short break while he figures things out.

- Initiate a breakup in which you still remain "best friends." (He means it.)
- Insist that a label not be applied to the relationship, because he can't have a girlfriend now—or he might take the label away but still act like your boyfriend.
- Suggest an open relationship, or that you both be allowed to date others.
- Check up on you from time to time after a breakup—or completely suffocate you with communication so you don't forget about him and move on.

Basically, a Mr. All That But cannot fully engage in your relationship, so he's going to lay down rules and hope you live with them. He's going to make you choose how to handle his need to be a little bit free. Most women have the *worst* time setting boundaries in this situation. They know what they feel—and their man feels it, too. But he isn't "ready." Giant sigh.

I know what you're thinking: *This sounds like a complete train wreck.* It is. Yet some of the smartest, most interesting women I talked to had a Mr. All That But in their past. It could be THE connection, but terrible timing thwarts the whole deal.

Modern men want to feel sure. Not just of who they are and who they want to spend their life with, but that they are in a place to fully commit and sustain a long-term connection of that magnitude. That's why he's Mr. All That But the Bag of Chips. There's still that "but."

## CHAPTER 7

# meet the real deal

**Real Deal,** *n.*—the holy grail, the manna from heaven, the diamond *not* in the rough—or a guy who's steady, sure, open, and ready for a real relationship; some believe such a man is but myth; if you find one in the wild, just don't panic.

⚙ **MO:** Recognizes connection and courageously pursues it.

🗂 **Category:** Ready

💰 **Emotional Investment:** Full

* * *

"When looking for a life partner, my advice to women is date all of them: the bad boys, the cool boys, the commitment-phobic boys, the crazy boys. But do not marry them. The things that make the bad boys sexy do not make them good husbands. When it comes time to settle down, find someone who wants an equal partner...These men exist and, trust me, over time, nothing is sexier."
                              —Sheryl Sandberg, *Lean In*

* * *

Lest you think every man has entered into a life phase where wishy-washy dating is his go-to method for driving women mad, I'm finally here to tell you about the manna of all prospects: the Real Deal.

This guy is "ready." He's mature. He's in control of his emotions. He knows what you need, and he knows what he's found when he meets you. And you can meet him anywhere. ANYWHERE. There is one superimportant catch: You'll need to determine your compatibility while simultaneously refusing to allow your typical "playing it cool" dating habits or a jaded attitude to get in the way. He's not going to date like the boys. He's in a league of his own—or at least of very few.

The beauty of meeting the Real Deal is that he really *sees* you, and he knows that you are worth more than a 2:00 a.m. text or a pseudo-relationship that you're never entirely sure will last 'til next Tuesday. He gets you. He's sure of what you could have together: the stuff of romantic fairy tales. Or, you know, you could be a 21st-century power couple. Whatever works.

Not every man is born a Real Deal, prepared to self-actualize right along with you. A "not ready" guy can evolve into a Real Deal when he conquers a personal issue or moves into a more stable moment in his life. I also don't think that having this smooth-sailing guy is a prerequisite for a successful relationship—not even close. You determine your own destiny.

However, I'm introducing you now to some signs that you've met a Real Deal, because I want you to see this: There *is* another way. If you're sick of the dropping out and orbiting around, wait for a man who is willing to meet you halfway, a man who will provide a safe, consistent stronghold for your emotions. He exists . . . but you'll just have to watch for the signs you've met that Real Deal in real life.

## Sign: It Looks Like the Wrong Time—and Yet It's Not

Lily was a "rules" girl. You can just hear the poise in her voice; she has the calm, direct candor of a therapist—and she even says she's treated as an informal one by friends and family. Knowledgeable, as you might expect, she had read all the books and literature on dating and relationships. She'd followed all the advice she deemed appropriate in nature. She'd created her own lists and litmus tests to figure out if she'd landed the right guy and the right relationship.

After moving from Seattle to Michigan, and then to Washington, DC, in her mid-20s, she finally landed the guy she'd been looking for. "He was a conventional pick," says Lily, now 30 and the global content head for an internet company. "He was stable. He was supportive. And yet I was constantly looking for emotional intelligence and maturity from him. Those deep conversations, he just couldn't really do. The bond just wasn't really there."

So they eventually went their separate ways—and Lily suddenly tore into online dating with some serious tenacity, before it was basically the go-to for every single in America. She was moving to San Francisco for work. She describes the process as a little harrowing. "I was so full of rules, [and there were] so many red flags in each profile," she says. However, she thought that if anyone could excel at finding a gem in the sand, *it was her*. She dated a lot of brainy types; she describes them as "guys in hoodies with emotional issues." Lily barely went on a second date with anyone.

But at least she had cool coworkers. One of them, Elijah, worked remotely from Los Angeles, but she always enjoyed interacting with him. Knowing he was married, she'd offhandedly tell people, "I'd like to date someone like Elijah. But not—obviously." Lily was a "rules" girl, remember. She would never dream of having an affair (or really, a relationship that deviated from the standard course *at all*).

But she and Elijah still interacted at company events; they had the same kickoff date at their jobs; and they shared a "weirdly romantic-feeling walk" in New York City once, where they opened up to each other. Lily passed this off as yet another instance of her informal role as therapist, until Elijah called her and asked her to dinner.

Yes, a date. He and his wife had officially separated, and he was moving to San Francisco (squatting with his uncle until he found a place). Lily was like, *Okay.* But she was very, very skeptical of just how cool

Elijah was with his current single status—and of his interest in her. "In my mind, the divorce narrative was that you need time to process," she says. "You go surf. You go to Brazil." Which she totally encouraged Elijah to do. He declined.

For years, Elijah had been trying to make it work with his now-ex-wife. She had made it big in Hollywood, actually, and had suddenly checked out of their marriage for the bright lights of Tinseltown. "Elijah is big into therapy," says Lily, one of the reasons she was always clearly drawn to him. "From a young age. He's been through a lot. So we've always been able to be very honest, supportive, and encouraging."

About the finality and closure of his marriage, he says simply this: "There's the time when your marriage ends, and then the time when you actually leave." For Elijah, this spanned three years. He'd done the emotional work. He was ready, despite what every dating rule and convention Lily had ever read about might have told her about men in his situation.

But dating always made Lily "uncomfortable, to the core." To get past that feeling, she credits the work she'd done reconnecting to her intuition the year before she connected with Elijah romantically. "I'd gone through a lot of emotions, and I worked on listening to my body," she says. "That helped me identify things in my life I needed to work on." She pauses. "I'm very analytical. I can poke holes in anything. I knew I needed to look not at the person on paper, but the person in front of me."

Elijah was everything her previous serious relationship was not. "I always liked being around him, even before we got together," she says. "We have this deep connectedness—both a physical connection and a true partnership. We have really deep discussions about life, about relationships. Nothing is off-limits. He is honest. He is emotionally intelligent. He was willing to dive right in with me and say, 'This is not a rebound; I intend to have a real relationship.' You can choose to believe bad intentions or good. We are secure."

Every other dating book might tell you that it was absolutely the wrong time. Due to a health condition, Lily was even worried about her *own* readiness for a real, vulnerable relationship. A "child of diet-ing," she was used to physically preparing for the perfect moment to enter into something serious. "People always wait for the perceived right time," Lily says. "Like, 'I'll lose the weight, then I'll get a boy-friend!' I had been losing my hair at the time we got together. It's not reversible, and I had been wearing a wig. I told Elijah. I said, 'I don't know how you're going to react.'"

His response? Pssh. "That is *not* a problem."

Lily has a new view on relationships and being ready. "I am now detached from the idea of having finally 'arrived,'" she says. "There is no safe, stable end point." You are *constantly* becoming; Lily has chosen to become *with* Elijah.

Oh, and did I mention they're now engaged?

## Sign: He Slowly Builds a Strong Foundation

Isabelle is an engineer in form but an adventurer at heart—so much so that this girl met her Real Deal prospect when they both signed up for an outdoor leadership class off the shores of Mexico. The then-22-year-old was still "figuring out her next steps" in life, but this particularly challenging getaway spoke to her.

Isabelle remembers first seeing her future husband, Shawn, at LAX and feeling this instant pull toward him. "I was dating someone else at the time," Isabelle says of her "happily stagnant" relationship—a state some twenty- and thirtysomethings believe to be the natural course of things in a best-case scenario. But the moment in LAX was magnetic.

"I wanted to find something to hate about him," she confesses. But that "something to hate" didn't materialize. Isabelle and Shawn spent the whole month sailing, enjoying the great outdoors, and hitting it off within the context of this newly forming friendship. "We had these amazing conversations," Isabelle says. "I felt so *heard* about my goals, and I was excited about what he was sharing with me. He validated ideas I had about life, traveling, going back to school. He was so sup-portive of me."

So, there, off the Mexican coast, Isabelle changed. Shawn knew about the boyfriend, and was respectful of that relationship—but when Isabelle returned home, she broke up with him, a very sweet guy. She describes that moment as terrible. "I had to do it immediately, and it wasn't about Shawn," she says. "I thought, 'If I can have this intense connection with a stranger, this can't be it.'"

After Isabelle cut those ties, she then plotted her future—which included a job interview in New York City a couple months later, where Shawn happened to live. The two went on a few "magical" dates over the weekend. If you think "magical" means "they lived happily ever after," you're wrong.

You see, Shawn knew that Isabelle was fresh off a breakup. He knew she was considering her future, what job she'd have or if grad school was in the equation. At nearly 10 years her senior, Shawn did not want to be a source of pressure or influence; he wanted brilliant, wise-but-younger Isabelle to choose her own path.

Isabelle wasn't exactly having a ton of fun going on dates with *other men* in NYC while Shawn remained in the back of her mind at a close-yet-not-quite-reachable distance in her life. Sometimes, she wouldn't hear from him for a week. "I used to tell my friends, 'Too bad the only guy I'd consider marrying is too good for me! It won't work,'" she recalls, knowing now that it was nonsense. But Shawn wasn't playing by the rules of past boys she'd dated.

This is where Isabelle departed from her own set of "rules" and constant friend check-ins to curb her anxiety. "Deep down, I knew this was special," she says of Shawn, who seemed to merge the traditional with the progressive. "So I'd force myself to be like—what if we didn't have cell phones? If I was thinking of him, I'd send him a thoughtful email. I'd take a day and think about it. This was a really special person, so I treated the interactions with care." Some bonds are worth more than a whatcha-up-to text, right?

Isabelle says she and Shawn entered into an intuitive relationship that transcended dating. As strange as it felt at first, she trusted their connection. And Shawn never forgot her—he hated texting, but he checked in steadily with phone calls and reciprocal emails. The two saw each other more and more. They even took a hiking trip to Japan—which perhaps crystallized their connection and their future.

Isabelle and Shawn spent four, five, sometimes seven hours at a time hiking and discussing everything from past relationships to the future, a scenario very similar to how they met. "No cell phones. You can't Google anything. You can't text your friend and ask what to say," she says. "You can't look in a mirror." It was just Isabelle and Shawn, practicing "dynamic openness."

Trusting the connection, continuing to foster a real relationship based on mutual respect and goals, and patiently hitting milestones, from moving in together, to surviving a bout of long distance, to an engagement, has led to long-lasting love. After four years, the pair married. "We committed to the person," she says. "Some just commit to the circumstances." And Isabelle keeps using the word "patience," which she credits her spouse with having.

In a hurry-up generation, Shawn refused to conform to a game that so often only leads to hookups and short-term flings. "He had unbelievable patience this whole time," Isabelle says.

## Sign: He Can Handle Emotions and Imperfect Situations

The day Cora met her now-husband, Daniel, a friend had to force her to rally and meet him. At the time, she was a 21-year-old student in New York; he was a 28-year-old LA entrepreneur visiting friends for the week in the city. They crossed paths at a bar in SoHo. "I met him on day two of his week here," she says. "The timing was not right for either of us." She was barely into meeting him, let alone dating him.

Let me explain: Cora was a "third culture" kid. She was born in the United States and raised in England and Asia because of her parents' work—constantly moving around, making bonds, and breaking them. When she and Daniel met, she was young and settling into what she hoped would be a permanent stay. Her *first*. "I was long distance with everyone in my life," she says. "I wasn't interested in a long-distance relationship."

However, she and Daniel had an immediate spark and saw each other a few times while he was in NYC, which led to a long-distance friendship. "It was somewhat flirtatious," she says. "The thought process was not there at the time, but looking back at some of the messages—which we had friends read at our wedding—it was clear we *were* trying to impress each other."

So fast-forward nine months. Both Cora and Daniel are checking in about twice a month in some fashion (text, call, email) but are dating others while growing their friendship. Then a natural disaster hit the country in which her parents were living.

Cora's parents were unharmed, but she still joined them in the country for the relief efforts. She was there for three weeks. "It didn't feel as terrible when I was there in it," she says. "But when I returned to school for spring semester, the first night there, I had never felt so lonely in my entire life—and that first night back, I was *really* alone."

It was late in New York, sleeping hours, and Cora had very few places she could turn. Daniel was on the West Coast, where it was three hours earlier. "I asked to call him," she says. "We talked for five hours, about everything."

This deeply honest yet comforting phone call changed everything. Although Daniel was open to it, Cora still did not want a long-distance relationship. But she continued to deepen her connection with him for weeks, accumulating phone calls, texts, emails, letters, and postcards. They continued to talk; she continued to date other guys—and she hated every second of it.

Catastrophe had changed her fun-loving live-for-the-moment mind-set into one that was seeking substance. "I was so bored," she says. "It seemed so hollow. I just wanted to talk to my friend—to Daniel. I stopped wanting to make new friends, too. Instead of more bonds, I wanted to retreat into stronger connections. I wanted to retreat into him."

Why Daniel? Well, slightly older and wiser, *he* was ready for

Cora—with her wild spirit of youth and newfound depths of maturity. Even amid her long-distance concerns, he knew they could make it work. Daniel made a couple more trips to NYC before, with almost "blind hope," she says, he moved across the country to pursue a master's degree in architecture, and into the same apartment.

"I didn't know him very well," she says. "It's strange. Even with the distance, I just felt so understood. We just had a friendship, with trust built there, and honesty. When we met, we had always been honest about other commitments."

A Real Deal connection doesn't have to take off like a rocket. Even with the distance, there was a positive trajectory. Sometimes, there are barriers—but there should always be forward movement, slow-and-steady ways of getting to know the other. Cora and Daniel gradually grew into each other, leaning into their foundation of friendship, trust, and honesty along the way. And sometimes, you've got reasons to be headstrong about your goals and your needs. Sometimes, *you* aren't ready for *him* instead of the other way around; that resistance won't deter a Real Deal.

Cora and Daniel are now married, with two children. They've had their bumps, even in that first year of living together, which Cora said was not exactly a honeymoon; she clearly remembers an embarrassing argument at Ikea about how they'd organize the cutlery drawer. "Real life and a relationship is not happily-ever-after," she says, "which is something I would tell my 20-year-old self."

All that said, Cora is keenly aware of the way Daniel is different from other men she dated. "All my relationships before him were extremely dramatic," she explains. "It was like a competition—each of us would feed off the other who was more invested. I was never secure, and I never went out of my way to make them feel secure. I was always afraid of getting hurt; love was a roller coaster, and safety was boring."

Daniel is sweet and kindhearted, confident yet humble—from the get-go, he was a departure from the men she'd met and tried to date in her late teens and early 20s. "I had such an erratic childhood. He seemed so stable and sure," she says. "I was still finding myself; he was sure he wanted to be an architect. Yet he was so passionate, so interesting. I always thought I'd have to be bored and safe, or insecure and in love. I thought I'd have to choose...Daniel opened me up to this whole new world, this middle ground."

Lastly, she adds the icing on the cake: "I did not *feel* like I was trying to impress him," Cora says. "I was just myself."

## Sign: He Knows (and Pursues) Exactly What He Wants

One of my favorite interviewees, 34-year-old creative director Harper, was a self-proclaimed New York City "fashion girl" before she moved to the West Coast. "I am the modern woman," she says. "I was career-focused, and I made all my life decisions while single. I only had one serious relationship during those years."

Harper says 90 percent of her dating was casual, even though she didn't realize it. She equates her unfocused patterns to "writing a book with no subject," while still thinking it would come out a masterpiece. "We all analyzed and obsessed about the guys we were dating—guys that had no potential," she says, noting *Sex and the City* hit too close to home at the time. "You lose sight of real love. You think you're heartbroken, but you aren't. Where I was mentally? I needed adventure and exploration."

However, adventurous or not, playing games of the heart with toxic bachelors can definitely lead to some subpar relationship strategies. Harper would meet a guy and assume he was going to ghost. When she moved to LA and downloaded Tinder (a first!), she went in fully expecting to have the same results she'd had in NYC, only amid palm trees and by way of a tiny iPhone. "I was operating from a mind-set of 'This will be fun. It will be exciting,'" she says of needing to adjust her sails toward a real, functional relationship. "I needed a *new* mind-set."

A friend of Harper's had recently married, and she made her this promise: When you meet the right guy *for you*, you will just have to sit back and enjoy the ride. Harper did not believe such a ridiculous notion. I believe it—that is, when you meet a Real Deal. And the only thing that could have shaken Harper from her crazy-chaotic, deeply ingrained dating patterns was such a man.

When Harper first saw her superattractive now-husband on Tinder, she thought he looked like just her type. At first, she did not take him seriously at all. "He was hot," she says with a laugh. "Like the type I'd date in New York. They'd pursue, and then lose interest." But Brody? Dude stepped up. "From the day I swiped right," Harper says, "he has never made me wonder. I never had time to obsess about him. I never had time to worry."

See, Brody, an entrepreneur in his late 30s, had been online dating seriously for a couple of years. He knew what he was looking for—someone attractive, smart, feminine, ambitious. A true match. He was on the lookout. Not forcing it, but ready. When he met Harper, he *knew* she was the girl.

He also noticed Harper's fear-induced bad habits early on in their dating life, and worked at making her feel safe. "He was an undergrad psychology major," she says. "When he first started seeing my patterns pop up early on, he told me, 'I have the special skills necessary to handle you.' I come off like a badass, but deep down I'm sensitive. Brody has everything I need. He is dominant, but sensitive and strong."

Brody called Harper the same day they matched. He has called or texted every day since, even when she jetted off overseas for a work trip early in their relationship. Their first date lasted for hours, as they did dinner, walked on the beach, grabbed drinks, and went back to the beach for a kiss under the stars. "We instantly connected," she says. "It was like talking, even texting, to a friend. It was so natural."

That first week would include four dates. After that week, Brody told Harper that he'd been single and dating for a while, and he knew what he was looking for—it was a "heart-to-heart," to which he said he required no reply. He just wanted her to know where he was at. He said he'd stopped dating other people. Soon after, he told her he'd cleared a drawer out for her at his place. "If I wasn't so excited and didn't feel it, it would have been too much," she says. Obviously!

But when you know, you know. When you're both ready, it's easy. Harper and Brody, by the way, continued on their Real Deal trajectory. She met his mom after three weeks of dating. "He's been doing this a long time," she told Harper. "He's overdue." The two moved in after a month and a half. They were engaged after only a few more months, and they are now married. "He said he needed to lock me down so we could travel together," Harper says. "I was so used to game-playing. He was so straightforward. It is so hard to believe it exists while you're dating—it is *so hard* to believe."

Harper and I discussed some of the indicators that a relationship will work out. "It's about being a team," she says. "When you put two chemicals together, do they explode? Or do they make a compound that works?" We also discussed timing. She and Brody, and friends, discuss this often. "I think for men, timing is such a huge part of it," she says.

## What You Can Learn from a Real Deal

In an era when timing is everything, guys seem to need to check boxes—playing the field, finding their career—before ultimately weaving their way to "ready." If you've dated a million "it's not you, it's me" guys, it feels like you will never meet someone to match your passion, drive, *and* commitment.

### Real Deals Are Different Because:

- They know who they are, where they're going, and what they want in a partner.
- The intensity and enthusiasm they bring as they pursue a relationship with you will seem mythic, perhaps even frightening.
- They are ready.

I think women like to say they're focused on career, or friends, or themselves. Sometimes, that is 100 percent true. It was for Harper, yet

Brody would not let her make excuses to get out of dating him—and now they're hitched, and she couldn't be happier. In our interview, I shared my guiding maxim with her: "Women aren't always looking for a boyfriend, but they're always looking for a soul mate."

"Yes! *Yes*," Harper exclaims. "You have to put that in your book." (This is me putting that in my book.) Please, while single, don't become a cynic. Stay open to a soul mate who never lets you doubt.

Real Deals are special finds—definitely rarer than the slew of guys who aren't actively ready. Brody knew this. He tells Harper frequently that every love story is *not* as seamless as theirs. "When my friends tell me about their guy problems," she says, "he always has to remind me, 'Don't scare them if the guys aren't acting like me.'"

Real Deals are unicorns that actually *do* exist. They also come with their own set of (non)problems—which we will discuss later. But right now, give yourself a pat on the back, because you made it through the profiles! (Woot, woot.) I know trudging through baggage can be tough, but it will pay off, especially as we start to hear directly from men. So turn the page—emotionally and literally. I'm excited to share what's next.

# part three

\* \* \*

# MINDING THE GAP

## CHAPTER 8

# what he's doing while he's not dating you

"I want someone who challenges me." "I want someone who makes me better." "I want someone who challenges me to *be* better." Lots and lots of my male and female interviewees expressed the same sentiments.

These aren't new refrains. Singles have been searching for their other half—the one who helps you become the best version of yourself—forever. But perhaps it's even more prevalent and sought-after today in an era where success is a moving target, the world is more competitive than ever, and men and women are both trying to forge their place in society.

When I first told my mother that I wanted a partner who challenged me, my monologue started with a five-minute explanation of my ideal future dynamic and ended with an excited, "Does that make sense?" Her response was a wide-eyed stare, followed by a line that made me feel deeply misunderstood as a millennial human seeking a high-level bond: "That sounds exhausting."

It took me a hot second to realize that a modern couple is slightly different from a couple of yesteryear. It's not that our parents didn't want great relationships, or work hard to create them. They just had fewer realistic options. For instance, we have apps to match with tons of singles, only a reasonable distance away, that we may have never met otherwise. Or we have Skype and social media to keep long-distance love alive. On top of that, previous generations had their future relationship roles relatively mapped out for them. Abandoning the "male breadwin-ner, female nurturer" dynamic is relatively new; even if women worked, a hefty pay gap often meant their careers came second.

Today, no one is telling us how to build modern relationships. The sky is the limit; if you can dream it, you can do it. It's not shocking that ambitious men and women would like to form ambitious partnerships with their eventual long-term mates. "Partner" is a term that emerged out of necessity—because relationships are no longer always traditional setups of husband and wife. Same-sex couples, while falling outside the scope of the gender dynamics we're investigating here, did help give us a new buzzword to encompass today's most desired relationships.

The essence conveyed in the word "partner" is something that women and men in their 20s, 30s, and 40s have taken up as a better description of the dynamics they desire. A partnership packs a deeper punch than a "marriage" or a "relationship," labels that can carry significant baggage. What if you desire to couple with the Real Deal, just not in a traditional marriage? (Hat tip to Goldie Hawn and Kurt Russell, whose nonvowed commitment has endured since, like, the Stone Age.) A partnership implies that both are equal, both have goals, both have merged their lives by choice, and both are working together toward mutual success as a team—that their lives are growing, and in the same direction.

Art Aron, PhD, a professor of psychology at Stony Brook University, has studied attraction, intimacy, and interpersonal relationships through-out his career. He concocted something called "the self-expansion model."[1] He and his wife were getting really into East Indian literature and meditation, where there is this sentiment about love: The love of a husband or wife isn't for the sake of the husband or wife, but for the sake of the self. "We have this goal of expanding, enlightenment—of 'more,'" he explains. "If you have more, you can accomplish more. We want to achieve. And what makes us feel good is the sense that we are *expanding*."

Today, it's not enough to just find a significant other. We want a part-ner who can take us to new heights we couldn't reach on our own. Certain people just help you grow *more*. You meet someone and can't get enough, because he helps you see the world from different perspectives, expands your horizons, carries different experiences that you find fascinating and valuable. With him, possibilities for growth seem nearly endless.

So, we know what we want. The question was, and still is, how do we get it?

## Webs and Laser Beams

With every opportunity available to us in life and love, we now set high standards for relationships: They must be strong and stable like our parents', but also full of romance, sex, and excitement, like the movies taught us to expect. This ultimate hybrid of a bond sits atop the Beacon of Lifetime Happiness, which men and women alike are all aiming for off in the distance. But the sexes may have different ways of getting there.

Research shows us that men and women may think a little differently; biological anthropologist Helen Fisher describes these differences best. Men tend to be compartmentalized, focused thinkers—think of them like laser beams. They complete one task at a time, do it well, and tune out much of their external world in the process. Fisher calls this "step thinking"—also known as linear thinking.[2]

Women, on the other hand, exhibit "web thinking," she says—also known as integrative or creative thinking. Much like a spider weaving its web, the female brain tends to multitask, contextualize, and form a holistic view of a given situation or data set. Women are able to pick up on more details from their surroundings and merge them together to understand the bigger picture. They also tend to be long-term planners, and better at living with ambiguity.

When I talk about how the sexes think, I am always talking about tendencies—because this is such a hotly debated topic.[3] Imagine the entire human race falling along a spectrum. In the case of web thinking versus linear thinking, more women are clumped around the web side of the spectrum and more men are clumped around the linear side. But there are always exceptions; some men will be great web thinkers, and some women will excel at linear thinking. Just like you'll meet women who are glued to timelines or need to play the field. Or men who will want to settle down early, or have been juggling life goals and building relationships since high school. On top of that, we can all learn to excel at whatever skills we want. Every day. All the time! Men and women alike are adaptable—and both are the product of the "nurture" side of the nature/nurture equation. However, for the layered reasons we've discussed—socialization, our inherent biologies, evolutionary factors—you will probably recognize patterns in how the sexes approach their lives, dating and relationships included. Considering how we think, for example, shows us where our tendencies (and perhaps strengths) might lie.

So, women weave weblike thoughts; men carry out tasks with laser-beam focus. Women take in the whole picture; men break down the parts. Men's brains are less in touch between the different hemispheres,[4] which tend to work independently; women's brains are not nearly as "lateralized," explains Fisher, meaning that perhaps these "well-connected brains facilitate their ability to gather, integrate, and analyze more diverse kinds of information—an aspect of web thinking." Boom! Gender solved! Just kidding.

But if we consider that the skills associated with web thinking can be used, strengthened, *or* learned to build stronger bonds with potentially compatible partners, they become a valuable asset in your relationship toolbox. I want you to trust yourself. You *are* socially in tune. You *are* mentally flexible. You *can* combine intuitive and analytical thinking, see the bigger picture, and make strong decisions for your life—and relationships.

Just don't forget that men, glued to their timelines, might be in a different, more linear, step-like default operating mode.

## What *Is* Happening Out There?

I can't join you on dates to tell you Guy X is not worth your time, Guy Y has commitment problems, or Guy Z is a player, so you should drop him right this second. This isn't that type of dating book anyway—there isn't a quick fix or a one-size-fits-all answer. Sure, I can tell you to wait 24 hours to text after a first date, but is that really going to make a difference with your complicated and nuanced real life? Probably not.

What I can do is arm you with understanding, so you can recognize what's happening out there in this incredibly confusing dating landscape, and make wise decisions for yourself. So remember that Maslow guy? Of course you do. I told you we'd come back to him and his hierarchy. Now that we've discussed different kinds of guys—those who are not ready, those who are—let's take another look at this hierarchy and dive back in.

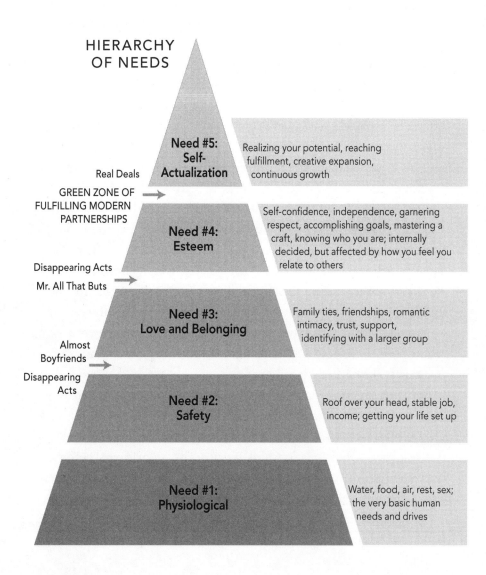

So, let's review. While you're single, you're working through each need in Maslow's hierarchy on your own. You start by getting good grades, so that you can get into a good college (and maybe a grad program after that). Eventually, you'll be putting a roof over your own head, with money from a paycheck you make at your stable job.

Next, your love and belongingness needs will enter the picture. This means you'll be adding people to your life who help you feel a sense of support and connection. That might be a boyfriend, but it also might be your mom, dad, cousins, besties, coworkers, and anyone else who helps you feel like you belong.

After that, you'll be working on yourself—your goals, your confidence, your self-esteem. You'll start to define who you are, where you're going, what your role is going to be, and what you want in life. You'll want to feel like you've accomplished something and you're respected by others.

Finally, you'll try for self-actualization, which is basically reaching your peak potential, finding fulfillment in your day-to-day life, achieving your goals, and working on personal growth and development. Sound familiar? It should.

While *self*-actualization doesn't directly relate to our mates, there's ample evidence they *can* play a significant role in helping us become our best selves—which is why I introduced you to Dr. Aron's self-expansion model earlier. Another study from 2017 shows that the most fulfilling relationships help you become more like your *ideal* self, not your *actual* self, defying the old wisdom that proclaims someone who "allows you to be yourself" is enough.[5] That way of thinking doesn't encompass the best relationships today.

Adults dating in the 21st century are typically idealists. We are more concerned than ever about having fulfilling lives with meaningful work and deep friendships. Our relationship requirements are also evolving as a result. The best relationships today really *do* help you become a better person, or help you grow closer to the person you ultimately want to be—they help you self-actualize.

Is this a lofty goal? Sure. Is it impossible to find? In a world where we have the ability to meet all sorts of people via apps, travel, random social connections, and far-reaching friend groups—and maintain those relationships with technology, near or far—I don't think so. While I certainly think there are *a few* daters who have outrageous requirements for a partner, lots of people are really just holding out for that higher-level relationship of positive influence and growth, or waiting for the right time to build it. This is related to the "Michelangelo phenomenon," where your partner can help shape you into the ideal, bringing out and affirming your best qualities.[6]

The major problem? These relationships are harder to find and maintain, because *all* the variables have to align; your ability to engage with the right partner has a lot to do with timing, the natural process of personal development, and the right perspective on the dating market.

If a person's overly occupied with Maslow's basic needs (#1–4), they're not likely to be able to find the fulfilling self-actualizing partnership that will make them better. They're still building the foundation. Plenty of "not ready" guys are still trying to figure out their jobs, put money in the bank, buy the house/apartment/condo, settle into a city, what have you. You are more likely to fulfill a supportive role rather than a growth-oriented role as you build a relationship with one of these guys. Growth might enter the picture down the line, as a couple's trajectory moves through the hierarchy *at the same rate*, but it's just not the main area of focus until life gets more "settled" for both sides of the equation.

Likewise, you need to know who you are and what your role is, and feel confident in that, before you can take on a partner who will help you to be the best version of yourself. That means personal growth and development—perhaps especially necessary for men, who don't build their esteem as interdependently as you do.

Remember that whole "basking in reflected glory" thing that psychologist Marisa T. Cohen told us about? If you're ahead of him and scoring bucketloads of achievements, a driven guy is more likely to feel pressure to catch up than to adopt your wins as his own—especially if the intensity of your connection rushes him along faster than he feels comfortable.

Considering that gender roles are often deeply ingrained, a full-package female partner's success may seem especially threatening.

Cohen points me to Abraham Tesser's "self-evaluation model" where our self-concept feels jeopardized based on how close the person is to us and how relevant their behaviors are to how we see ourselves.[7] In cases where he's feeling less than stellar around your high-achieving aura, man has a few options to protect his self-concept:

- He can distance himself.
- He can try to reduce the relevance of your behaviors to his self-concept.
- He can work to improve himself.

Do you see your latest Almost Boyfriend, Disappearing Act, or Mr. All That But in those descriptions? Men will do *all* these things with girlfriends (or potential girlfriends)—a.k.a. the person whose behaviors and traits matter to him the most—to regulate his self-esteem.

I want you to see the key point here: *Sometimes, many times, it isn't you; it really is him.* We women are so quick to adopt blame. Understanding how a guy evaluates relationships can stop you from jumping to incorrect conclusions, thinking your relationship probs are all your fault. I want you to file this information away, and stop the all-too-familiar "But why did he leave me?" cycle of questions. You now know. You can now recognize the men who aren't ready faster, and move on without analyzing the crap out of your dating misfires over a pint of ice cream. It's done, baby.

Thankfully, there are also ways to understand differences in where you fall on the hierarchy—and why you're so often ahead. Let's see how the sexes move through it.

## How Men and Women Move Through the Hierarchy Differently

One of the biggest critiques of Maslow's hierarchy is that it's obvious that you can work on some higher-level needs before completely fulfilling lower-level needs—and people have different paths through the hierarchy. They do not always simply move directly from one need to the next.

Maslow himself said the hierarchy is somewhat flexible. The basis of his theory is that unmet needs are "activated," and we are thus "motivated" to work toward meeting those needs until they are finally fulfilled.

I see the sexes working through their needs in different ways, which may be a combo of societal pressures, our biology, inherent tendencies, and social norms—but it often comes down to the way we think through our problems and work on our goals.

| CAREER WOMEN | CAREER MEN |
|---|---|
| ○ Lay out all their goals and work through them in a more flexible, interconnected manner. | ○ Decide which goals are most important, and work through the hierarchy linearly, shooting from one building block to the next as they fulfill each task. |
| ○ Are future-oriented and better at long-term planning. | ○ Live in the here and now, and tend to be more concrete. |
| ○ Mature quicker, so they desire relationships and know what they're looking for earlier. | ○ Mature slower, so it takes longer to know who they are and what they're looking for in a partner. |
| ○ Derive esteem from many sources and different relationships, which gives them fulfillment. | ○ Derive esteem independent of others, from their own achievements and successes. |
| ○ Are holistic thinkers, who are constantly gauging prospects to determine if there's potential for a future. | ○ Are compartmentalized thinkers, who tend to categorize different relationships as fulfilling various needs based on what they're looking and ready for at different phases of their lives. |

When web-thinking women are working on their needs, it's often in a multitasking, overlapping manner; we dart around the hierarchy, checking boxes as it makes sense to us, working toward the bigger pic-ture. When linear-thinking men are working on needs lower in the hierarchy, they're often focusing on one major need at a time.

If you're ahead of a guy, checking more boxes, it might be hard for him to keep up and maintain a relationship with you. Trying to do so causes a deep sense of unrest, a feeling that you may not necessarily experience in the same way or as much.

Settling that unrest may hinge on building esteem.

## How Women Build Esteem

Where do you derive esteem as a woman, really? You, me, your mother, your grandmother, your best friend, your younger sister, and your hair-stylist might set forth a list of completely different criteria. A life well lived, as it is defined by and for women, depends on the era in which you grew up and what you personally consider most important.

That might be raising a gaggle of high-achieving children, balanc-ing both family and career until you retire at age 60, starting your own business, becoming a doctor or lawyer, checking every box on your vision board, or carving a new path all the way to the U.S. presidency. According to sociologist Lisa Wade, women today have the freedom to set and achieve goals like no generation before. "As an individual, a woman can create herself in any way she wants," she explains. "She can blend the masculine and feminine; we like women who have some elements of masculinity—whether she's a CEO, likes camping, or has a great [traditionally male] name. Women have all this freedom."

When there are, oh, I don't know, 38,205+ ways to define yourself as a successful modern woman, you eliminate some of the pressure attached to what fills your cup. Success, mastery, and confidence are more personal. They are whatever you define them to be; what makes you happiest and most fulfilled; where you derive a sense of achievement, independence, and respect, better known as esteem (#4 on Maslow's hierarchy)—whether that's building and maintaining relationships within your social network, getting married, raising children, doing good for humanity, building a brand-new career path, or climbing the ladder in an established industry.

And because of your forward-thinking, weblike mind, you're likely to start self-actualizing (or even just thinking about it) before the average guy. Men today arguably have a tougher, more rigid, more hyper-focused climb toward realizing their full potential.

## Why Men Are Delaying Serious Commitments

Women, with tons of options for self-definition, are building esteem left and right. We're checking off boxes of achievement throughout the hierarchy and deriving joy from multiple sources. We, as our moms and dads told us, can truly be whatever we want to be. While modern men have a lot of other things going in their favor (hello, pay gap?!), they don't seem to have that same luxury of openness.

Men are also falling behind. In 2015, for the first time since the United States Census started collecting the information, more women than men in this country held bachelor's degrees (30.2 percent versus 29.9 percent), all thanks to an emerging set of 25- to 34-year-old females who are outpacing their male counterparts. The data shows that 37.5 percent of these young women have at least a bachelor's degree; just 29.5 percent of men the same age do.[8]

The story behind these numbers begins at an early age, according to Art Markman, PhD, a professor of psychology at the University of Texas at Austin. "Boys typically need to move around more, and education has become less and less physical, which is one of the reasons women are outperforming men," he explains. "Getting out and getting exercise causes dopamine to spike and enhances the brain circuits that focus on attention. There are mood-stabilizing effects to exercise—and in the current setup, generally speaking, there's a lot more that can get boys into trouble." I'm sure you're heard "boys mature slower" a million times, right? According to Markman, "early success influences later success," so boys who struggle in the classroom when they're children may be a step behind for many years.

As such, lots of men have a longer road to personal stasis (stable job, steady paycheck) than women, and men in the career-driven set, in particular, may want to bear down and find their place in an increasingly crowded career environment during their 20s and early 30s—or beyond, if required, since life is long. Many of the most ambitious among them—your entrepreneurs, doctors, scientists, and finance gurus of the world—are making sure success is secured before locking down (or even thinking about) a high-quality, long-term partner. They want to be *ready* for love. In 2014 Pew research, "not financially prepared" topped the list of reasons never-married singles ages 25 to 34 had yet to tie the knot.[9]

As they find their way to compete and survive, so many men tie esteem to success at school and work, and they understand that the entirety of their teens and 20s (even 30s for some) is devoted to their climb to the top, according to 28-year-old banker Tim. "I remember getting cut from my first hockey team at age nine," he says. "There is just this insane pressure for guys to be successful. From the time we're young, we're trying to be the best, the smartest, advancing the fastest."

Research hints that men are indeed more *obviously* competitive.[10] In trying to explain male versus female ambition, Sarah Blaffer Hrdy, professor emerita of anthropology at the University of California, Davis, explained to *Time* magazine in 2005: "Primate-wide, males are more directly competitive than females, and that makes sense. But that's not the same as saying women aren't innately competitive too."[11] Women are more inclined to use teamwork, think big-picture, and "split the difference if they don't get everything they want"—that holistic web-thinking in action. This effect is also evident in the way men and women look at career trajectories and accomplishments.

According to a 2014 study of 25,000 Harvard Business School graduates, high-achieving women expect egalitarian marriages upon graduation, where careers and housework are viewed equally, but frequently end up in relationships where they take on the brunt of the childcare.[12] Many more women than men also *expect* to shoulder this burden of caring for kids, even with their personal ambitions in mind.

Having a well-rounded and fulfilling personal and professional life is complicated; there are tons of variables and decisions. But in that flexibility women have, it makes sense that many EGs want the best of both worlds and may adapt to get there—even if that means succeeding as a partnership and a team. They can bask in their partner's reflected glory, too.

Driven men are different. That emphasis on success and rising to the very top is still pervasive. Even among the brightest pairings, men presume their role is to be the bigger breadwinner in a couple. As journalist Derek Thompson puts it in a 2016 article in the *Atlantic*, "The cultural expectation that men be the top providers proves to be an insurmountable force, even (or especially) among the best educated households."[13]

Think about these attitudes of competition in the chaotic romantic landscape, where daters feel they need to compete with other singles to stand out. Women are less likely to enjoy the process of fighting it out with their female peers, and would rather team up with a compatible partner to "split the difference." Men are more likely to explore their options, and may even enjoy the battle for prospects as they gain confidence and (hopefully) score the best long-term mate.

While women start to feel the pressure of a ticking biological clock, men are still competing. With options in the career realm, men are going to find their place in society at many different rates. Maybe they'll do their undergrad and work for a couple years, then decide to go back to grad school to gain more career leverage. Or maybe they'll need to switch majors, and it will take three additional semesters before they enter the competitive career market.

Maybe they'll decide to start their own business—possibly as a side hustle after their nine-to-five gig, eating up most of their free time. Or maybe they'll want to fill a traditional pathway to success and become a doctor or lawyer, meaning they are unlikely to enter the workforce until their mid-20s or early 30s at the earliest, once they've finished a residency or taken the bar. Dating and relationships might be important, but less so than career achievement (at least for some time).

These career-driven men often take the longest time to become "ready," all while romanticizing the bond they will one day have. Sometimes, their ideals are even less realistic than women's. As 24-year-old Noah, a Brooklyn-based engineering grad student, tells me about the girls filtering through his dating life and some of his shallow desires: "There's no reason to make compromises right now." Not that he's telling dates that.

## How Men Build Esteem

While they build their careers and climb the hierarchy, men are figuring out how to operate in an increasingly chaotic dating scene—and how to compete with other men for the best prospects. Some date excessively, turning themselves into charmers to have some fun—or they get on those apps and devote $x$ amount of time to personal romantic objectives.

Sometimes, they are looking to fulfill physiological needs (#1) by scoring sex, and sometimes even love and belongingness needs (#3) by falling into relationships. Early dating success can also create a growing semblance of dominance and status, à la Maslow's esteem (#4)—perhaps something they didn't have in high school. Dating, in some ways, plays into their sense of self.

Dating expert Susan Walsh, who has a background in business, tells me this: Men legitimately looking to find a prospect to settle down with before the age of 26 or so are the exception and not the rule. "Right now, the age of marriage is hovering around age 29 for men," she says. "Add a year for college education, and another year for each additional degree. Don't assume he's going to lock it down." Even if he *is* commitment-minded.

When Walsh's daughter was in college just a couple of years ago, a bunch of her friends were in relationships. "She thought all the couples were very serious and headed toward marriage," she says. "All had broken up after graduation. The odds against it lasting are so strong." Today, we simply want the best of everything. "This generation is very idealistic," says Walsh. "They want to have meaningful work that they're passionate about, that is also financially rewarding, *and* find their soul mate. Human beings have never asked for more—especially in love, where historically marriage was an economic transaction."

With that in mind, it's not unreasonable to want to "test the market" and determine your mate value, Walsh says, and maybe men feel the need to do this more than women. When the options today seem endless, they have no biological clock, they're socially encouraged to "play the field" instead of find relationships (at least according to what *women* hear from the peanut gallery), and their esteem somewhat hinges on feeling attractive to the opposite sex, few men are willing to pass up the opportunity to explore—or they may feel paralyzed until they do so.

A lot of men talked to me about the art and science of attraction. This had nothing to do with any one particular woman, and everything to do with the process of getting women interested in them, thus allowing them to fully explore their options and ultimately nab the catch of their dreams—a step-by-step process of development.

Before we get to that catch-of-your-dreams thing, though, let's take a look at my handy-dandy (un)scientific equation of male esteem.

$$\frac{\text{Peak physical attractiveness} + \text{Confidence with women} + \text{Career success}}{\text{ESTEEM}}$$

Unlike *your* esteem, which is more relational and personal in nature, male esteem is more independent and concrete. As one guy put it, it's based on the "successes I feel I've accomplished through my own deliberate efforts." Pretty much the opposite of the interdependent myriad sources of esteem women often experience, right?

You'll see plenty of men in their 20s and 30s working on their physical fitness. From running to strength training, most of my ambitious twentysomething guy friends are fine-tuning their bodies. This leads to a sense of confidence, which theoretically allows them to get the girl.

William, a 25-year-old former race engineer, is pretty obsessed with the approach. By that, I mean he has always wanted to master the art of walking up to a girl, getting her interested, getting a number—and maybe hooking up, but not necessarily. "It's not about taking a girl home and sleeping with her," he insists. "I just have a problem with the approach—and so do a lot of people. Think about when you're the master of your craft. Each time you flawlessly execute, it's like a high. But since I can't execute flawlessly myself, I constantly seek the feeling that I see other guys experiencing."

Men want to feel attractive, in the same way women do—most men just don't walk through life garnering attention, like tons of young women (as complicated an issue as that is). Yet they know that a lot of their appeal hinges on their confidence, which is self-initiated and self-created. "You remember when I told you about wanting to be a player?" William says. (I do.) "My failures at that challenge always make me want to keep trying." Perhaps the longer he sucks at the "approach," William says, the more "potentially perfect girls" he'll miss out on. (This is, of course, mostly a wild illusion, folks; guys like William just don't realize it yet.)

In addition to that, the "lifestyle" is also a source of excitement while waiting for the right girl (or *time*) to come along. Resident physician James, who is definitely also playing the field, tells me something extremely similar to William—that wielding those powers of charm can lead to sex, which is exhilarating in itself. "It can be a status thing," he says. "Everyone knows the guys who get laid and the guys who don't... It's a sense of validation." He might enter a relationship for a bit, too, if it *feels* good and supportive—he's just not thinking toward growth or the future. James will end it when it stops working or serving a purpose.

Right or wrong, many men seem to like the power, the intrigue, the sense of the unknown—all of which delays strong commitments. That lifestyle that William so aptly referred to can be a source of entertainment. James even says that the process of casual dating can be a thrill or adrenaline rush. They're competing, not knowing when or if they're going to win a woman over. "We like the in-between. We like the messy," he explains. When was the last time one of your girlfriends said THAT over brunch?

## Boxes and Lanes and Tracks—Oh My!

Men's romantic lives seem to mimic their life stages—which is why they are all about timing, and timing is all about *Am I the man I want to be yet?* Even Brody, happily married in his late 30s to a wife with a kick-ass career, does not think he'd have been in the place to court his wife had he met her only two years earlier. "I wasn't settled," he says, explaining that women seem far more capable of maintaining healthy relationships both earlier in life and when key variables are still in flux. "With the psychology of men, there's something about sowing those wild oats, feeling confident in who we are and what we're doing."

This is also a key reason many men who are still working on their esteem are not great relationship prospects. They're "not ready," and you are, EG. You are chilling further up the hierarchy than they are. Once they get a sense of who you are as a person, and where you are in your life, you're a reminder of a woman they're just not quite ready for... not someone they'd feel comfortable pairing off with now.

Another interviewee, Landon, a 30-year-old journalist, echoed a similar sentiment, from back in his early dating days. With the exception of one slightly more serious relationship, he says much of his 20s were composed of "a series of ill-fated dates and short-term girlfriends," girls he couldn't see as long-term fits. Landon remembers getting on the phone with his buddies to discuss some of these girls—true train-wreck relationships, with the dramatic highs and lows you might witness over popcorn at the movies. Then one fine day, when he'd reached stasis in his career and competence in his adult life, he finally called Kaitlyn, the girl from college he'd always felt a strong connection to, and sought out the long-term relationship he genuinely wanted.

Maybe "liking" the mess is a strong way to say it, but Landon says his misfires certainly gave his otherwise ho-hum not-ready-for-The-One-yet life a sense of adventure—not that he was particularly conscious of this process. He was still learning himself. He was trying relationships on for size, to make sure he knew what he wanted. (Hindsight is always 20/20, with deep-seated feelings unearthed upon examination years later.) "I didn't try to psychoanalyze the bad, dramatic relationships," Landon explains. "Part of me thinks I entered into them because I knew they wouldn't work out—which is the worst. At the time, they were just fun and wild. It's a break from the mundane, like a movie with car crashes and explosions." Even his short-term but more significant relationships involved a level of *self*-deception. "I always entered relationships knowing if there was going to be a future there," he says. "Sometimes, I think I'd convince myself to keep going because the alternative was being single and alone."

Landon says he always determined rather quickly which lane he was operating from—hookups were hookups, short-term relationships were temporary distractions, potential girlfriends were firmly that. And Kaitlyn, that EG from college, had a special spot in the back of his mind as the type of connection he hoped to one day find and foster.

The point is this: Men have boxes, lanes, compartments, tracks, and probably a bunch of other organizing tools for the women they encounter. Very often, how you're slotted has nothing to do with you, and everything to do with where you're at in your life, where he's at in his life, and the type of prospect a guy is open to at that very moment. You could be amazing, even perhaps a little *too* amazing for his preoccupied mind...and perhaps he's subconsciously aware you won't help build his esteem anyway.

I tell you all this because men have so many reasons for dating besides finding a potential long-term partnership. I don't want you to start dreaming about wedding bells and babies when he's at home watching television, not planning on calling you ever again. I want you to take each date as it comes, and wait for positive signals that will ultimately manifest in the relationship you want.

## Why Esteem Matters for Men

Maslow noted one *key* flip in the order of his hierarchy—between needs #3 and #4, love (and belongingness) and esteem. "There are some people in whom, for instance, self-esteem seems to be more important than love," he wrote in 1943. "This most common reversal in the hierarchy is usually due to the development of the notion that the person who is most likely to be loved is a strong or powerful person, one who inspires respect or fear, and who is self-confident or aggressive."

Okay—I'm not saying that most modern men want to be feared more than they want to be loved, but I do think more modern men seem to feel their careers and personal goals need to come *before* their relationships—or before The Relationship, a.k.a. capital *L* Love. Love with the great and magical "it" factor. Love that helps you become *better*.

In a world rapidly evolving to include more women who can provide for themselves, men are learning what they will bring to the table in a relationship. High esteem may well come *first*. "Satisfaction of the self-esteem need leads to feelings of self-confidence, worth, strength, capability and adequacy of being useful and necessary in the world," Maslow writes. "But thwarting of these needs produces feelings of inferiority, of weakness and of helplessness."

There's a rising generation of twenty- and thirtysomething women who have been kicking butt since grade school—you're a part of it— and who may be inadvertently causing men's high-strung vibes. As women began to climb the corporate ladder, things began to change— and that change will continue to accelerate. Feminism is here to stay. We're going to keep talking about the gender wage gap until it closes. Women are going to break one glass ceiling after another. And men will keep watching this cultural shift go down with quizzical gazes and (secret) mixed emotions.

As modern men tell me firsthand, the trajectory of men's success and their journey to manhood has not really changed. Men respect the emergence of a forward-thinking feminist generation—but they've also shifted their attitudes away from relationships to counter an increasingly competitive career front. Gendered expectations lead to a pressure cooker for men; if the ideal is still masculinity, women embracing masculine qualities has led to men pushing to be hypermasculine, says sociologist Lisa Wade. "Men are constrained and feel the pressure to fit into a much smaller box," she explains.

Wade says that as men mature and get older, some get more accustomed to choosing the path that suits them best and embracing some elements of femininity. Down the line, they can more easily decide, often with a relationship partner, how to pursue the life they want and get the most out of it—which could be deeply egalitarian in terms of gender roles. But that must come from a stable base of personal esteem, self-worth, feeling respected. Men need to know who they are, where they're going, and who they want beside them. Maybe they can handle some relationships. But partnerships? *Forever* love? Don't count on it. They are glued to their timelines.

"Am I ready?" will be the question that precedes every type of relationship, because the current culture is leaving men with a bit of paralysis. For women, success is the icing on the cake of esteem, and we're poised to lick the excess from our fingers. For men, it's pretty much the whole cake—and they're not making their cake nearly as fast as we are. "I see more powerful women in the sciences, engineering, and technical fields all the time," says Noah, the 24-year-old engineering grad student. "Any guy who doesn't admit that it feels slightly threatening is lying."

As Tim, the 28-year-old banker, explains, there are lots of snide comments about the women in his male-dominated industry. Women who put their heads down and get the job done are often seen as cold, domineering, bossy. Then the hard performance numbers arrive on everyone's desk. "There's a lot of ego involved working with women," Tim says. "But when their successes enter the picture, everyone shuts up."

If single women are surging ahead in personal fulfillment and self-definition, men may have the natural edge when it comes to dating and relationship options—where they do not feel the pressure of a biological clock, and where they are ready to compete for prospects. Men still hold the keys to commitment in heterosexual pairings. "As individuals, women have more freedom—but as a group, men are still in charge. They are constrained, but they are constrained into the more powerful roles," Lisa Wade says.

Arguably, dictating when and how relationships form is one of the most powerful roles in any society.

# CHAPTER 9

· · · · · · · · · · ·

# why men let you go

Let's talk about what happens when a man meets an End Goal woman. Because there are tons of smart, kind, career-focused women who can provide exactly what men want. "The question is, what can a woman provide that I can't get elsewhere?" Tim says. "Part of that's caring." (Hey, Maslow's #3!) "Part of that is that she inspires me to be *better*." (Classic Maslow #5.) Men need support first, growth potentially second.

Noah has totally dated an End Goal woman, who showed him what a relationship could be in its very best form. She tested his paradigms and changed the meaning of a relationship in his eyes. "She challenged my moral views, the way I spent my time—a girl like that is bold enough to make observations that force you to change how you see your world."

That's serious stuff—right? It also starts to encompass what that "intimidating" label really means. "We know that long-term, this is what we want," says Tim. "It will be better. But we have to be willing to give up our short-term desires to spend our time however we want. It's selfish. But an intimidating woman forces you to confront the problems you know you need to change."

Guys want to rise to your level. They really do. But sometimes, they think their selfish desires—playing the field, building a career, etc.—really are more essential than the End Goal woman. Sometimes, it's because they haven't grown up enough to have the right kind of foresight; other times, it's because they really believe their focus needs to be elsewhere.

The whole should-I-or-shouldn't-I decision-making process men undergo is something psychologists, sociologists, and economists use. It's called "social exchange theory"[1]—and it works in many types of relationships, whether you're friends or business colleagues, roommates or dates. Basically, a relationship forms when Person A subjectively looks at Person B and assesses the potential costs and potential benefits of a relationship, while at the same time comparing Person B to alternatives. Let's think dating.

For a standard guy dating today, undecided on his level of readiness, he's going to look at the (many!) potential benefits of dating you, Ms. End Goal. He's also going to look at the cost to him in terms of investment of time, energy, resources, independence, and long-term viability: Can he keep you around and happy, maybe forever? Will the relationship go the distance if initiated right now? Then he's going to look at his other options, from sporadically dating other girls on his Tinder list to staying single, to see if it's worth pushing play *right at this very moment*. We all carry out this cost-benefit analysis on a continuous basis. You do it too—it isn't a one-sided game. But with added time, perspective, and life changes.

"You know you're going to have to sacrifice to obtain that girl," Tim says of the modern EG. " 'Ready' is simply finally coming to the realization that the changes you'll make will be for the long-term betterment of yourself and your relationship." Sometimes it is; sometimes it isn't. That's how the cookie crumbles.

"Ready" is a word men harp on a lot, so it's right here that I'd like to pause and explain a long, storied phenomenon oft repeated to young women. Many of you have probably heard the saying "For a man, it's the right time; for a woman, it's the right guy." There is some truth to that statement. It seems "the right time" is a prerequisite to meeting "the right girl" for your average career-driven guy. As 27-year-old John, an engineer in Michigan, tells me: "You will *never* meet the right girl if you're not ready."

Until they've grown and have their feet set in life, they have an inability to settle down with someone who seems like a potential huge commitment. It often has nothing to do with you.

That is why they let you go.

## It's the Wrong Time and Place

It is a truth universally acknowledged, in book clubs and happy hours across the country, that men make some really befuddling relationship decisions. If I had a nickel every time a girl told me an emotional dating story that ended in, "But seriously, WTF," I could take a trip to Ibiza. Let's take a look at a case study, from the male perspective.

Resident physician James met Lindsay when they were 25-year-old med students in the South. A nurse introduced these two at the hospital where they all worked. They went out on a date, and butterflies ensued; it was the meet-cute plus perfect-first-date setup you always wanted if you were a kid who could never let a rom-com pass you by if it was on cable.

Basically, the first six months went incredibly well—and James was counting his lucky stars he'd met such a catch. "I thought she was better than me," the now-27-year-old tells me. "Kinder, pretty, smart." And their feelings for each other were mutual, as such things so rarely seem to be. "I think we both just felt incredibly lucky to be with each other," he recalls.

Life is not a rom-com, though, and you don't always get a happily-ever-after—or even more than a brief reprieve from the realities of our fragile human existence. This budding med-school romance was shaken to the core when one of James's college friends died in a car accident, opening the door for the discussion of deeper issues, like faith, marriage, and kids. He and Lindsay had been together only about seven months at the time, which—let's be honest—in the best relationships is still the sunshine-and-roses honeymoon stage.

Welp, until the slap of reality. "We had a fight about religion—we had never talked about religion before," James explains. "And this made her question things. She started pulling back, and then she asked me, 'Where do you see yourself in two years?'" His thought: *Whoa there.*

The reality and the potential of their relationship was suddenly front and center, and the relationship was rocked. They were on totally different timelines. Lindsay wanted to be married and starting a family in two years. James knew he was going to be in the toughest part of his residency during that time—a.k.a. intern year, a prestigious form of servitude. He'd never imagined having kids until way, waaaay later.

They quickly reached a standstill, and after a week or two of contemplation, Lindsay pulled the plug. "She had this idea in her mind that she wanted a family and kids *now*," he says. At age 25, that was a little too real for James—but that didn't mean he loved her any less.

So what happened in the immediate aftermath? Normal stuff. James consulted friends, who swore he was better off without Lindsay. He played the field for a while. "I went back to doing the things I couldn't do while I was in a relationship," he says. "At first, it was great. I was like, 'Don't have to worry about her!'"

That carefree, emotionless shtick lasted about a month. Then his latent feelings reared their ugly head and went, "Psych."

As so many exes do, James retested the waters—first mentally venturing back in time, asking himself if it really had been that good. Answer: Yes. "I started missing her," he says. "I was thinking, 'She was everything I wanted. Really nice girl, conservative, great values.'" He let this thought cloud run on and on until he went to Washington, DC, which gave him a reason to text her a photo. "She loves Kennedy," he explains. Aha! Perfect convo starter! Now, he was taking active steps to make this work. And Lindsay texted back, which is when the floodgates began to open and, frankly, all hell broke loose.

The duo convinced themselves they could get on the same timeline—after all, James *did* want all the family-oriented things Lindsay wanted, just maybe not quite so soon. So they got back together for like a week. "We decided we were both really into it and we wanted to try again," he says. "But things were really dramatic this time. She even went and got her parents' approval for the relationship."

Talking abstract babies and family someday (in like maybe two years)? Doable. Getting parental okay, which feels like an impending prerequisite of marriage? Too much.

Let's not forget that at the time, James and Lindsay were still in med school. James was also studying for boards, and as the serious vibes of this second-chance relationship began to crystallize around him, he started to have a silent, but very real, panic attack. "It had been less than a week, and I already couldn't study, I couldn't sleep, and I couldn't think," he says. "I started overthinking everything—like, could I really do family and kids in two years?"

Remember when I said men are linear thinkers? Suddenly, James's relationship had slid ahead of that other big goal in his life: med school, a career, becoming a great doctor.

James wound up ending it with Lindsay in a very messy split, flew home to Florida, studied for his boards, and then reassessed his life. "The timing was wrong," he says. "I couldn't do it—and it suddenly felt toxic. After that week of suffering, I couldn't come back to the relationship anymore."

Now, all relationships require compromise—but there is realistic compromise, and then there's compromise that will cause you to resent someone because your desires are worlds apart. Lindsay is now engaged, James is about to graduate from med school and enter residency at a top hospital, and they're both on their separate timelines.

From a third-party perspective, this is probably the happiest long-term scenario for both of them. However, James still has lingering "the one who got away" feelings, and he admits, now that he's nearly finished with med school and entering a more settled state of mind, he may have reapproached Lindsay to try again had she not gotten engaged in the meantime.

## LESSON 1: *There are two timelines in any relationship.*

Lindsay is a classic EG. Convinced she can do it all, meets a guy she clicks with and, bam, ready! He suddenly or slowly begins to see the future—depending on how much *time* is emphasized at the beginning of the relationship. There's a lesson for readers here: EGs are used to getting what they want, and they want it when they want it. I know that works in business and any other achievement-based thing you've ever done in your life, but that does not always work in relationships and dating. There's a fine line between knowing when to walk because the relationship isn't right, and walking because you're unwilling to bend your desires at all. You have to decide what's most important to you: your timeline winning out, or the guy in question.

## LESSON 2: *Sometimes, it's not a good time for one of you.*

I know that "I'm not ready" and "It's a bad time right now" sound like the biggest cop-outs ever. But for most men, who have lived in a bubble where the emphasis on success has been extreme *for their entire lives*, timing is a very real issue that messes with their brains.

Sometimes, they just can't be in The Relationship at that very moment—or at least they can't give 100 percent to the gravity of dating and committing to an EG. You should respect that, but know that you may need to make a hard decision accordingly. Lindsay ended up happily engaged to another man on her timeline, and I'd say that is a win, even though James was left wondering, *What if?*

## You're in the Wrong Lane

In dating, men may seem to embrace a lot of chaos—but it's organized neatly, and energy is expended accordingly. Men who compartmentalize talk a lot about lanes or tracks or boxes in dating—one-night stands, hookups, short-term girls, long-term material—which was news to me, as a woman. "I seem to always get put in the boyfriend lane," one of the guys told me with actual confusion. See, men don't always understand women—just like we don't always understand men.

If a woman is going on consistent dates with a guy, she's considering him as a potential boyfriend. She's either interested or she's not. The guy is in the boyfriend lane. There is *only* one lane. (Don't worry; I told him.)

Women, in fact, are all about assessing potential. We are forward thinkers, often working on self-actualization or thinking about it—Maslow's fifth and final hierarchy stop, the "growth" need—before we have our lives 100 percent figured out. Men measure potential, too, but they will botch a great connection with great potential if they feel they are "not ready" for it—because energy needs to go elsewhere. Take it from Max, the 33-year-old tech entrepreneur. "Maybe the longest relationship I've had is six months? Eight months?" says the director of digital strategy, who recently skipped town from LA to Indonesia to take a new business opportunity. "For various reasons, I have just not been interested in committing myself to someone long-term."

The self-proclaimed "serial dater" tells me he experienced his first "love" during freshman year in college, where he played baseball on scholarship, smack-dab in the middle of a small Iowa town. "I ended up transferring," he explains. "I did not even consult this girl—but I was very attached. She's the first girl I told that I loved her." Nevertheless, Max did break it off with this girlfriend, just knowing *he could not spend four years in Iowa.* (Sorry to any awesome Iowans out there; *I* love you!) But now, ever since experiencing the drug of real love and attachment, he calls women he dates "crushes" instead. "I'm a tech guy—I like new things!" he says with a laugh. Then he adds, "In reality, the crushes are innocuous. You can't really get hurt."

See, he's been dedicated to maintaining a driven mind-set. "I have major career goals, and I've been very stubborn in believing that a relationship could keep you from those goals," Max says. "You have to put time into it. You have to make sacrifices. I couldn't imagine trying to juggle the stress of both at once."

That is why there are two types of relationships: a relationship that fulfills your need for love and belongingness (#3), and a relationship that helps you self-actualize (#5)—otherwise known as The Relationship. Max is only doing the former right now.

Still, if you ask Max to define his "type," he'll say smart, funny, focused, and mature every time. "I say that I like women who are confident, who know what they want and where they're going in life," he says. "I definitely see myself with a Sheryl Sandberg or a Tina Fey versus a Kate Upton." Max's career is constantly evolving—he up and moved to Indonesia "for a new adventure," and not permanently.

During this more unsettled period, he tends to date women who are younger, or less mature, or less focused, or women who are "still trying to figure it all out." They're not thinking marriage, he *assumes*. They're not his type either, he thinks; they're in the short-term box. "I think I choose the wrong women on purpose," Max tells me. Why on earth would he do that? "I never have to answer the hard questions."

See, he's vetting specifically for women he thinks won't work out.

## LESSON 3: *For reasons beyond your control, you might be in a short-term lane.*

Men might approach you with a specific agenda—especially if they're "not ready." They might not want to get attached, so they're not screening for women who have their ideals and they slot you in the "short-term lane." Do not bother trying to figure out what lane you're in by reading signs of interest. Max told me he once rented out a vacation house on a tropical island for a woman who was "just a fling." They had a great time, and he was still super respectful; during their entire weekend stay, he says they only cuddled!

Also, if a guy like Max assumes his desires and timelines won't align with an EG's, this may rule you out for a relationship entirely.

## LESSON 4: *Move on if the connection doesn't feel right.*

Can you jump lanes or build a potential long-term relationship with a guy who has initially tossed you into his short-term box? Sure. But it *is* riskier, if you're looking for a relationship with a great guy, so it's important to recognize whether he's ready or not ready early on. (That's why we spent all that time on the profiles, amiright?) That way, you're not blindsided.

In the case of guys who aren't ready, much like Max, your gauge of connection is crucial. The strongest relationships are built on *real* connection: shared interests, shared long-term goals, complementary strengths and weaknesses, the same sense of humor, same passion, whether or not you can talk forever...Look for it early, within the first couple months. If you don't feel its potential, or if he's got walls up to prevent connection from fully blossoming, don't delude yourself. Move on. You could invest in better prospects.

## He's Not at Your Level

Like Max, Isaac is a moving target. He's currently on a 40-city tour with a fairly well-known band. "I know what kind of girl I want to end up with, and I don't think it's ever changed," the 24-year-old tour manager tells me. "But I don't think I'm ready to be that kind of person yet."

The way Isaac sees it, there are the girls men date and see where it goes, and then there are the girls men see a future with immediately— because those women seemingly have it all figured out. And whatever secret sauce they're conjuring up and consuming, men want a taste. They respect these chicks. They think they're amazing. "It's inspiring," he says. "Perhaps 'aspirational' is a good word." They want to lock that down. Just not yet.

"Who I want to end up with is different from who I want to be with *right now*," he explains. "The girl I want today likes to hang out, drink, is into music, binges on *Game of Thrones*. The girl I want to end up with has real interests and real hobbies—like running or something constructive. She has a real career. And the other girl, the one I want today, is still working towards a career."

Isaac's life is up in the air. He's still trying to make enough money to set up shop in his chosen field: the competitive music management industry. Another guy not at your level might still be playing the field. Another could be considering a cross-country move. Yet another is perhaps contemplating a career change or grad school. If you're ahead of a guy in the hierarchy, he often won't be "ready" to pursue you.

William, the 25-year-old former race engineer, is considering grad school and his next career steps, and isn't sure how "ready" he is for a relationship. William says it's really a mind-set that indicates the level of risk versus reward a given guy is prepared and willing to adopt when he invests in a given woman. "From a supernerdy engineering standpoint, it would be like this," he says. "Say 95 percent career plus 5 percent casual sex means that 95 percent of his effort is going into making his career better, with only a 5 percent loss going to time spent sleeping around. Or you can spend 80 percent on career and 20 percent investing in relationships, trying to find somebody who is attracted to you. It's...stressful. Or perhaps inefficient."

Feeling "ready," for William, is all about his personal assessment of opportunity costs; it's basically the social exchange theory, without calling it out by name. And as Isaac tells me, when he does the choosing, he is looking for someone "at the exact same place in life." An EG? Pressure he doesn't need right now.

Young guys, especially, feel that investing in challenging relationships may slow them down at best, and completely derail them at worst—and on top of that, they often haven't built the esteem to feel they're in your league and on your level. Esteem is developed, and it's further up the hierarchy than basic love and belongingness.

Max has always thought he'd be "a late bloomer," and he has become an Almost Boyfriend to more EGs than he can possibly count—those "closer aligned to Sheryl Sandberg—educated, ambitious, working through real *life* issues." And he always has one EG in his life; he talks to his current female best friend every day.

He invests in these women, who have become great friends and good contacts for business. He calls them his "platonic girlfriends" and truly enjoys their company. "These are girls that I pursued, but probably not very well," he laughs. "My pursuit ended up coming off as 'just this cool guy who wants to hang out.' But I'm supportive of them. I do boyfriend things—I'll go shopping with them, go hiking, get drinks on the patio of a little bungalow!" If you see yourself in Max's EGs, take heart: Max says he frequently loses their companionship to their eventual long-term boyfriends or future husbands.

For many men, they're either on the path to being the guy they ultimately want to be—or trying to venture back to their best self. "I am progressing," says Isaac. "I am closer to being ready for that girl I want to eventually end up with—I'm evolving. But I'm *not* where I want to be."

And thus, if a guy is not exactly where he wants to be, it's easy to stand in front of an End Goal woman and freak TF out. "She's harder to pursue, because there's something to lose," Max explains—a potential future, her respect and good opinion. "I'm a little more timid, not as aggressive. So I might like Sheryl, if I'm perfectly honest—she's beautiful, has her shit together—but I'm way too nervous and intimidated to pursue that on any real level."

Max even confirms my Love Gap theory from the male perspective: "I believe that, for a lot of people, even the majority of the time, what people want in their head and what people go for are not aligned," he says. "It's just—are you aware of it, or not?"

## LESSON 5: *Being at your level is another type of timing problem.*

Guys aren't actively looking to couple off with someone who has her life totally set up while they're still establishing themselves as modern men. They may really love your company, but they may not even see you as a real option. Like Max points out—many of his besties are EG women he can't quite bring himself to pursue. He perceives them to be higher up Maslow's pyramid, further ahead in life, wanting *more*.

Sometimes, these guys might hang around. Sometimes, they'll ghost and come back—zombie, as the kids are calling it. "They like you, but they're not 100 percent sure that they're ready for a relationship with you," says Isaac. "Sometimes, I want multiple things that contradict themselves." (Do not ever let someone tell you men are simple.)

## LESSON 6: *Relationships evolve.*

This is why men couple off and marry some women and not others; the two paired off when they were both on similar planes, and they grew and evolved *together*. Those relationships are oftentimes easier for men, rather than trying to date an already-established EG—who they really do like but perceive to be ahead of them.

It's not that you can't date someone who might have it less figured out than you, but it's trickier. We'll talk about strategy later.

## "Just Going with It" and "Mitigating Expectations"

We humans often vacillate between two romantic mind-sets: "thinking about the future" and "living in the present." They're both important. And both men and women alike engage with each mind-set—albeit, I'll argue, a little differently.

When you start dating someone you like, you will probably want to enjoy the chemistry, forget long-term compatibility (for a *liiittle* bit), and "just go with it." You're gathering data in the here and now anyway, figuring out if this person might make a good partner.

Men like to "just go with it," too. They're definitely lured by *how they feel* when they are with a woman, *how she looks* in that black dress—and "not ready" guys especially would rather block out how they might feel 10 years from now. They figure, if she fills a companionship need and it feels good—why not? As long as they don't have to think about the future, they're fine. Problem is, they often do feel the apprehension of what may lie ahead.

The faster the future comes into the picture, the faster a guy is going to make decisions about your lane, box, or track. He needs to figure out what you're all about, and how that meshes with where he's at in life, so he can determine how to relate to you. Often, the future looms way too quickly for "not ready" guys who encounter EGs. Here's why:

- You're ahead of him in the hierarchy, so he's *naturally* looking forward as he sees where you're at.
- Imagining the future, and discussing it, is just how you live your life.

You probably don't even realize you're thinking about the future at all—because, really, you're not doing anything unusual. This is just your normal operating mode! You love talking about your goals and dreams! And if you're ultimately looking to find a relationship partner, you're entertaining a maybe-future with any guy you're interested in enough to actually date—or you simply like to think any guy *could* have long-term partnership potential, ambiguous as the present may be.

Herein lies the problem.

Guys notice how many EGs like to talk about future stuff—a big ol' theme among the men I interviewed. One of my older, more seasoned single interviewees, a man in his 40s, laughs and perhaps puts it best: "I've never met a woman who didn't need specific plans for the future." Pssh. You've just got goals! You're growing! You love thinking about how it all might play out! LOL, but really. This wigs some men out.

Maybe you love discussing what it'd be like to live in Europe someday, or own your own vineyard. Maybe your goals just seem eerily compatible with long-ranging desires, and that's triggering "What if?" or "Am I ready for that?" thoughts. Or perhaps you just seem to know exactly who you are and have your whole life together...in a way that does not stack up to his current life stage, and your mere presence is forcing him to acknowledge that.

Ruby, a 29-year-old book editor, is one such EG woman. She's smart, she's quirky, she's cool with herself and *she's future-oriented* in the way she dismisses men who aren't at her level. She says she's encountered a bunch of men "who don't know what they want to do with their lives," even "party types." She also has a solid idea of what she needs in a partner. Ruby ultimately just wants someone who gets that she's a "special, weird creature with layers and foibles." (Don't we all!)

She also recently ended a long-term relationship, so she's been out of the dating scene for nearly a decade. Ruby isn't necessarily looking for something serious right away. She'd like to meet some interesting guys, feel a connection, and "just go with it"—but she's been forced to notice this bizarre, unexpected trend among modern male daters.

They won't let her just go with it. "I never expected how much they'd be trying to mitigate my expectations," she tells me. "Literally, it's the second date and a guy is going, 'I want to let you know that I don't want to be exclusive yet.'" Ruby is frustrated by these premature declarations. "I just got out of a relationship; I am not trying to lock it down," she insists. "If you really listened to me, you'd realize that's not what I want."

It's not that men aren't listening, per se. They're just noticing you're an EG. You tend to operate with an eye toward the future. As such, they're suddenly *looking ahead* toward your spot on the hierarchy. You're an End Goal; they're not *there* yet. So, they'll acknowledge what they see, hear, and sense: They're still dealing in the here and now; you look like the future. They're just dating around; you seem like a relationship.

So, while you're just going with it, not overthinking your behaviors, trying to see if you like a guy enough to go on another date, he's gauging your connection, assessing your spot on the hierarchy, projecting "commitment" upon you, determining your lane, putting up walls, and trying to keep just enough distance—all so he *can* "just go with it."

Here's the point I really want to make:

- Men frequently like to *just go with it* when there are zero expectations or pressures about the future of the relationship.
- You like to *just go with it* when you're allowed the possibility of a maybe-future in a given relationship.

When a man tries to tell you he's not ready, explains why he can't focus all his energy on you, or even lets you know that you two will someday end (yes, some say this), he's often trying to stay in that expectation-free zone. He may mitigate your expectations in some way, or he may just shut it down.

Mitigating your expectations doesn't mean he isn't into you enough; in fact, he may really like you. He might even continue to date you if you let him. But when a man tells you he's operating in that short-term lane, recognize that he is giving you an essential data point: He is telling you, straight up, "I am not ready" or "You're ahead of me." He's warning you that he'll be doing his own thing, playing the field, building his life, maintaining distance, or whatever. He's not thinking long-term, because he's still figuring *himself* out.

I'm not saying you should never date a guy who tells you he's "not looking for serious," "does not want exclusivity" right now, or "can't be in a relationship" at this moment, etc. Engage with him as you see fit, and invest in a way that's mutually agreeable—but with eyes wide open. *Don't simply ignore what he told you up front*, because *you* like him and feel chemistry or potential. He is telling you that he doesn't feel he can give you that.

When a guy tells you his position on the hierarchy, listen. Don't get so caught up in his weird behaviors, or winning him over, that you forget what you want—which could very well be "just going with it."

If you eventually want more from him, you have to vocalize that. But since he mitigated your expectations right away, you can't claim you didn't know. This is a higher-risk guy, and there's a stronger chance he'll bail. Invest wisely.

## Bucket Theory

Here's another problematic side effect of livin' in the future. Let's imagine that a "not ready" guy meets you, EG, and he feels that "click" of connection. He thinks, *Wow! That's amazing. She has all these awesome qualities.* Then "the future" starts to loom, as you talk about your goals, plans, fears, dreams, and everything *you* want in the future.

Think of a situation where you and your hypothetical significant other each have 100 energy points to fill as many 100-point buckets as you want in your life. At minimum, there are two buckets: One is labeled LIFE; the other is labeled CAREER. Now think about this: If both of you decide to pour *all* of your energy points into the career bucket, said bucket will runneth over—you will have no outside life, and the relationship may suffer. Kind of depressing, right? Look at all those wasted energy points...

You have to split your energy appropriately, and it's a decision uniquely made for each couple. You can have as many buckets as you want. One might be labeled TRAVEL; another might be labeled KIDS. The guy I concocted this theory with even excitedly suggested "a sex bucket!" (I'll let you decide.) But you never get more than 100 energy points each, no matter how you split your time as a couple. Guys are fairly levelheaded creatures. They know this.

That's why issues like when to have kids, where to live, and how to divide household labor have been causing tension—and breaking up couples—forever. You have to find a person you can reach a mutually acceptable compromise with about how to allocate your energy. This "bucket theory" is another reason why EGs are hard for men to handle: When you've got big, well-planned aspirations, men fear that some of their life goals, like kids and family, just won't jibe with yours.

It's not necessarily the case that it won't work, of course. But it's one reason why talking early and often about the unknown future with "not ready" guys is such a bad idea. Remember, they are on timelines and glued to their goals, so they start to worry you aren't compatible instead of asking, "How can we compromise?" Compromise is an absolute must, but it's *long-term relationships* that are built on it. The early phases of dating? Far less so. Without it, men can veto the whole type (EG), and stop looking at the person (you!) and the connection you have.

* * *

Sometimes men bolt because EGs can trigger an evaluation of *current* relationship desires. An ideal-checking woman with whom a guy feels a great connection forces him to assess himself—as in, he's asking himself, "Am I actually *that* guy today?" or "Do I actually want *this* kind of relationship today?" (Isaac's words.) Oftentimes, an EG looks like the future, and maybe not the present.

Just like engineering grad student Noah said, men connect on a deeper level right away with some women, typically those who possess a slew of their imagined "girlfriend traits." They're confident, bold—the full package. But they still have to check that esteem box (#4).

Interesting research has found that when men know they want a smart significant other, they endeavor to up their game. Case in point: In a 2016 study published in the *Journal of Applied Social Psychology*, researchers found that men with a desire for smarter relationship partners performed better on math and science exams than men with a lower desire to end up with such a superintelligent woman.[2] These men also performed better when they were primed with romantic thoughts before taking their tests versus men who were asked to think about neutral thoughts (say, about their ho-hum commute to work or what they had for lunch). Ah, the power of modern love that keeps us self-actualizing.

This self-actualizing bond is part of the badass, exciting, inspiring, supportive hybrid partnership I want for you. But it's superimportant—for women, and perhaps especially for men—that we grow independently, too.

part four

\* \* \*

# A RADICAL PLAN

## CHAPTER 10

# why you should never settle

One of our generation's greatest female pastimes is discussing love. We were raised on *Sex and the City* (or the reruns), and we watched the bonds of friendship forged over Sunday morning brunches that were often better than Saturday night dates.

I've sat across the table from many a girlfriend dishing about dates and dilemmas. I nodded along and mentally filed away the recurring themes. You want to know what all my amazing, beautiful, independent girlfriends often ask me about?

Settling.

That's right. Each woman will sit across the table, taking sips of coffee and reflexively smiling in a way that I can tell means she's not fully happy. I'll ask her about "that guy" she's been seeing—the very same guy I know she is dying to discuss at length. Instinctively, I can tell something is off.

Many times, I have watched said woman bite her lip in rumination, then look up from her mug and say, "It's still early," "Things are going okay!" or "Haven't found anything wrong with him yet."

No one ever says, "He's *fine*, so why isn't this working?" to me outright, but I'm an expert in female guyspeak. The unspoken words embedded in my friends' body language are: "Dating is superhard, and I'm maybe ready to settle for something safe and cozy... This guy seems like he might be a candidate. Why isn't he worshipping the ground I walk on? I was promised this would make my life easier!"

In a 2008 article in the *Atlantic* (and subsequent book), writer Lori

Gottlieb proclaimed that we should all be doing it—and by "it," I mean settling.[1] "Don't worry about passion or intense connection," she writes. "Don't nix a guy based on his annoying habit of yelling 'Bravo!' in movie theaters. Overlook his halitosis or abysmal sense of aesthetics. Because if you want to have the infrastructure in place to have a family, settling is the way to go. Based on my observations, in fact, settling will probably make you happier in the long run, since many of those who marry with great expectations become more disillusioned with each passing year."

Not only did this opinion kill the dreams of American women everywhere who have been in search of a soul mate for the vast majority of their lives, but it played right into their logical sides. Many friends of mine read Gottlieb's advice (or heard something quite like it elsewhere), looked at the chaotic pool of suitors in front of them—becoming ever more chaotic with the dawn of each new dating app—and actually said, "Yeah, okay. I'm tired, so I could maybe do that."

And then they tried it. They tried to settle. And it didn't work. Instead, it depleted their self-esteem.

## Women Don't Like Settling

I remember reading *Cosmopolitan* back in the summer of 2012. The issue was bright orange, Demi Lovato was on the cover, and there was an article inside called "Why He Should Love You This Much More Than You Should Love Him."[2] As a voracious consumer of romantic knowledge, I thought this one sounded like a winner.

The story proclaimed that some relationship experts say you should date the guy who is 10 percent more into you than you are into him. "Let's be clear: We're not talking about settling," the article reads. "But...picking a guy who digs you about 10 percent more than you dig him is smart." The piece goes on to say that if you follow this advice, you will "check all the will-he-or-won't-he anxiety at the door," according to one expert. He won't "eff with your mind," and he will continue to act thoughtful and caring for the duration of the relationship. Hefty promises.

I remember thinking many, many things about the 10-percent notion, including:

- I wonder if any self-respecting modern man would be okay knowing his girlfriend thought she could do 10 percent better.
- I've met some guys who should theoretically feel #blessed to be dating their girlfriends, but don't act that way.
- I've met some guys who have acted super into a girl at the start of dating and then proceeded to lose interest over time.
- Come to think of it, this 10-percent thing sounds an awful lot like settling.

It's not that I have an issue with the "10 percent more" dynamic but, rather, that someone felt the need to quantify that balance of power in the first place. In the end, I decided that article was well-intentioned but faulty. To this day, I get why it was written. You do, too. Dating is hard. Finding a man to invest in long-term, who won't break your heart, is tricky.

Three years later, I sat across the dinner table from a friend of mine. Nearing 30 and craving that long-term relationship that would fill her cup of satisfaction to the brim, she was engaged to the right guy "on paper." She had only dreamed of the kind of connection they had. Their courtship had started brilliantly, and she quickly thought she was dealing with the man she'd marry, Then everything devolved.

The connection was still there. But he was in his 20s, and unsure if he was truly ready to settle down for the rest of his life. He was there for her only when he wanted to be. To stay together, they started to negotiate what their future would look like, each compromising their ideal views of a relationship—a little more freedom for him, a little more space for her. It wasn't what either of them really wanted.

She wasn't sure she was in the right relationship anymore. She was dealing with almost right, or "once was right," but not all-the-way right anymore. His erratic behavior was wrecking the entire dynamic and foundation of their relationship. "How do I know if I'm settling?" she asked over dinner. "I have thought about this forward and backward, left and right, and maybe this is all there is."

My advice wasn't complicated, and can apply to life as much as it applies to love. I told her, "You're settling if you feel like you are."

It can be that simple. Your conflicting, mixed-up feelings all lead to this conclusion. It doesn't matter what settling means universally, or what it means to your very best friend. In this arena, settling is what you, and you alone, feel.

You should be looking to commit, forever, only to the guy who doesn't make you weigh the concept of "settling"—and if you're letting too much slide. I promise, you are not too complicated to find everything you're looking for all in one package, and you will know the difference between settling and compromising. You will and should question every single lingering emotion that doesn't make you feel right about the relationship you're in. Relationship-building is a process, a climb, and a journey—one where intuition plays a real role.

I am sure a light went off if you read Gottlieb's advice, as she warned against ignoring the tick of your biological clock in favor of waiting for a soul mate. Time passing is a scary prospect to an End Goal woman who has set her sights on a happily-ever-after that includes kids. So you thought, *Maybe I can settle! Perhaps not a lot, but a little bit.* And you sprinkled fairy dust on that wish and hoped to dream your 10 percent man into fruition. If past generations of women have asked themselves, "How will I know when I've found The One?" the current generation is asking the question, "How will I know if I'm settling (or at least settling too much)?"

Frankly, you're smart. I don't believe in this The One nonsense, and you probably don't either. You think, *Out of the billions of people on planet Earth, there are probably at least a few partners I could be truly happy with—but at the same time, I want to meet one of those guys, not settle before I do.* Yes. And ultimately, you keep working at relationships until you *choose* your One.

As End Goal women, we can't always define what settling is, but deep down we know that we are repulsed by it. Settling goes against absolutely every inclination we've been taught to let guide us since childhood—that we have the power to create a world in which we can obtain the best of everything, and love is the most idealistic of all our goals. However, the longer you are single, the more you start to question your strategy.

I told you that I would never issue strict rules, since dating and relationships aren't one-size-fits-all, but I do believe in key principles that everyone should base their dating life around. With that said, I'm here to tell you the first one: Never settle in love.

Settling is a way of life. If you settle with your love, you settle with your life.

## Equal Marriages and Sortin' Off

With the dawn of app dating, we've seen the rise of an interesting phenomenon: assortative mating. More often today than in the past, we're seeing a marriage of equals. As a 2016 article in the *New York Times* explains, "Assortative mating is the idea that people marry people like themselves, with similar education and earnings potential and the values and lifestyle that come with them...People are now more likely to marry people with similar educational attainment—even after controlling for differences between men and women, like the fact that women were once less likely to attend college."[3]

Husbands are still earning more than their wives on average, but that gap is shrinking. According to the *NYT*'s evaluation of recent Census Bureau data, wives make 78 percent of their husbands' salaries—up from 52 percent back in the '70s. For opposite-sex couples where both partners work some of the time, women bring in more than their husbands 29 percent of the time, up from 23 percent in the '90s and 18 percent in the '80s.[4] The pay gap between husband and wife is closing with each passing year.[5]

Assortative mating is on the rise for a number of reasons. Dating apps support pairing off with someone similar to yourself in looks, education, background, and interests. This isn't necessarily a bad thing. Entering into a relationship with someone who is similar to you in important ways often throws a magical veil of positivity over your bond.

You each think your significant other is pretty hot. You were educated in similar settings, and likely have similar interests as a result. You come from the same socioeconomic background and likely make similar incomes—so it doesn't feel like one person is pulling *all* the weight early on, and you can jointly decide how to make your careers coexist as the relationship progresses. You probably "get" each other.

There is also a feeling of mutual regard within the relationship. Each partner feels like they bring a lot to the table. No one is a dependent. It's love formed and maintained by *choice*, not obligation, societal expectation, or necessity. Basically, both people feel really freaking happy to have found each other.

From the outside, assortative mating seems to be the antisettling. Just pick someone exactly like yourself and, voilà, you can stop reading here. But when put into practice, it isn't that simple, because obviously there are some bigger issues at play here:

- You need to find a person whose personality and life goals mesh well with yours.
- You need to find a partner who is ready to be in an honest relationship.
- You may have misjudged a partner who was not right for you in the past.
- Our generation, on the whole, is delaying marriage.

Take it from dating expert Susan Walsh, who understands the unique predicaments of the current generation. "Among the educated cohort, it's really a bimodal distribution," she explains, which basically means there are two "coupling" age peaks. "An increasing number of women are realizing all these great career and growth opportunities exist to explore. Rare guys get a lot of interest early, but for most, it's natural to delay commitment." The stock for these young men is rising. They have no biological clock. So why would they settle down now?

Also, the closer you are to the top of the pile in terms of earnings and education, the fewer options you theoretically have to "sort off" with and be similarly matched—and more women are bringing more to the table today than ever before. You don't have as many equal matches. Everyone is pairing off in other arenas, and there you are searching for the needles in the haystack who "get" you and fit your life. You are single for long periods of time, because it's harder to find a guy who can and will really date you.

Now, this is where the plot begins to thicken. You're a catch on paper, and all your friends tell you this. Guys tell you this. Your grandma tells you this. Strangers tell you this. You are accused of being "picky," hard to please, overly critical—and you start to believe all those people. You'd be married by now if they were wrong.

*I must be picky,* you say to yourself as you internalize this negative dialogue. (This is actually BS, of course, because nobody is even asking you out, and you're getting ghosted left and right on dating apps. But you still think these people must be onto something... right?)

Eventually, you get restless and think, *Nothing is wrong with me! I'm getting a date, dammit.* And so you find a way to force the issue with some guy who seems like a *safe* slide into the Realm of Official Coupledom—you even sort of pursue this dude, because this is the 21st century and no guy takes action anymore (amiright?).

You choose some guy you think could maybe, possibly, fit the bill. He's pretty cool! Perhaps he's your guy friend/acquaintance, or your electrician, or this guy at your coffee shop who has watched you order a skinny cinnamon dolce latte for eight months now. He seems safe enough—a solid option. He's nice to people, and doesn't strike you as a heartbreaker. He's even cute!

All this is okay, so far. In fact, it might even be good. I don't think a paycheck, paper checklist, or set of physical characteristics should define anyone or any relationship. But the important thing to emphasize here is this: *You really feel no connection with this person.*

But everybody tells you that you're picky, so you think it must be so. You ignore the inherent pull of modern assortative mating and think (deep down) you're not settling *that* much. *This is doable,* you think. The chemistry isn't fireworks or anything, but you have a reasonably good time hanging out and a couple things in common. He is not exactly what you imagined for yourself, but he's not a bad option either. So, you decide to go full tilt with dating and give it a go.

At first, he seems pretty receptive to you. He sets up some dates (or allows you to set them up), takes you out (or goes out). He doesn't even make a move at first! (Which must be some sort of respect thing, right? He's just nervous; he'll get over it, you convince yourself.) He doesn't call or text you much in between either. But you're busy anyway, and it's not that big a deal, you think. You go on one date, and then two, and it's all fine and not so bad, and you think things are going okay... You're not sure, of course, because you've been out of the relationship game awhile, but you *think it's okay.*

But that's exactly the problem: It's just okay.

As you're starting to see this guy, you are mentally adjusting your expectations for a partner—how much is enough, and how much you can let slide. You are creating an image in your head of what you two *could* be in the best of circumstances, fashioning some sort of future time in which this will work for both of you and you'll be madly in love.

You are now talking yourself into a relationship, by way of hopeful daydreams, rationalizing that this connection will one day blossom into the one you've always imagined. You are getting attached to that idea, too. So when he starts to pull back even more, you begin to panic. Because you were told this could work—by experts, and the media, and your grandma, yet something is going awry!

You try harder to keep your dream afloat. But unfortunately, the connection is off; it was never there. Not just for him, but for you too. See, this guy you're dating has put up the Great Emotional Wall, and there's no getting past it. Forcing a connection is an easy way to get slotted into the short-term lane.

Don't settle for "meh" connection or pursue a relationship just to have one. Those men will stay at arm's length; they can feel when they're not fully pleasing you, and they do not want to feel like they're being settled for, so they often refuse to even get close. That's why chemistry will *never* bloom in a forced environment.

## Settling Is a Way of Life

Still, the longer you're single, the more you start to consider settling as a viable life course. You start making compromises about what you once considered "big things." Someone with passion becomes enough, even though he doesn't have a real career focus. Someone with a real career focus becomes enough, even though there's no spark. Someone who doesn't share your desire for kids becomes enough, because maybe at least you'll have love.

Over time, you get jaded. You start to forget what it feels like to be really, truly to-the-core excited about someone—and the great and terrible thing about that is that it's like muscle memory. Your heart seems to remember the sensations of something greater, but your mind continues to play tricks on you the longer you don't find it. You've cauterized yourself to what *greater* really feels like—because it was amazing, but it ended. It hurt once, and badly. So everything you come across seems not quite right, even though you don't know why.

I'm not sure that I believe in love at first sight, but I believe in undeniable connection. It's the "click." It's that moment when two people converge in such a way that they were just meant to be. Maybe for a moment. Maybe forever. But that click is powerful stuff and tends to brew the best relationships; it's based in excitement and a certain "fit" that's driven by synchronous connection. On the other hand, any relationship where you struggle to connect from the very start is not the right relationship.

When you're in a relationship like this and you feel the pull of settling for less than you deserve, I want you to stop and reflect. I want you to remember that our generation is delaying marriage and that you are not alone. I want you to know that you may not find a mate who has all the earnings and success that you have—but you will find a complementary partner with whom you connect strongly, who fills the gaps in your life, and who has the self-esteem to understand how special your dynamic is.

Eventually, you will meet this person, who will shock you back into the reality of your desires. And you want to be single when you do.

## Be Selective, Not Picky

Lots of single End Goal women are accused of being "picky"—a label assigned to them by their mothers, their best friends, the men they're into (men they would date, even though they won't ask them out). The sentiment is "You're amazing, and single, so it must be *your* fault." Meanwhile, you just want a guy to show up for you! (And maybe put the toilet seat down.) Hard to find? You really wouldn't think so.

Now, it's not like I've never met a picky EG. I've met a few. Maybe it *is* you. Whenever I ask a picky EG why she isn't going out with Mr. X again, her response is always "His laugh just bugged me" or "He grew up in a small town—ugh" or insert another inane reason here.

Women who are constantly told they're catches, but who are unlucky in love, have some of the highest walls and expectations I've ever seen. No one gets why you're single. You've had your heart broken by men you've "settled" on in the past, or ones who were amazing but not at all ready to commit. You think you deserve the best, yet you're terrified of worst-case scenarios. So you analyze the crap out of every date you go on, looking for reasons to stop the train if there's the slightest sign it might not reach its destination at some future point.

A lot of pickiness is a defense mechanism. The more time and energy you spend on prospects that don't fit your life, the more you want to create reasons to dismiss someone early, or set up hurdles for men to jump. *You only need one man,* you tell yourself. *Just* one. So unless Mr. X fits a very specific list of criteria that indicates likely-forever compatibility, you throw him out. You forget what you need from a relationship, and start creating "if *x*, then *y*" rule systems, looking for men who pass a surface once-over. However, many of the factors that can keep you forever-happy are not ones you can gauge at first glance. The "best" person for you might be someone you are not expecting, who your rules do not account for, and you are missing out on him because you're gauging long-term compatibility with the wrong criteria. You're being picky.

At this point, I know you are thinking, *I have every right to be picky! I've earned it!* And I've told you before that you shouldn't lower your standards and head down the road to settling. But it's a fine line. If you want a relationship you're actually at peace about, you should be selective, not picky.

It's a competitive world out there. As an EG, you're not in the market for a man who bleeds you dry emotionally and exhausts you during all the hours you're not at the office (and even some you are). You want to expend your energy on relationships that might actually be supportive and fun, not dead ends or duds.

I want you to really know the difference between picky and selective. Let's take a closer look (see Exhibit A).

*Picky is critical. Selective is discerning. Picky is obstinate. Selective is wise. Picky is insecure. Selective is confident.*

---

## EXHIBIT A

| PICKY | SELECTIVE |
|---|---|
| O Looking for reasons to dismiss him | O Looking for reasons to like him |
| O Having ridiculous dealbreakers | O Having realistic dealbreakers |
| O Investing energy in dating only to obtain your perceived ideal | O Investing energy in dating to obtain a mutually supportive long-term partnership |
| O Focusing on what you *want* in a relationship | O Focusing on what you *need* in a relationship |
| O Focusing on getting the most from a guy | O Focusing on giving your best, and whether a guy recognizes your specialness |
| O Having a closed mind | O Having an open mind |
| O Having insanely high expectations | O Having high standards of treatment |
| O Living by a rigid set of rules | O Using positive and negative reinforcement |
| O Trying to change an ill-fitting ideal guy instead of walking away | O Accepting when it's not a good fit and walking away |

See the difference? I thought so. Throw out your rules (are they really working anyway?), make decisions you can stand by, have a willingness to be vulnerable and open to new ideas and people, and be receptive to love in a form you may not have initially imagined.

I also want you to be a good gauge of personalities that mesh. While I absolutely love the principle behind assortative mating—and psychologists back up the fact that we choose partners who are similar to ourselves, and are happier for it—you don't want to date *you*. A good relationship blends similarities, to bond over, with differences, to make your life interesting and growth-oriented. You need to live and breathe growth—both as a person and as half of a future partnership. Let's take a look at exhibit B.

---

## EXHIBIT B

### GREAT SIMILARITIES FOR COMPATIBILITY

o Educational attainment

o Religion and values

o Communication styles

o Long-term goals

o Family desires

o Career desires

o Travel

o Interests (to bond over)

o Reasoning (asks, "Why?" vs. "Why not?")

o Home life and raising kids (you agree on division of labor)

### GREAT COMPLEMEN-TARY DIFFERENCES FOR COMPATIBILITY

o Energy (high-strung vs. laid-back)

o Job lives (creative vs. analytical)

o Decision-making (considering logic vs. considering others' feelings)

o Structure (planned vs. spontaneous)

o Interests (to learn and grow from each other)

These are just examples. Your partner could embrace any number of these differences and similarities, creating a unique, interesting, and growth-oriented relationship that will help you self-actualize. You want your partner to "get" you on some level but also to push you outside your comfort zone so you are constantly learning more about your potential. Seek out that right balance of similarity and difference—whatever feels fresh and exciting.

But how do you find this person? Good question. I actually believe that you are uniquely designed to recognize potential—your ideal, your spark, your soul mate—if you can get in tune with your own internal guide. Remember, you're intuitive. You can feel what is interesting, exciting, and complementary. Now, I want you to act on it in a way that seems organic and natural, fostering a connection that could last.

## Exercising the Power You Hold

MacKenzie Bezos, by all accounts, is a woman who pursues what she loves. She attended Princeton University to study under Nobel Prize–winning author Toni Morrison, intent on becoming a writer of fiction; she graduated with a degree in English in 1992.

Unfortunately, writing doesn't always produce immediate success—or a lot of funds to survive. (Not that I'd know anything about that…) So her first job out of college wasn't in writing at all. The 23-year-old freshly minted college grad worked at hedge fund D. E. Shaw to pay the bills and put a roof over her head, writing on the side.

While at D. E. Shaw, she met this guy named Jeff. He interviewed her for the position at the company, actually. "My office was next door to his, and all day long I listened to that fabulous laugh," she recalled to *Vogue*.[6] "How could you not fall in love with that laugh?"

The way Jeff tells it, lots of people failed to fall in love with him. He asked tons of people in New York City to set him up. "The number-one criterion was that I wanted a woman who could get me out of a Third World prison," he told *Wired* magazine, implying that he was looking for someone smart and resourceful.[7] "I'm not the kind of person where women say, 'Oh, look how great he is,' a half hour after meeting me," he said. "I'm kind of goofy, and I'm not"—he trills off an infectious round of laughter—"it's not the kind of thing where people are going to say about me, 'Oh my God, this is what I've been looking for!'"

Yeah, sure, Jeff. MacKenzie knew. This smart woman thought he might be exactly what she was looking for. She saw a lot of potential for a marriage of the minds, and quickly became smitten with the bright go-getter who worked at the desk nearby. She asked him out, in fact—she suggested they do lunch. Fast-forward three months, and they were engaged. Another three months, and they were married.

When Jeff suggested they move to Seattle to pioneer some e-commerce book thing, MacKenzie went because she saw his sheer enthusiasm. Although she had zero business knowledge, she believed in his judgment and dreams completely. She trusted her gut and banked on Jeff.

Today, MacKenzie is a novelist and Jeff is the titan of Amazon.com (in case "Bezos" didn't give that away). She is the anchor of their home, while he is off engineering the way we buy. They also balance personalities: Jeff is the extroverted mogul while MacKenzie is an introverted bookworm.

They are a team; they've built not just an empire together, but a life. "Theirs is, by all accounts, one of those complementary marriages in which the two parts come together to form an even stronger whole," writes *Vogue* journalist Rebecca Johnson.

All because MacKenzie noticed Jeff, the "goofy" guy with big dreams. He counts himself a lucky man. "I think my wife is resourceful, smart, brainy, and hot," he told *Vogue*, "but I had the good fortune of having seen her résumé before I met her, so I knew exactly what her SATs were." (Not that he'd ever tell, he insists. Props.)

Sometimes, making moves, showing interest, and recognizing the potential of a bond pays off—something I will argue that relationally minded women are naturally better at. You just need to sense it, deep down in your core, and *not settle* before you feel that tug of electric madness. And, yes, it's okay to make a move! Knowing what you bring to the table and confidently displaying your worth can throw even the most committed bachelor for a loop. I want you to start attuning your-self to potential growth-oriented partnerships, adding those men to your circle in a way that feels mutually comfortable, and growing each connection.

Jeff Bezos was looking for a partner in crime—but just because a guy isn't on the market for a serious relationship doesn't mean he can't change course. Maybe he will be tomorrow, maybe in a few years, or maybe never. You will meet men creating unpredictable lives. Some you'll date; some you won't. Dating is not the goal. Building a relation-ship, and finding a life partner who will eventually be ready, is.

Today's relationship landscape is sort of like the stock market. It has evolved into a new beast, with no firm rules or guidelines. You are allowed to invest your time and energy however you'd like—but that said, investing wisely and with discernment will help you eventually reap the long-term rewards of an amazing partnership. It takes only one investment to pan out and make you wildly successful.

Also like the stock market, modern-day relationships are both an art and a science. I've given you a lot of the science. Now, we need to start talking about the art.

## Connections Are Rare

I met my first real boyfriend in 2014. It was summer, I was on the cusp of graduation, and this zany inventor just kept showing up for me—asking me on dates, asking me questions I'd never thought to ask myself, and continuously teaching me new things about humanity and science.

He was impressive on any level. At 26, he had founded two start-ups. He was breaking ground and trying to change the world. I couldn't *not* notice, despite my goals. As such, it was the first time in my life I wanted to invest in a relationship at all.

He did make me better in some ways, but he also made me worse. We were too young to sustain a relationship and our goals. We would spend 15-hour days trading ideas instead of doing work. And because he was my very first boyfriend, I felt deep down like there was something else out there for me—something more stable, something more sustainable.

While he was everything I wanted in terms of connection, our long-term goals were vastly different. I craved both tradition and expansion, whereas he wanted to be free and uninhibited at all times. In my mind's eye, I could see our lives diverging rapidly—and so I walked away. If he ever reads this, he should know that I still consider our relationship a major positive in my life. I credit the seeds of my success, in part, to him. Even if it wasn't "it," our relationship ultimately made me better. He made me want to work harder to achieve my goals and simply to know *more*. I started to wake up in the morning craving knowledge and understanding. He had accomplished so much at 26, and I thought, *Why not me?*

What I lacked in experience, I made up for in drive. I had no backup plan, and I laid the foundation of my career one brick at a time. I had started writing listicles for blogs and websites as a side job in college, while only dabbling in the work I wanted to do, but now I endeavored to write strictly on topics that mattered to me—whether that was examining the media's influence on mass shooters, or speaking up about the domestic violence rates against men. Slowly but surely, I whittled down the percentage of work I did "just to pay the bills" until I was writing 100 percent only what I wanted to write.

I also thought that finding another connection like the one I'd had with my ex would be easy. It wasn't. After more dates and "almosts" than I can count, I still haven't found anything quite like it.

I say scarce little about my personal dating experiences unless it really counts. This is one of those occasions—and what I'm trying to illustrate here is twofold:

1. Connections are rare. When you find one you believe in, trust your gut and invest.
2. The right person should inspire you to be a better version of yourself.

Because many men are on those strict career timelines, they might not be ready for you when you notice a palpable connection. But don't be afraid to invest in them in a way that feels mutually satisfying and enjoyable—maybe you're long-distance email buddies, or maybe you're in an undefined relationship where you're emotionally and physically committed (you just don't have the label that everyone else thinks you should). Whatever. Seek to fill your life with connections that make you want to be better, that help you grow toward becoming the best version of yourself.

One day, you'll feel IT. You're going to know. There will be someone you can't quit, because you believe he could be The One and he's worth the time. Or maybe there will be someone who absolutely scares you with his level of certainty *about you*. Or maybe that ex from your past, who you originally believed was The One, resurfaces and says he always felt the same way.

At the end of the day, I want you to keep asking yourself this question: *Does this connection feel rare and different from any others I have found in the past?*

If yes, to keep your levels of delusion at bay, ask this: *Is this relationship helping me become closer to the person I ultimately want to be?*

In any relationship, you should weigh the energy you put in against benefits you derive—your give versus get. This isn't selfish. When two amazing people come together in the right relationship, they are greater than the sum of their parts. They get more than they give, because they create a *net positive* as a couple.

Whether you're just getting to know a guy, investing slowly in a friendship with him, or he's your fiancé, the answer to the question of whether you are better because of him should be easy. I once heard, and fully believe, that great relationships are easy. *Not effortless, but easy.* As in, even in your ugliest moments, you'd still easily choose your partner. You'd say, "Yes, I choose you." Every time. No hesitation. That choice needs to start in early days, and extend after years.

Like Jeff and MacKenzie Bezos, you're looking for a "complementary" partnership, where "two parts come together to form an even stronger whole." With that in mind, here's a listicle with *actual value*.

## Poor Reasons You Hang On to Relationships

Since I want you to start gearing yourself toward finding the best relationship of your life, I need you to let go of the relationships and prospects not ultimately meant for you. And I know, EG, sometimes that's a hard pill to swallow. Relationships can actually be shockingly hard to come by these days. And you deserve one. I just want you to have the right one.

A short-term loss may very well be a long-term gain, so here are reasons that are no longer good enough for you to hang on to a guy/relationship/dream.

### 1. It's yours.

Remember 26-year-old Samuel from NC? He has learned a very valuable skill: knowing when to walk away. "I think even though I spend a lot of time and emotion in relationships, I'm always okay regardless," he explains. "I can recognize if the compatibility isn't there long-term." He's noticed that women, on the other hand, seem to view every relationship as an investment—some of which turn out to be meh, or poor.

In behavioral economics and psychology, "the endowment effect" explains the tendency of humans to assign more value to the things that they own *just because they own them.* Not only do people tend to be reluctant to trade their items for items of equal value (which they may even need), they also tend to pay more to retain their items than they are worth.[8] Once you associate yourself with the item or person in question—maybe it's an old concert T-shirt, or maybe it's your assistant who is about to leave you for a higher-paying job—you're going to have a harder time letting it go.

Maybe your T-shirt is really too small these days anyway. Maybe Janet was always just an okay assistant. If your BFF was struggling with either of these decisions, you'd say, "Donate it! Get the tax write-off," or, "Let her go! You could hire another Janet tomorrow." But it's not your BFF. It's you, and these are your things. You're reluctant to let go because you chose that T-shirt and you chose Janet. There's psychological value in that. It's a loss, and humans are loss-averse.[9]

We also see an endowment effect in relationships—whether it's early days and he's pulling back, or you've been together for years and can't reconcile differences about a wedding, marriage, and future. You probably overvalue what you have, simply because it's yours, and forget there are tons of people in the world who are potentially a better fit.

## 2. You have history together.

History is a powerful thing. For as much depth and character as it can provide a couple's story, history also keeps us hanging on to relationships way past their expiration date. Samuel deftly points out that women are "more astute and perceptive," but he says we also seem to suffer from "blind spots from an emotional intelligence standpoint."

This is why you should consult your gut early and often—and especially before you take another step in the relationship, like making it official or getting engaged. When you are young and relationships are bright, shiny, and new, you need to amass experiences. You may have had a long-termer with someone who was totally wrong for you, and that's okay. You were learning.

As you get older, though, you should get more discerning. You know what's out there, what works for you, what feels wrong. You are aware of the unsettled feeling in the pit of your gut that says, *Don't go further!* History can blind you to that feeling or rationalize it away. That is why you are going to ask yourself these two questions before every "big step," or whenever you feel like something is wrong for too long:

- Does this relationship feel rare and different from any others I have found in the past?
- *Is this relationship helping me become closer to the person I ultimately want to be?*

You have to know when to walk away, cut your losses, and find the person who is actually right for you. This takes getting real with yourself. This takes knowing what makes a strong partner, acknowledging what you like and can't stand in a guy, and recognizing that rare person who contains the "it" factor—the one whose long-term goals and desires line up with your own, who inspires you to be better, who values what you bring to the table.

Some mistake history for connection. It's an offshoot of connection that can add to its beauty, but is *not* connection itself. History creates attachment, not connection. And if you're clinging to history, you might never find the great and elusive "it."

Positive experiences that greatly outweigh negative ones can sometimes bring couples back together when the timing is right. Negative or ho-hum experiences, which vastly outweigh the positives, are just history that you should learn from.

### 3. He fits an ideal.

Some women say the darnedest things—like they will date only African American finance guys who are six foot four or taller and have an athlete's pedigree. Or that they will date only Southern men with scruff who own farmland or are in possession of oil money. I kid you not. I have had real conversations with women who have told me the above.

Not only are these types of ideals a hindrance to finding a great guy in the first place, but they can keep you holding on to a guy who is totally not working for you. They can also keep you from asking the hard, real questions. Delia, a 29-year-old magazine editor in NYC, recalls dating a guy when she was in her early to mid-20s. "He was objectively great—attractive, ambitious, a wonderful person," she says. "From the outside, people think you're the perfect couple."

Delia thinks she probably hung on to her ex simply because he seemed ideal—even though inside her relationship, he could not open up emotionally and they were never in sync with their humor or goals. "I tried to bring fun into our daily lives," she says, to no avail. When

Delia "added up their relationship on paper," after years, it finally did not work. "He wanted to get married, have kids, and stay in DC," she says. "He had always assumed that path. For me, it was the bonus, but not the goal."

Delia broke up with him, moved to NYC, and got her current job. Oh yeah, *and* a relationship built on connection. Of all my interviewees, Delia speaks with the most excitement about her guy—after about a year together. "He already gets me on such a deeper level," she says. "He's thirty-five. He's been through relationships. We think about the world in the same way. He's a great storyteller, and very creative. We love to hear about each other's lives."

This guy had so shifted Delia's paradigms about a good relationship I couldn't help but smile while talking to her—as if it were happening to me. "I feel like this is everything you hear about!" she explains. "The person makes you want to be your best self, you never get jealous...and you're not crying all the time." (That's a good box to have checked.) "I think I bought into the older generation, who said, 'Relationships are hard,'" she says. "So I was always thinking, 'Well, *how* hard?'"

In reality, relationships aren't hard. Life can be hard. A relationship with a person you deeply love and are compatible with should be easy.

## 4. You feel external pressure.

You get pressure from every side to find The One—Mom can't stop asking, Great Aunt Sue always brings it up at Thanksgiving, societal norms say women in relationships > single women, and there's that silent-yet-deafening tick of the biological clock. But pressure is no reason to settle.

Lydia is one cool EG. Not only is this DC 23-year-old working in communications, she just has an impressive *life* résumé. "I'm really interested in politics and international affairs, traveling," she tells me when I ask her about her life. "I've lived in hostels in Australia and Europe. When I was in London, I met a lot of people who were like-minded."

She is a smart, upbeat person who speaks with kindness and who can discuss just about anything—the kind of girl you'd definitely want in your squad. But Lydia is also perpetually single, and confident as she is, she's not immune to the pressures of singledom. "Society doesn't exactly help," she says. "There is this woman at work who keeps asking me if I have a boyfriend—and it's really hard when you *want* that companion."

Recently married to Isabelle, 37-year-old Shawn, can also attest to this. When I ask him to name "traps" singles should avoid, he mentions only one: "If you are feeling external pressure to move forward in the relationship, be skeptical," he says. This includes pressure from your friends, your family, societal expectations, on-paper ideals, your dog... whatever. "You should feel an internal push to move things forward," he says. Internal pressure is your desire, which feels organic, exciting, and full of potential. External pressure is other people's desires for you, which can feel uncomfortable, confusing, or even terrifying if you form relationships based upon it.

## 5. You're lonely, and dating sucks.

It's okay to admit that you're lonely. We are created for connection; a 2013 Gallup poll found that only 5 percent of Americans have never been married and say they don't want to marry, meaning that most others have been married, are currently married, or want to marry in the future.[10] But just because we're basically all looking for connection, that doesn't mean we find it whenever we desire it.

Hunkering down with the wrong person is only a barrier to meeting the right one—so you have to learn when to stay and when to leave. Take Landon, the 30-year-old journalist, for instance, who admitted to remaining in multiple relationships beyond their expiration dates when confronted with the alternatives of staying single or dating around—one vaguely sad, the other exhausting.

Lydia is similar, but she's taken the opposite approach. She's holding out *until* she meets a worthy candidate. "I've met and talked to lots of guys, but it always seems like just first dates or hookups," she says. Deep down, Lydia knows she's a relationship kind of girl, and she's always had the courage to admit she wants something real. "I've never been in a relationship!" she says. "I want someone who cares about me— a partner, a form of support. When you go on dates and get ghosted repeatedly, you have to act like it doesn't faze you. But I've spent whole mornings crying."

Lydia meets plenty of guys. She's been on apps. Even while she was abroad, she hit it off with multiple guys back to back—like one night at a speed-dating event, and another at a poetry reading. However, she has had no luck in finding a long-term connection.

While Lydia's hunt for a real connection hasn't been easy, it puts her in a better position to meet the right person, because she's not expending tons of emotional energy on guys who don't call her back, guys who only want a regular hookup buddy, or guys who just like the thrill of keeping multiple girls in rotation. She knows what she wants, and she's keeping her eyes on the prize.

And remember: Settling is a way of life. It's insidious, and it will catch up to you once you start down the path of making small concessions. So keep asking yourself those two questions—and don't hang on to a relationship out of comfort, history, fear, pressure, or loneliness.

You're not being picky; you're remaining selective to find long-term compatibility. Don't let anyone tell you otherwise.

## CHAPTER 11

# your relationship toolbox

It has never been a more complex time to find a relationship, with more potential for BIG LOVE and more potential for heartache than ever before. So I asked Art Markman, PhD, the University of Texas at Austin psychologist, why relationships are so confusing today. He is one of the broadest, most in-depth psychological thinkers I get to interview, so I knew he'd help me find some answers. He immediately brought me back to childhood.

Our first relationships of any kind are typically with our parents. Markman, a boomer, remembers getting a key to his house in fourth grade. When he arrived home from school and let himself in the door, there was a list of chores for him to do if he wanted to go hang out with his friends later. He'd leave a note saying where he was going to be if neither of his parents was home when he wanted to peace out for the evening, and they had no way to check on him, since there were no cell phones. Markman remembers biking by himself to Little League at age 10.

By the time Markman had kids, encouraging children to have a sense of independence and fostering their decision-making skills wasn't the social norm. His peers in the baby boomer generation were raising their kids in what he thought was a crazy-overprotective sort of way. "I remember none of the kids were doing things on their own," he says. "My kids' elementary school was literally right around the corner—and yet all the parents in our neighborhood were walking or driving their kids to school every day."

While we can thank Mom and Dad for the overabundance of love and guidance, it positioned us to have some extreme repercussions. "Those first relationships do set beliefs about the relationships you're going to have," says Markman of hands-on moms and helicopter dads.

And we leaned into our mothers and fathers for a whole lot longer than past generations, creating a new not-a-child, not-yet-an-adult "in-between" time—a.k.a. "emerging adulthood," a term coined by psychologist Jeffrey Arnett.[1] To be real, lots of you probably still call Mom and Dad before you make a big decision. I do, too. "This is a huge shift," Markman says. "The expectation in relationships is that someone else is looking out for you, and is the source of your enrichment—that is what a close relationship *is*. And some amount of that has transferred over into the relationships people are forming now."

Obviously, it is not a bad thing to derive enrichment from your relationship. But our standards today are insanely high—which is something social media enforces, says psychologist Marisa Cohen. "Just look at the 'relationshipgoals' hashtag," she says. Add in the idea that we're supposed to explore all these so-called options for dating, relationships, *and* career fulfillment, and it becomes easier to see why relationship standards feel different today than in the past—and why we're all so paralyzed by the possibility of doing life wrong. "My generation did not have this word 'adulting,'" Markman says. "But this generation has this expectation that you have to be qualified to do anything, to take the next step. The entirety of your schooling from K through 12 was teaching mistake minimization." (Oh yeah. You mean, A+ = zero mistakes? I was great at that. As to whether it was actual understanding or just perfect memorization, I plead the fifth.)

If you've taken pause to think it over, life is not actually about mistake minimization. It's about growth, reaching for goals, actually *making mistakes*, and learning from those mistakes.

Both men and women can fail to understand this, but I'm more concerned about you, EG—someone who has probably been achieving, in part, by way of mistake minimization for a good, long while, and may be stuck in a mindset that's hindering relationship-building. This is why I decided to create a toolbox for you to use. Employ accordingly.

## EG Tool
## Trust Your Intuition

I am fascinated by the power of intuition. Karla Ivankovich, the clinical counselor and psychology instructor, explains it as "that gut feeling—a sixth sense, inner voice, or uncanny wisdom that allows the hardwired internal defense systems of the brain to reveal a greater truth." Sounds mystical. And kind of badass.

That truth might be whether a decision is right or wrong for you.

Our brains process information via two different pathways. One is conscious, and the other is subconscious, the latter evaluating situations based on external cues and past experiences. There are lots of cool studies on the intuitive pathway, but let's look at a recent gambling study.[2] Each participant chose cards from two decks. One was set up to dole out minimal gains but no losses (the "safe" deck); the other had big gains followed by big losses (the "dangerous" deck).

Around 50 cards in, participants intuitively figured out which was the safe deck of cards—but they couldn't explain the phenomenon until around 80 cards in. Even more interesting, however, is that only 10 cards into the game, the sweat glands in participants' hands began to rev up whenever they'd reach for the dangerous deck.

Our gut is a live wire of neurons and regulation. It is sometimes referred to as our "second brain,"[3] and we're just learning all the ways in which it communicates with our body.

Good decisions, investments, and choices are often felt somewhere deep in our core—and women might be uniquely wired to have a stronger sense of intuition, perhaps especially as it's related to the realm of human emotion. Ivankovich says the intuitive skill set is typically linked to those who are more attuned or sensitive to others, an area where women seem to have a leg up on men. Historically, women have had to look out for their children's interests as well as their own, all the way back to prehistoric times, when we had to evaluate threats quickly or risk extreme dangers—like decide which direction likely held resources, or how best to ditch a saber-toothed tiger. Women might have developed those stronger gut feelings as a result.

Or perhaps a woman's keen intuition is biological in nature. In a study of nearly 90,000 people, published in the journal *Molecular Psychiatry*, women consistently scored higher on the so-called "Eyes Test," which tallies people's ability to correctly predict what someone is thinking or feeling by looking at the eyes alone.[4] The researchers showed that women might have "genetic variants on chromosome 3," which may result in a better ability to read others.

No matter the reason, I want you to remember that your intuition is a powerful tool. I want you to trust your decision-making skills and make choices that sit well on a gut level.

We've been taught to rationalize absolutely everything in society today, so we often ignore "gut feelings" when we cannot identify the reasons that we have them. But sometimes, your intuition is thinking and processing invisible information that does not sit at the forefront of your mind. Especially in relationships, which feel so hard to begin with, I don't want you to ignore your gut. You don't need a specific reason to break off an unsatisfying relationship; you don't have to pinpoint why you've been unhappy or unsettled for months on end, just so you can defend your decision to others. You don't have to justify your investment in a guy who keeps making "silly" decisions to others (and sometimes *to yourself*) if you believe the potential of the connection might bear out over time.

You know yourself. You are self-actualizing! You know the kind of relationship that will ultimately make you happy, and you can often feel the right decision before you can explain it—or, at least, the risks you need to take or moves you need to make that could lead to something wonderful. Sometimes, *you feel the right path in your gut.*

# EG Tool
## Keep Standards High and Expectations Low

In love, we are looking for a perfect match all too often, instead of a realistic, awesome partnership. Modern relationships do take work—just like your mom said. Perhaps they even require more investment than in past generations, simply because we have such high standards of excellence for the connection and its benefits. But don't forget that standards are different than expectations. Let me illustrate:

### EG Standards

- ☑ He treats me with respect.
- ☑ He's inherently trustworthy, and his stories always add up.
- ☑ He follows through on his commitments.
- ☑ He prioritizes time with me.
- ☑ He is honest, open, and transparent.
- ☑ He handles his emotions well, and does not lash out or hold grudges.
- ☑ He handles conflict well and effectively communicates his opinions.
- ☑ He shares my values and goals.
- ☑ He stays in regular communication.

### EG Expectations

- ☑ He sets up dates with me at least twice a week.
- ☑ He calls me every night after work.
- ☑ He tells me he loves me every single day.
- ☑ He texts me first thing when he wakes up and last thing before he goes to bed.
- ☑ He's at least six feet tall.
- ☑ He never loses his cool or brings work home with him.

Much like being selective versus being picky, standards versus expectations are an issue of confidence versus insecurity. List number one contains goals for a reasonable relationship. List number two is a hyper-sensitive, borderline-petty list of relationship self-sabotage, which will lead you to feel unsatisfied, and your man to feel like he can't satisfy. That's a breakup in the making.

A man—even a Real Deal—cannot possibly fulfill a detailed list of desires in a relationship. There may come a day when he doesn't call you as usual, or a week where he can't see you at all. He might not be six feet tall! Life. Is. Messy. And the world doesn't revolve around your budding relationship, important though it may be.

It's okay to have high standards. In fact, insist upon it. If a guy doesn't meet your standards, you have every right to break things off. It's grounds for immediate dismissal. But for now, I want to zero in on what you are actually looking for—which is more abstract than specific expectations, more meaningful, and there are many ways to get there.

## EG Tool
## Use the Connection Trifecta

EGs often like to "résumé date." Some résumés read like, *He's passion-ate, he's a creative when he's not working his 9-to-5, and he'd be up for taking one international vacation a year!* Other times, that CV is like, *He's a Rhodes scholar with an Ivy League pedigree and an entrepreneurial spirit.* It depends on the girl. But I know you've idealized some qualities of the dream man you'd have this "on fire" connection with.

While it's wise to date men who are similar to you, assortative-mating style, that's *a whole broad category* of men. I want you to stop reading profiles and questioning men like you're filling the position to be your boyfriend. I want you to stop hypothesizing so much about hyperspecific traits that will work for you, and start using your gut as a gauge. I want you to set your sights on a new, simpler set of standards. I want you to look for the Connection Trifecta:

1. **Emotional connection.** *You are attracted to his emotional energy.* Sometimes, warm and cool create a delicate balance. Or laid-back

and high-strung. Sometimes, two friendly, bubbly people find solace in that safety net. Or two independent, driven folks share less time together but have a strong bond when they do meet. Whatever the energy, it needs to feel homey and positive to both parties.

2. **Intellectual compatibility.** *You are attracted to his mind.* You always want to know what he's thinking—about big decisions you need to make, how his day went, the latest debacle in politics. You share a sense of humor. You have at least a few interests in common, and enough differences to keep it interesting. You think on the same wavelength and can pick up each other's thoughts.

3. **Physical chemistry.** *You are attracted to him.* No matter his look or what others think, you're wildly into him. He turns you on. You think he's sexy. You also have similar sex drives and are open to discussing each other's preferences. He needs to feel desired by you as much as you need to feel desired by him.

These three facets of connection are the cornerstone of a great relationship. Discovering "it" is nonspecific—a more intuitive process than a rational one. Stay open-minded about the packaging; don't scan résumés to find a man.

## EG Tool
## Seek Certainty Before Sex

When should you have sex with the guy you're dating? This is one of the oldest questions in the book, because there is no established right answer. When to have sex is a deeply personal choice. Naturally, you're a modern woman with her own mind, and you're welcome to have sex whenever you'd like with whomever you'd like (as long as terms are mutually agreeable and healthy, of course). However, always remember that there's a difference between sex for pleasure and sex that furthers a relationship. That's why it's important to seek certainty before sex. There are a couple of questions you can ask to get there.

First, consider, "How do *I* feel about *this guy?*" If you don't feel much for him beyond the physical, you *want* to engage casually, and you're up front about it, then do whatever! He'll likely fade away as soon as you meet someone you're more compatible with. However, if you think he has Connection Trifecta potential, then you may want to delay sex for a while. There's good reason for this. Guys I surveyed were far more prone to say that to have sex, they need only to feel physical attraction, whereas women were far more likely to claim they need both the emotional and physical to truly enjoy sex. Since relationships are best built on equal footing, I want you to make sure he's developing real feelings for you before you go there.

This brings us to our second question: "How does *this guy* feel about *me?*" Only time and observation will inform your gut. If he keeps planning dates with you, keeps contacting you, is open with you, asks thoughtful questions, remembers small details, and sticks around for four, five, six dates—or whatever feels right to you—you're good. You're good when you feel safe and happy with the decision. Guys want that emotional connection with the potential *right* woman. In my chats with them, many say they feel it's one of the biggest misconceptions among women—that men are only out for sex, and not intimacy. One says he and his friends are all seeking "substance, across the board," despite how guys are often pigeonholed. If he sees that in you, and he's ready and open, he'll let that intimacy develop. It'll come with time, cool dates, great conversation, and mutual effort, so don't rush.

Now, it's okay if the emotional components grow *in tandem* with the physical side. In fact, that's good! One guy tells me the key is that the relationship always has a "positive trajectory," even if it's slow. Guys just want to feel like sex is on the table, eventually. Plenty of guys say they'd wait months or years for the right girl—or, as one guy even tells me, "as long as it takes." I think one of my late-20s interviewees puts it best: "If you want to build a relationship with someone, it's okay to say no to sex. See if the guy sticks around." We're not reinventing the wheel with this one; the point is to make sure he wants your mind and your heart as much as he wants your body. Delaying sex is still the best strategy until you're certain that you want to build a relationship with him (or not) *and* that he's emotionally invested in you.

## EG Tool
## Put On Your Oxygen Mask First

I've never understood why women are the relationship builders and social connectors of the world yet we seem to let men drive relationships. Yeah, yeah. I get it. Men have this innate drive to "pursue and obtain." We're told men are wired more toward sex and attraction, instead of real love and bonding. Really? In the end, don't men want the same deep, long-term connection we do?

When I embarked on this mission, I had one major goal: to explore female agency in modern relationships. What works? What doesn't? How and where do women control the process of building and working toward reaching the potential of our relationships?

Relationships are undeniably important to both men and women—but women are the more relational sex, and men can be a step behind, that is *until* they meet someone who shows them that a healthy, meaningful relationship is safe, exciting, and beneficial. We therefore hold the power to build, foster, and nurture relationships that are founded on deep connection and directed toward continual growth. But you need to put on your oxygen mask first, before helping others.

This is self-actualization in action, something you may well be working on *before* the men to whom you're most attracted bloom into the marvelous flowers they could one day be. So, first and foremost, we have to discuss what that looks like. Maslow identified some key behaviors that lead to self-actualization.[5] When we apply these to relationships, they are exactly what we're going to use to build strong, authentic bonds.

You can employ these strategies almost anywhere. In fact, you probably already are using them when it comes to your career, friends, family, hobbies—whatever. With dating and relationships, it's trickier. It's like all you can think to have is "rules" or "commandments" by which you live your life. There is nothing more emotional than relationships—and that scares people. But I'm not going to give you a list of rules. Instead, I'm going to teach you skills, and trust that you'll know which investments are most worth your time and energy.

Lots of men talk about wanting someone to challenge them, or simply someone who complements their strengths and seems to naturally make them better. Well, you are going to see if relationship prospects rise to your level simply by practicing Maslow's self-actualizing behaviors within romantic contexts.

> *Soak up words, actions, and patterns; tune in to *exactly* what's happening.*

You are going to plug in to the male mind, on every date, social gathering, and ice-breaking meet 'n' greet. This means listening to a man when he tells you he's "not ready" or he's a "heartbreaker," or when he gives you a list of reasons not to date him. This means you will believe the negative narratives he offers up, and wait for positive actions instead of positive platitudes before investing deeper in a relationship.

> *Break old habits and try new strategies, even if they lead you off the well-worn path.*

Insanity is often defined as doing the same thing over and over again, expecting different results, right? If you see a pattern in past relationships, amend it. If you notice traits that don't work for you, look for the ones that do. Maybe you need to start choosing healthier relationship qualities, like consistency, follow-through, and honesty. Maybe you need to take more risks, and date a charismatic man, who doesn't seem like your usual shy-guy type. Don't be so desperate for a relationship that you'll take any one that is offered. Don't look for safe; look for right.

⚑ Make your own decisions about where to invest your time; don't just listen to past tradition, authority figures, or what friends and family think.

It's really nice to have your mom, dad, big brother, and best friend on board with your relationship. It's also nice to see your social circle embrace someone. But guess what? That doesn't always happen, and having a gold star from society doesn't mean you'll be happy or fulfilled. Your close friends and relatives will have opinions about each guy you date—and for guys who aren't "ready," the ones you may have vented about to your mom and BFF, they might not all have glowing things to say. Your job is to listen to yourself, your gut, your feelings, your needs, and your desires in determining if a man is worth your investment. Every relationship is a risk, and you're the one who will live with the consequences—be they positive or negative.

⚑ Refuse to play games with men; remain honest, even if it's hard.

It's easy to get sucked into games to maintain the upper hand. And men claim to like the game, even though they really just like the intrigue. Usually, they haven't met a woman who rises above it all. Don't play hard to get; simply *be* hard to get. Don't be a "catch" in the game; be a "catch" in real life. A catch in the game is elusive and difficult to read. A catch in real life is the living definition of mystery—intrigue that never runs dry for the right compatible man. This will extend even after you're in a relationship, because you are smart, deep, and curious. You don't need to fake your value. Any guy who's worth your time will see that you command respect, and know you are hard for anyone to obtain.

All that dating and hookup culture have taught men and women is how to play games and gain the upper hand. Whoever cares more loses, right? Wrong. That isn't how we self-actualize, and that isn't how we create strong relationships. Any relationship that's going to last will be built on authenticity. You will be sincere in your needs and your effort in getting to know a man. You will be transparent and honest in what you're looking for. You will come at each potential match from a place of confidence, telling yourself: *This is me. This is what I ultimately want. You can like that or not—but either way, I'll be okay.*

🍸 **Stand up for your choices and actions, even if others disagree.**

Along the lines of being entirely authentic in your relationships, I'm going to ask you to make hard decisions about your love life. Down the road, you may be considering getting back together with an ex— perhaps one who broke your heart years before. You may be investing in a man who has potential in your eyes but who others think is so not worth your time. You may want to date someone who doesn't look *at all* right on paper but who makes you happy every day—even if others don't understand the dynamics of your relationship. They don't have to. This is your life, and your relationship. You make the decisions.

🍸 **Own your decisions, take responsibility, and constantly strive to realize *your* potential.**

While choosing your partner should ultimately be easy, relationships still take effort, and you're going to need to put that forth for the rest of your life; it won't stop even when you've met Mr. Right. So start now. Take responsibility for your faults and failures. When a relationship or prospect goes south, look for the lessons. What did you miss in him? Maybe there was a lack of honesty, but you wanted to believe his words over his actions. Where did you contribute to the demise? Were you too demanding early on, or perhaps overly accommodating…right into pushover territory? Not only do you need to work hard to meet new people, you also need to work hard on yourself—learning what works for you and what doesn't, what you want and need in a partner, to avoid repeating toxic patterns.

🍷 Figure out your walls and defensive tactics, and be brave enough to surrender them.

This is perhaps the hardest behavior of all. In a world that encourages women to be independent, and conditions us to compete in tough academic and career environments, we have become naturally defensive—which is the opposite of allowing the vulnerability required to build a deep, honest, lasting relationship.

I want you to take a hard look at your defensive tactics. Maybe you adhere to traditions or rules to keep your heart safe. Maybe you want men to put in all the effort while pursuing you before you'll consider reciprocating with attention. Maybe you're holding back your true feelings, for fear that men will run. I don't know. But I need you to think about your walls, write them down on a piece of paper, and remind yourself that great relationships are not built from a place of defensiveness.

Remember that you are gorgeous, smart, successful, and talented, and you deserve a great relationship. You have self-esteem in many other facets of life. You know what you're looking for. You have great friends, a family to fall back on, or both. And if you put yourself out there and some guy doesn't see your worth...you'll survive, and you'll learn some valuable lessons to file away for the future. I promise.

Every single one of Maslow's self-actualizing strategies should be employed in creating relationships that will help you and your partner reach your highest potential—individually as two unique human beings, and together as one long-lasting unit. Because some guys are not ready, and you'll need to employ these strategies to help you sort through the noise.

## Activating Your Tools When It Feels Like Men Have the Power

By and large, the men I interviewed for this book tend to compartmentalize love and relationships more frequently than women do—or in a systematized way women do not. Maybe they're conditioned to do it, maybe it's ingrained, or maybe it's a combination of the two.

Whereas women tend to live in potential, projecting the possible ways a relationship will evolve, I found that men tend to assess the women they see in the here and now—especially those younger, developing guys, who may still be living, breathing dating stereotypes.

They talk about tracks, lanes, boxes, and categories. Even sex, dating, and relationships seem to occupy three separate spheres instead of being viewed as three intricately intertwined parts of a larger whole. That's why a man can meet a woman he thinks is great and yet not pursue her. Or he can have a no-strings fling and walk away devoid of emotional entanglements. Or he can meet the love of his life and decide that maybe he needs to date some more (?!). To most women, that's baffling.

This makes some sense, of course. From a young age, men are taught to be detached from their emotions as a way to declare their masculinity. Some are also taught that separating sex from love, and short-term from long-term, makes dating more emotionally manageable. Society encourages this, too. I talked to Harris O'Malley, a.k.a. dating blogger and relationship coach Dr. NerdLove, about this very male phenomenon of compartmentalizing. "Yeeeeah," he says with a sigh. "One of the 'greatest'—and I mean that sarcastically—things to come out years ago was 'ladder theory.' "[6]

The idea behind the "ladder theory" is that women basically have two ladders—a ladder for friends and a ladder for dateable guys—and those ladders never cross. Men have one ladder, and they just stack women on the ladder in terms of sexual desirability. But there are zones to this ladder. Top-tier, outta-my-league zone; really-like-her zone; would-hook-up zone, etc.

There's also something called the "Madonna-whore complex," which suggests that there are two types of women, categorized based on their perceived sexual experience: those you sleep with and those you marry.[7] "This sort of thinking is a self-inflicted wound," says O'Malley. "Why would a woman who's willing to sleep with you on the first date be undateable? So it's like, 'This girl likes me and wants to spend time with me, therefore she must be crazy.'" (I don't get it either.)

Like it or not, men are often wired to compartmentalize women, until they realize that doesn't work, or they stumble into a great connection by way of their crappy systems (luck happens). There has never been a lot of serious literature for men on how to build real relationships, simply advice on how to pick up or attract more women—so a lot of these toxic ideas come from online message boards and pickup artist communities, because they fill a need, says O'Malley. "All of this stems from the idea that women play games and are hard to understand," he explains. "To be fair, I've seen stuff on the cover of [women's] magazines...that says, 'Do this—test your guy!' But someone who 'follows *The Rules*' and is never available is not who you want."

Basically, we've created a detrimental back-and-forth: Women follow rules prescribed by bad dating literature. Men don't understand the weird behaviors. Then they seek information and put women into boxes to try to better make sense of these behaviors or of women in general. Perhaps this is yet another reason why it seems men have the power: They control your box, and thus the script. Like I discussed with two of my interviewees, a man and woman in their early 30s: In the teeniest, tiniest little mental space, you approach each date thinking: *Maybe he will be The One*—you never know! Meanwhile, a guy approaches each date thinking: (1) *Where am I meeting this girl for drinks?* and (2) *When should I leave the office to get there on time?* You're hoping that maybe he'll be "it," while he will be more or less *laissez faire* about the whole deal.

I'm not suggesting that you play games. In fact, I'm suggesting you rise right above playing games, while *still* knowing the rules by which others are playing—and the scripts others are following. I'm also suggesting you use your tools to attract and invest in the right connections.

While you might not have the advantage over men when it comes to dating as you know it, because you're less likely to have a very specific short-term lane, a long-term box, a one-night-stand compartment, and a "good for now" bucket (gah), you do have the advantage when it comes to relationship formation. You've been primed to form relationships from an earlier age. You know who you are and what you're looking for. You are intuitively aware of what sort of connection will probably make you the most happy.

So I want you to learn the rules of the dating game—and then I want you to flip the script, acting out of authenticity and looking for reciprocity.

I'll show you how to win in love without ever "playing" at all.

## CHAPTER 12

# dating effectively: how to stop playing the game

I had a major revelation upon writing this book when one of my interviewees told me about his dating life—you met Landon, the journalist, earlier. I'll get to my revelation shortly, but here's what you need to take away *now*: Landon did not like dating. But he became skilled at playing the game and reading his script.

When Landon was dating a few years back, he had actually already met the girl with whom he saw a future and would eventually enter into a long-term relationship with serious potential. But it had been initially complicated; windows opened and closed without a real relationship forming, and he wound up in the competitive NYC dating pool for a period of time.

It's not that Landon did not take each date as it came. He planned it. He showed up. He engaged. He just didn't necessarily have specific *intent* to form a relationship. He wasn't really ready to settle down. He wasn't necessarily looking for The One. He was operating with his own agenda—which may not have matched his date's.

He also wasn't going to have a bad date regardless of how he felt about a girl—even if he wasn't at all interested. Over time, he just got really good at dating. "I'd put on my best performance," Landon says. "I'd be the funny, charming guy—I didn't want to be a letdown. So that's the expectation. That's what you do!" Some of these men deserve Oscars, right?

If you've ever met one of these guys—you felt sparks, he was the best date ever, yet then he ghosted you or gave you a thanks-but-no-thanks vibe as you headed to your car or followed up the next day—now you know: *Sometimes, guys are just really good at dating.* Sometimes, they are skilled at the art of creating chemistry. Some men even practice this; they consider it a form of self-improvement.

There is an important lesson to be learned here: Dating is *set up* like a game, especially if you're on apps—a.k.a. the modern version of Hot or Not, but with higher stakes. More than that, you're figuring out how to unlock each other, and mutually determining if you want to know more—without ever saying it outright.

So in the aftermath of any date, you're still maneuvering, asking yourself, *Does this guy want to see me again?* It could be an objectively great date, and the answer could still be no—he could be dating three other girls, and one relationship is progressing faster. He could have determined this was a one-night gig going in. Everyone dates with a different agenda:

- One guy might be getting over a breakup.
- One guy might be bored on a Thursday night.
- One guy might be in town for the weekend and just want a little fun.
- One guy might be dedicated to the search, looking for the love of his life.

You just don't know what you don't know! And agendas may change. But oftentimes, they don't. And since he may not be evaluating the date in the same headspace as you are, I don't want you to take rejection personally. You do not know anyone well enough after one date for the rejection to be truly personal.

And you still can turn dating from a game into an exercise in real relationship-building—because that's what dating should be.

## Smarter Dating for a Full-Package Woman

My greatest desire for you is to embrace your agency in the process of finding The One, right alongside living your already fabulous life. I want you to treat every guy you encounter like a *potential* investment. Some men are worth a little of your time and may prove themselves worthy down the line; some connections are worth all your emotional energy almost from day one.

You get to decide. That is your right. I won't take it away from you or tell you who's worthy. I just don't want you to waste time on any men who you haven't personally decided are worth your investment.

The great thing? Men will generally tell you where they're at in their life. They will also reveal a lot of their intentions in their actions. Initially, all you need to do is read the situation effectively and decide how to make your investment—which, as I said, isn't fixed and can change over time. First, though:

- Gauge the three levels of connection (see the Connection Trifecta in chapter 11), then decide whether to veto or pursue.
- Determine if he's ready or not ready.
- Invest accordingly.

I'm going to assume you can decide whether or not you're interested. We've already discussed what you're looking for in a connection, and the different types of guys out there. Now, we'll get into the deeply personal decision-making process behind how to make relationship investments.

But first, where do we meet these guys?

### Offline

There are three primary methods for meeting dates offline, where you'll be put in a position to form real relationships of sorts: through activities, friends, and work. While dating apps are a legitimate way to meet potential matches (and we'll go down that rabbit hole, too), I want you to focus more of your energy on meeting prospects offline for two reasons: (1) You're better able to gauge the connection in a natural way; (2) you're more likely to be doing something you enjoy in the process.

Before meeting his now-wife, Isabelle, Shawn remembers reading an article on relationships that stuck with him. In it, the advice for meeting the love of your life was simple:

- Do the mundane things you do every day that you enjoy.
- Try new things you'd want your best self to do.

So Shawn started to do that. Exactly that. And before long, he met Isabelle while taking a leadership/sailing class in the middle of the Pacific. Those long talks, late nights, and new experiences in person set the foundation for the deep, lasting bond they have today.

Besides taking part in activities, the other methods for mingling with new people are through friends and work. Meeting dating prospects through mutual friends has been going on for decades—there isn't much new territory to tread here. However, if you're single, don't be afraid to ask people you trust if they know anyone who would be a good fit for you. Today, we basically think it's shameful to act like we're looking. Stop thinking it's shameful to look for love! It's not; it's proactive.

Dating in your field of work could be amazing, yet it could also be terrible. You both likely entered the career for a reason, so you'll have tons of interesting conversations about topics you enjoy. The flip side is, your success and position will go head-to-head with your partner's. I've talked to plenty of men who say that they might feel those flames of inferiority the closer a person's achievements align with accomplishments or skills they actively desire.

If you've always dated within your field, and you've frequently felt competition with or jealousy from partners, I'd encourage you to try dating off the job—or wait until you find a man who seems very secure with his position.

Bars are another great place to flex your meet-and-greet muscle, although I have a couple guidelines to best operate in these settings.

First, choose bars where *you* like to hang out, not bars where you think the most men will be. This accomplishes two purposes: (1) You are not changing your life to find guys, but rather meeting men within the context of your already-fun life; (2) you're meeting people who have similar taste. Chances are, if you like to breeze into a swanky cocktail joint in heels and a floaty dress, meeting a dude who lives at a local dive will only lead you to question if you have enough in common.

However, it could be a good idea to vary your bar, according to your interests. If you're up for playing games, find a place with darts or a pool table and challenge any nearby boys to a round. If you want to watch the game, see who else is cheering for your team with the same fervor. If you're dying for a mixed drink after work and want to show off your new shade of lipstick, choose that trendy joint downtown—and ask whoever is sitting next to you at the bar what he's drinking or reading. The best bar connections are usually made in the context of already having the kind of fun you want to have, with your friends or even alone. Do you.

My last suggestion? Notice *everyone* in the bar, not just the loudest, cockiest, won't-take-no-for-an-answer bar star. That guy might be fun to banter with, but he's also probably pulled his lines on a hundred other girls. The shy guy who's been checking you out from the corner might be a better, hidden prospect—and is often open to an approach. Remember that men get harassed endlessly by their guy friends if they try to talk to you and then you bat them away. Most guys aren't used to getting approached either, and find the attention flattering. Even in the worst-case scenario—he isn't interested, or he has a girlfriend—he'll probably be supersweet about it. My friend once approached a guy on the dance floor of a folk bar, and although he was taken, he was so flattered. "Keep doing that!" he encouraged her. Men like being noticed.

## Online and Apps

Apps and online dating are the way of the future, but I don't want you to throw 100 percent of your dating energy into them. While I do believe many great connections are made on Bumble and Match, the swiping setup has a psychological coloring to it: Since there is no investment or risk for men (or women) to nab that date, prospects seem easy to discard and shuffle.

If you're using apps or dating sites on the regular, try not to focus on any one single prospect early on. No matter how awesome your first date, or even your second or third, force yourself to spend emotional energy on other guys. Go on other dates. Meet up for a quick drink or appetizer. No matter how tough it is, even if you're thinking about Amazing Dreamboat Prospect, date other men.

Remember what Landon said: that there was a point in his mid-20s when he just got really good at dating. He knew how to charm virtually every woman he went out with and make her feel special, regardless of whether or not he ever planned to see her again.

Do not invest up front; slow your roll. You've been there. You've seen guys fade out, or drop off the grid completely with no explanation. This is the 21st-century landscape. Technology will allow guys to ghost unless they feel they owe you some firm ending—even if you've invested emotionally. So pace yourself. Assume he is dating other people. Respond positively to his gestures, but continue to pursue multiple leads.

Many of us have developed this terrible abandonment complex, and it's exhausting to fret about each exciting prospect to cross through our stratosphere. It can lead to burnout long before you actually connect with someone promising. So date multiple prospects at once. You don't have to hook up with them! Millennials are less sexually active than Gen Xers or boomers,[1] and there is an app for every style of dater. It's how people meet and connect. So go on coffee dates. Suggest a walk around town. Meet for a drink during happy hour. Then, if one guy ghosts, you'll be much more Zen about it than if you were focusing only on him the whole time. You will also have been cultivating some other prospects, and you can line up another date the next weekend.

Get to know a handful of prospects and keep dating them, until one emerges as the clear winner or locks it down. You are single. So act that way.

## Strategies for Successful Swiping

I used to be the worst app user of all time. The old me would swipe, get a bunch of matches, focus exclusively on the guy I found most interesting, get into long back-and-forths over text, ignore all other options, meet up with said interesting man, and realize he tooooootally wasn't a fit... But by that time, I'd usually lost all my other prospects and need to start swiping again. Don't be like the old me.

Swiping on an app is a mindless form of consumption. You can over-swipe just like you can binge-eat when you're not thinking strategically, when you're not trying to optimize and enjoy the experience. You might waste good options swiping away out of boredom instead of trying to rock out a game plan—which there are plenty of.

I have two friends who were simultaneously dating using apps to meet guys in the winter of 2015; within a month of each other, both ended up with boyfriends who have lasted to this day. However, through discussions, I figured out that each of my friends had a markedly different strategy.

Fiona was a first-time app dater, and she put up a tough filter from the get-go. She had only six prospects on Tinder. She was talking to all of them, and actively going on dates with three of them for a couple of months. She had a type—nerdy, alternative, Eastern European—and she stuck to those criteria when choosing. For her, this seemed to make things fun and manageable. Eventually, Boris emerged as the clear winner among her three real suitors. Exclusivity was felt before it was expressed; after a month or two, she told the others she was seeing someone. After three or four months, he asked her to be his girlfriend.

Rose's strategy was almost opposite. She would liberally swipe right, saying yes to anyone she felt had potential. Then she let the guys sort themselves. She talked to those who messaged her first and let them move the relationship forward. She was dating two guys for a while, before one finally emerged as the clear winner. Her now-boyfriend was consistently the most in touch, most interested in setting up dates, and the most willing to lock it down. They DTR'd relatively quickly; I'd say within six to eight weeks.

My strategy these days is much different than it used to be. I don't swipe endlessly; to get around the "paradox of choice" (which suggests that too many options will cripple, instead of liberate, us), I swipe until I am messaging with three guys I'm genuinely excited about. And then I stop. Once those options have fizzled or been vetoed, which might take a couple of weeks, I go back to swiping. This never feels overwhelming to me.

If I feel particularly strongly about a guy, I'll message first. I think most men and women are blind to the opposite sex's experience on dating apps—but my guy friends have let me take a peek at their match queues. Ladies, oftentimes these guys have *way* fewer matches than we do. So, if you find one you like and message him first... well, I cannot think of a time it didn't end in a date for me. Just saying: Please feel free to make the first move! Like in the bar scene, he'll be flattered.

What's the ultimate lesson here? There is no one way to use apps, and you can adapt your strategy based on: (1) your personality; (2) how you want to engage. But there are certain things that are going to make life easier on you, and some suggestions to think about:

- If this is your first foray into dating recently (you've been off the market because of work, just broke up with a guy, etc.), perhaps try Rose's strategy. Opt for a wide field and figure out what you like. Shop around.
- If you've been dating for a while and know what works for you, try Fiona's strategy, selecting a small field of suitors who intrigue you. This will save you time and energy on the actual apps.
- You want enough prospects to take the heat off any one guy. Aim for dating about three men at once, à la my personal favorite strategy. Three is a really good number of prospects to keep in rotation until you DTR—whether that's three months into your app experience, a year, or five.

- Get off the app in a reasonable amount of time. If he's not somehow getting you into the real world, he's on there only to toy around. If you'd be interested in meeting up, give him your number (or set a time and place) and make it happen.
- Assume he's dating other girls by default—just like you should be dating other men. Don't expect a guy to commit early on. Don't expect him to stay in touch with you a certain amount right away. If he ghosts, do not take it personally; he doesn't know you well enough for it to be personal. You're an awesome EG, lady, so go out there and meet some dudes.
- If you're getting overwhelmed with too many prospects, stop communicating on the app. Give three guys your phone number and then shut the in-app communication down for a while.

If you absolutely hate app and online dating, do not feel pressure to date this way. I know some men and women who've literally never downloaded an app in their entire lives, and they're perfectly content. However, apps are good for a few reasons:

- To get yourself back in the game after a breakup or drought
- To test the market, see what's out there, and figure out what you like
- To feel like an in-demand woman

App and online dating does take persistence, and has the tendency to feel gamelike. That is why, perhaps more than with any other type of dating, it's wise for you to keep standards high and expectations low, and to be authentic at all times.

## Filters Aren't Just for Instagram

Every single guy you consider as a dating prospect will pass through a "filter" in your mind. He will land in one of several camps, and which camp you filter him into will determine how much you can likely expect from him. While it might seem like we're taking a page from the boys' book of compartmentalization, that's not the case. The sole point of filtering is to make sure you're not deluding yourself. When that guy you shared fireworks with isn't beating down your door to hang out, or calling you every night, I want you to know why. If you filter him into the correct group up front, there won't be a string of disappointments. Based on the signs a guy is exhibiting, you'll have two basic camps: "ready" versus "not ready."

How are you going to figure this out? Well, it's easy: Men tell you who they are. Most women just selectively listen. (Don't feel bad; I've fallen victim to it, too.)

This is where we *stop* selective listening, though. Knowing where a guy's at in his life will ultimately help you feel more chill about dating—and unlike men's lanes and tracks, these groups are fluid. A guy can easily transition with a few life changes, or putting in unexpected effort to build a bond.

This is not an exhaustive list, but an idea of what men who are ready and who are not ready for relationships will mention or say.

### *READY*

- ☑ He has a stable career, with no plans of moving in the next couple years.
- ☑ He listens attentively; he follows up on things you've mentioned previously.
- ☑ He does not pressure you.
- ☑ He explains information that might give you pause. Like "I'm considering jobs in another city—unless, of course, I have a reason to stay here."
- ☑ *He says he's looking for something serious.*

Mature men are as wise and discerning as you are. They know when a woman is an amazing EG—she's smart, she likes many of the same things he does, she has the same values, she operates with integrity and authenticity despite a world that has given her every reason to feel jaded. She rises in the face of challenges and disappointments.

With a man who's ready and open, you can be sure that he likes you—one misspoken word or faulty move won't change that. You're operating from a place of relative safety, and he wants you to know that.

**LESSON:** *He will make it clear he is focusing on finding a partner, or is seriously open to it.*

### NOT READY

- ☑ He says he's about to move.
- ☑ He says he just moved to town and he hasn't even settled in.
- ☑ He says he doesn't know what he'll be doing in a year.
- ☑ He says he's about to embark upon a months-long travel excursion.
- ☑ He says he's "really slammed at work right now."
- ☑ He got out of a serious relationship less than six months ago.
- ☑ He talks about love and relationships in a skeptical or jaded manner.
- ☑ *He says he's not looking for something serious.*

Guys who are not ready typically play the field—by accident or by intent.

- They've been taught to expect games from women. Some even come to enjoy them over time.
- They seek the upper hand. They want to control the speed of the relationship and to engage without pressure or expectation.
- They often act to inspire certain feelings *in* you, instead of acting on their own authentic feelings *for* you—those come later and slower, and are usually accompanied by an "OMG, I care" panic moment.
- They are somewhat insecure, which can inspire petty reactions; they withhold emotionally (effort, encouragement, information, support) when they don't get their way or don't like your reactions.

- They're selfish with their time and energy. They are focusing on themselves, not actively looking to give to a partner and relationship.

A man who behaves this way is not fully ready for a relationship right at that very moment, and you should plan accordingly. He may panic. He may think *you're* too much work, or he'll want to stockpile his freedom by building emotional walls. He may disappear because he's bored that you're not playing his games or reacting with enough *feeling* when he pulls back. He will be working on his own timetable. He's out there *dating for himself*, not to give back to a woman. He's not trying to fall in love. Sometimes, he's actively resisting it. Tons of people don't date to fall in love; they date for companionship, or fun, or ego boosts. If love happens, it's pretty accidental in nature.

I'm not saying you can't (or even shouldn't) date guys who are not ready. But if love and bonding is your ultimate goal, he's a higher-risk guy with a longer timeline to commitment. "I don't think he's aware he's playing those games," you tell me. He may or may not be, but I don't care about that. I care about *you*. So, I want you to know that "not ready" relationships are inherently fragile. Realize this. Accept this. You are going to need to work around his rules and games, or it'll be no dice, right from the start—until he decides he's ready to be his authentic self and take himself off the market. And even then, he could still panic.

## LESSON: *He will make it clear he is focusing his energy in a realm other than relationships.*

Guys may make a bid to transition to a new category, but you are not going to force them into any box they don't naturally belong in. In essence, you're going to read the signs and let guys sort themselves. The best-case scenario is that he *is* ready—or gives every indication. "Not ready" *can* be grounds for an immediate rejection; dating is an odds game, and I would never suggest you invest time in a long-term *project* if you are ready for a real relationship *prospect*. However, if you feel that he's a connection worth exploring right off the bat, but not ready, then simply proceed with caution and keep expectations low.

## Good Filters Versus Bad Filters

Filtering doesn't end after the first date—although oftentimes we think it does. He's cute? He's funny? He's got a good job? Set!…Eh, no. Until you're in a relationship, you need to keep assessing the situation to determine if a guy is worthwhile. And after confirming that basic set of attraction and connection filters, you have to ask yourself about the bigger set of compatibility filters. "Good Filters" are smart, legitimate ways to tell if he's potentially right for you; "Bad Filters" are signs you might mistakenly think prove a prospect is worthwhile, but actually aren't enough.

### Good Filters

Honesty. You want someone honest (with himself and others). Does he tell you what he wants, clearly and transparently? Does he divulge information when asked, even if it doesn't make him look the best? Are there inconsistencies that don't *feel* right, in your gut?

Alignment. Do you have enough in common? Ah, the age-old question. Do you have similar moral values, political ideologies, and religious beliefs? Can you have deep, substantial conversations (especially if you're a person who values "talking")? Do you like some of the same activities (especially if you're someone who values "doing")?

Patience. In a relationship, there are tons of timelines—how fast you get physical, how fast you talk about personal beliefs, how fast you talk about your past, how fast you communicate your desires for a relationship, how fast you lock it down. You both will have personal preferences, and you'll engage when the slowest person gets to their comfortable place, their place of "go." A man's ability to handle a "no" or a "not yet" is one of the best qualities you can filter for—it is the mark of being able to delay gratification, and it goes beyond delays in the moment to what he does afterward. Does he punish you? Does he withdraw emotional support or attention when he doesn't get what he wants?

**Reliability.** So simple, but frequently tossed by the wayside early on. We make excuses for the people we like *all the time*. How many times has a guy said he'd call or set up a date with you but didn't, and you said something like, "Oh, he probably just forgot," or "He probably just had a busy week"? No more; that's a sign of unreliability. Does he do what he says he's going to do? Some men are all talk. Everyone slips up—but not three, four, five times in a row. In dating, words mean nothing, actions mean something, but patterns mean everything. Patterns of reliability are the foundation of *trust*. It will be a very frustrating relationship if you can't count on him.

**Listening skills.** A guy who really cares about you will want you to be happy and comfortable—he'll want you to feel seen and heard. If you say something bothers you, like that you don't hear from him between dates, does he try to correct it? If you mention that you can't get enough coffee in the afternoon, does he pick one up for you on his way to your place? It's the little things that make a relationship.

## Bad Filters

**Strength of pursuit.** I want you to recognize that coming on strong right out of the starting gate is just a tactic of pursuit. It's not the only tactic. It's not even the *best* tactic. It is one tactic, and should have very little impact on how you assess a guy as a potential partner. Here's why I dislike using this as a filter:
- It is one-sided.
- It's not necessarily authentic. You know you're great, but how does *he* know this soon into dating you?

- This excitement often wanes over time; the strength of interest and frequency of communication should grow in accordance with the intimacy of a relationship.
- A busy, quality guy may not be able to text you all day long. That should be applauded, not discount his relationship viability.

**Alpha qualities.** If you've dated around and decided that you like alpha qualities, great! But unless you've put why you like those qualities under a microscope, don't use them to assess a man's value. Today, there are oodles of male incarnations—from the nerdy alternative guy who is a massive NFL fan to the business guru who spends evenings songwriting. Seriously, pulling out his Amex to pay for your steak isn't the only measure of a good man.

**"Nice guy" qualities.** We are grown-up women looking for soul mates. If you've had your fill of bad boys, you may have a tendency to go in the other direction and look for "nice." Oh, how I hate that word. "Nice" should be a baseline for how you treat people; it is a tenet of basic human decency. If your bar is so low that "nice" is the sole identifying characteristic for which you've chosen your mate, there are problems with your filter—or that guy is not being fully honest about himself and his intentions. If you never see a flaw, it's not real.

**Sex.** Sexual chemistry is important. I can't tell you the number of women who discount physical attraction, claiming they'd feel superficial if they put too much stock into it. (Um, hello...Feeling physical urges around your guy is what elevates your relationship from friendly to romantic!) That aside, great sex is still an incredibly poor filter. Physical chemistry is only *one* part of the Connection Trifecta. As alluring as it can sometimes be, sex does not a relationship make. In fact, insisting that your hookup buddy is a great relationship partner just because you two have amazing sex is sort of like claiming chocolate ice cream is the same as Neapolitan. Someday, you're going to need your partner's advice, crave a deep discussion, or want some emotional support—and if you've filtered only for sexual chemistry, that day will be a bummer.

## Authenticity 101 and the Problem of Playing Hard to Get

There are some men who will play games with your heart for sport, perpetuating the claim that all is fair in love and war, and how you play the game "signals your value." This is what *The Rules* tries to teach and preach, actually: If you play hard to get, you're showing a man that you're high-value and he'll need to work to prove he's worthy of you.

So much to dissect there.

- If you "play" anything, you're operating from a place of inauthenticity.
- You are high-value because you're an EG. A guy will either recognize that or not. If you feel you need to act a certain way to prove your worth to a dating prospect, you'll always feel like he's one step away from disappearing.
- A man will want your time if he's interested in getting to know you. If you act like you don't care, he'll suspect you aren't serious about building a relationship with him at best, and are totally uninterested at worst.
- There will be no maneuvering or playing around with guys who are worth your time. They invest in you—at the pace they are comfortable, with the level of enthusiasm the intimacy of the relationship warrants at any given time.

So, forget all that *Rules* stuff. What is our motto? Hint, hint: There are no rules. You don't need to play hard to get if you *already are* hard to get.

You are an EG: You make people earn your time at work and at home; if someone isn't treating you with kindness and respect, you call them on it. You invest your energy wisely in people and projects that feel genuinely worth your time. You have all the qualities of a great long-term partner for the right guy, and you're not going to attach yourself to anyone who doesn't value you. You know you'll be as successful in the right relationship as you are as a boss or business owner, or as a friend or daughter.

You're a catch. So simply act your value—no games required. That means you are kind, open, and ready to get to know a dating prospect, but also capable of caring for yourself and maintaining a full life with or without a relationship.

So here's my crash course, Authenticity 101:

- Your attention and investments are always selective in nature; you will not date just anyone. Classic research actually shows that an effective strategy for dating is to be hard to get for the majority of prospects, but moderately easy for the one person you're most interested in.[2]

- You make an effort, but you have a sense of balance in your life. Your career, friendships, values, hobbies, and personal development are just as important as dating (if not more so).

- A man will earn more of your time and attention when you decide he's worth it through his investment of time and energy and your assessment of compatibility and connection. He meets you at least halfway, he shows interest, and he doesn't punish you if you have a busy calendar and a lot of people you care about.

- Every guy must rise to the same standards of treatment; you do not set the bar differently according to the guy. He has to observe basic tenets of kindness, respect, and thoughtfulness, and a genuine desire to know you and make you happy—because you are doing the same for him. No placing the bar higher so he'll prove himself, or lower because you really like him. Your bar is your bar.

- He is welcome to set his own pace in getting to know you. You are also welcome to walk away and make the final decisions about your time and energy. You do not need to identify and state a detailed reason for ending things either; your reason can be that it doesn't feel right anymore. The tug in your gut is enough. Don't let anyone convince you otherwise.

- Refuse to play games. "Playing" any game signals that you are trying to establish yourself as someone or something you are not. If a guy falls for *that*, the day will come when you can't keep up the facade of mystery and intrigue. He'll either like what he finds under the mask, or not—which you should have shown him from early days.

If you don't feel inherently hard to get, you need to address that. Ironically, on a personal note, feeling like I'm #undateable is actually my internal signal to stop dating—code for "Take some time off and do you." I ask myself, *Okay, why do you feel so undateable and worthless as a partner?* Answers, by way of my internal dialogue, have ranged from:

- You feel like it's been a long time since you've met a guy who "gets" you—the real, deeper you.
- You've gone on a string of dud first dates. You're tired.
- The last two guys you really liked were Almost Boyfriends, and you didn't know how to deal with that at the time.
- You were in an emotionally manipulative relationship with a Mr. All That But; you need a breather to find your value again as a kick-ass, independent woman.

Dating from a place of high self-esteem is best. Remembering what you're looking for in a partner is best. If you feel emotionally healthy and confident, you are in the best place to actively date. Not only can you more readily notice men who embody self-actualizing relationship potential and invest wisely, but you're also ensuring that you won't make a decision based on low self-esteem and the pressure to be coupled simply to prove your worth. That's a recipe for long-term misery.

So actively date only when you *feel your value* in your bones. When you don't, revisit the places of joy, fulfillment, and meaning in your life—from reading your favorite authors to doing volunteer work to traveling. Who knows? In the process of rediscovering your worth, you might meet a soul mate in the most unexpected place.

## The Three Cs, Making Investments, and Keeping It Real

Okay, so where does this leave us? Your time and energy are valuable, and you get to decide where and how to spend them. That is your agency— but never "play." Pay attention. Look for the three *C*s, in this order:

1. **Connection:** Can we talk easily? Do I feel a spark? Is this enjoyable and exciting? (Living in the present.)
2. **Compatibility:** Do our lifestyles and goals align? Do our personalities mesh? (Looking toward the future.)
3. **Character:** Is he a man of integrity and honesty? Does he know who he is, or is he actively figuring it out? (Looking toward forever.)

The three *C*s make up the Commitment Trifecta. When you settle down, I want you to be batting a thousand in these categories. However, you can't get all this information on one date. And even though many men won't be "all the way there" yet in their growth—that doesn't mean they aren't worthwhile, or won't ever get there. That is for you to filter, risk, and decide. (You're not always "all the way there," either!)

Now, let's take a Real Deal into account. Multiple mature, "ready" guys have told me that if a girl plays hard to get, they are automatically going to think she's not interested or she's toying with their time and emotions (not cool), so they cut their losses and bow out. That's how real, mature men act: Their time is valuable, and they do not have extra energy to spend "figuring out" your games.

This is another great reason to be authentic and show interest, especially if you are looking for a "ready" guy versus a "not ready" guy, a Real Deal versus an Almost Boyfriend. Guys who aren't "ready" are sort of turned off by too much authenticity. They don't like your lack of dramatic intrigue and can completely miss how interesting you are in your natural state. You're no longer "fun," mysterious, elusive—a game to win, a conquest.

Which is amazing. When one guy in the "not ready" camp told me, "My interest drops off a cliff when she texts me first," I knew I was onto a great filter for men who just want to play games: *Text him. Call him. Ask him out.*

In equal measure as he communicates with you, of course. We've all had someone OD on expressing their interest in us (yikes). You should both be working for places in the other's busy calendar. But the point is this: Any guy who is remotely ready should be excited you want to spend time together and build a relationship—whether he initiates that time or you do. If he's not interested, he'll be unresponsive. If he's not ready, he'll distance himself to the place he feels comfortable. If he's a player, he'll disappear. If he's ready and interested, he will respond positively. Every time.

If you text him, he'll answer in a timely manner.

If you call him, he'll pick up or call back.

If you ask him out, he'll say yes—or, if he can't make it, propose an alternative time.

It's not that a guy who plays games can't end up in a relationship—some men are more misguided than actually manipulative. (According to Dr. NerdLove, they've been taught that women are confusing creatures who are basically walking paradoxes.)

However, you need to filter the misguided men from the manipulators. Here's what I know:

- The right guy will be authentically interested in you.
- Guys who are not ready are way more prone to letting you walk away.

Investments should be made taking these two realities into consideration. I wish that every guy you instantly felt the Connection Trifecta with would easily recognize the potential of your connection and display the Commitment Trifecta, but that's not life. You have to learn to read the situation as it unfolds around you. You don't need to play hard to get, but you can use positive and negative reinforcement. You get to decide how important it is that you find a compatible guy who is *ready* versus one particular guy who seems to have all the qualities and connection that you've always wanted but is *not* ready.

Learn to relax and explore different kinds of bonds. Take risks when they feel warranted, so you don't have regrets. Realize what sacrifices you're willing to make with a partner—putting off marriage, having a long-distance relationship if he moves for work, waiting for him to get over a broken heart—before you settle down with a given guy.

Each time you're interested, figure out what kind of man you're dealing with, and then ask yourself: How important is this specific guy? Also ask yourself: Is he trying?

Effort is important. Establishing the appropriate dynamic is important. Lots of people have dating all wrong—you're building a relationship, not trying to snare a mouse in your trap. Men have been told many incorrect dating "rules," just like you have. It's okay to be patient if he's figuring out there could be a better way.

We often teach others how to treat us. And you can teach a man how to have an authentic relationship—but don't pretend and don't play. Make him rise to your level. You are a self-actualizing woman, and you need a self-actualizing man at your side. He can operate from a place of "I want to be a better human being, and there's something *different* about this person," or he can think, *No, thanks.*

Either way, you're being you.

## CHAPTER 13

# the case for waiting

There is this enduring myth that when you meet your lifelong partner, that guy will have it totally figured out. He will "just know." He will see you across a crowded room and think to himself, *That's it, she's The One!* Interestingly, I've heard very few love stories that begin that way. Okay, I've heard *zero* stories that start that way. And I've talked to a lot of people.

Today, most love stories begin in a somewhat messier manner. Take model, TV host, and social-media funny girl Chrissy Teigen, for example. She met her future husband, musician John Legend, on a music video shoot back in 2006. It was a long day that ended with In-N-Out burgers and some canoodling in John's room.

Of course there was a connection—and both (silently) felt it right away. But then, you know, John left to go out on tour. Instead of crying or sulking around, Chrissy simply chilled out and lived her life. Hokey though it may sound, Chrissy just *trusted the connection*.

And later, she didn't push John to commit. Over the course of a year, they texted and talked on the phone. Chrissy was aware John was playing the field—but such is the case with most men and women in the early stages of dating, and they couldn't realistically date right at that moment. The timing was wrong.

So Chrissy let John come to realize what an amazing woman she was slowly, and with concerted effort building a longer-range bond. "I let him be himself for a while," she told *Cosmopolitan* magazine in 2014.[1]

"The worst thing you can do is try to lock someone like that down early on, then have them think, 'There's so much more out there.' I played it cool for a long time. Never once did I ask, 'What are we?'...I was just happy to be with him." She allowed their bond to blossom to its full potential, because she waited. She gave John the necessary distance to feel "ready" and sure of himself in order to pursue their relationship.

Yes, if a guy doesn't seem instantly sure about your relationship it can feel scary! Early on, John was still reticent. "I was on tour with him and he'd gotten sick," Chrissy told *Cosmo* in 2016. "He was feeling really bummed and stressed out. He was like, 'I can't be in a relationship right now,'" she recalled. "That lasted for one day. Literally, a day. I knew it came from a place other than us not working...I always joke, 'Remember when you tried to break up with me?' He's like, 'Yes, sorry. *Big* mistake.'"[2]

We can all learn from Chrissy, who gave John the space to grow on his own—so they could *both* choose each other from a strong, stable place. And now that he's settled and stable in his success, he can be an equal partner to Chrissy. "One of the coolest things is how supportive and happy and proud he is of my success lately," she told the magazine. "I'm with someone who is totally secure in himself. He's not trying to be anything other than what he is. The confidence he has brings it to me."

These two are a modern couple, two halves of a better whole, merging two timelines and finally growing together. But—again, hokey saying alert—good things take time. And many relationships are no exception.

Ever the more relational, more intuitive sex, some women see what others cannot: the connection, the character, the way a certain special man could make them happy long-term. They invest, leaving themselves open and vulnerable, but fully believing in the potential they feel with some unsettled guy.

Since there are a lot more men in the dating pool who are *not* ready to date an EG than men who *are* ready to date one, extended relationship timelines and nonlinear trajectories are common, and they're totally okay—as long as you're cool with how things are progressing.

EGs with whom men connect on a deeper level can trigger thoughts of the future. Guys might not see how you're going to merge your time-lines and goals into one plan. Or they feel you're a "higher investment" of time, energy, resources, and *ego* anyway, a perfect storm that "not ready" guys may not be sure they can weather.

Sometimes, though, they just need to see how you fit.

## When to Wait: There's a Foundation of Trust and Friendship

Remember Jillian and Zeke, her Mr. All That But—a.k.a. her best friend/nonboyfriend, because the relationship was label-less? I swore we'd get back to her. It's time to reveal her *full* story.

Jillian was 24 years old when she married Michael—her good friend's older brother, four years her senior. They'd been dating since she was 20, and she thought it was a healthy bond. "I remember that he was quite mesmerized by me," she explains. "I thought, 'This is how it should be, right?'"

In fact, Jillian had a lot of misguided ideas about love and romance. She'd had a tumultuous relationship with her mother and a weak rela-tionship with her birth father, so basically her only concept of what a solid relationship *should be* was a product of pop culture—Disney, rom-coms, and happily-ever-afters had formed a lasting impression.

So despite the fact that she and Michael broke up *a whole lot* before they ever got married, she thought they could make it work—after all, heroines always had relationship trouble before they had lasting success, and he was "mesmerized." "Honestly, when we had broken up a couple times, I had dated a couple other people, and I had moved on—but one day he called me and he wouldn't let me see the dog that we shared," she says. "And somehow, it took about three months, but we ended up back together." He convinced her to come back. "Of course, I had seen all these movies. I thought loving him was enough."

The two married, but Michael's family, who was actually *really* involved in his life, did not like Jillian for cultural reasons; they didn't approve of the marriage. However, she tells me, "he kept coming back to me, so I just figured he would fight it out. It still felt like a movie." Besides, she says, "Somewhere along the line, I had heard that a husband should love his wife more than she loves him." (OMG, did she read that *Cosmo* story?!)

As we discussed before, theories like the "10 percent rule" allow us to cling to faulty logic. Even though Michael pursued her strongly before marriage, and *was* in love with Jillian, he didn't stand up for her in front of his family. And the lack of acceptance and support from Michael's relatives was a huge burden for her to bear.

In the meantime, Jillian had gone to work at a start-up. Start-up employees tend to be a tight-knit crew, and most everyone at their small-ish company knew that Jillian was contemplating a divorce. Among them was her boss, Zeke, who was invested in her success—both professionally and personally. "There was mutual respect and friendship there," she says. "He gave great advice. I told him that I didn't think I was happy in my marriage. I suddenly realized that if I was having this open dialogue with another man, something must be wrong."

At home, Jillian was miserable. She'd moved farther from her friends to be closer to her husband's relatives, and when they couldn't fix the familial tension, the couple had discussed a move elsewhere. But one New Year's Eve a few years into their marriage, Michael refused to budge. "He said, 'I'm not moving,' and I said, 'Okay. Then I'm leaving.'" Jillian methodically packed her bags and went to a friend's place a week later—where she subsequently started to freak out about what she'd done. One day, she was at work (completely losing it) when Zeke asked her a very basic question: Was she *happy* with Michael? Her answer: "Not at all." Zeke always seemed to know just what to say, simple as it might be. "He said, 'If you're miserable, there's no point in going back,'" Jillian recalls.

She didn't. Zeke also reminded Jillian that she was capable and competent—on her own—and secure and financially stable. In fact, Zeke was suddenly Jillian's "shoulder through the divorce," making sure she showed up to work and focused on her job. The dynamic with Zeke was vastly different from her dysfunctional dynamic with Michael. "We were soon best friends," she explains. "We were the same age. He listened to me, without judgment, and didn't look down on me. He pushes me to be better and to grow, but still respects me for me."

Maybe you can see where this is going. Over time, Jillian and Zeke caught feelings for each other. However, neither was necessarily ready for a commitment. Jillian was coming off that taxing divorce, while Zeke was "a committed bachelor," says Jillian. "He regularly mentioned he was in no position to have a girlfriend. He even joked that he'd help me find a husband one day, when I was ready." He said that even *after* the two started seeing each other. Jillian took this all in stride, though, because she knew, with him, something was different.

I asked Jillian if she thought Zeke was "mesmerized" by her in the same way Michael had been—thinking perhaps *that* was what had allowed her to chill out and trust the connection from the beginning of their relationship. "No!" she says with a laugh. "*I* was mesmerized by *him*. I was so impressed that someone my age had started a company and traveled the world already. People loved working for him. I was attracted to his brain, and how he could motivate and inspire people to do their best work."

Jillian says she fell hard for Zeke's character. She also knew that, although he didn't feel he was in a position to have a girlfriend, the foundation of friendship the two shared was stronger than the lack of label. She remembers having to tune out a peanut gallery of friends and family members who told her to cut it off. "He wasn't ready to commit right away, and that was frustrating, but I knew he was not a person you push," says Jillian, who also insists she never felt disrespected. "I never saw anyone else for those two years, and he didn't either. It was a felt understanding. Having him in my life was most important. I wanted *him*."

Zeke and Jillian were only 28 when they began seeing each other, and he was still in the process of making big career changes and creating companies. For Jillian, who had done it wrong before, marrying a guy who had pursued her directly into a problem-plagued marriage, this relationship felt drastically different. It felt like the merging of equals, despite its strange, quirky trajectory. Slowly but surely, even silently, Zeke took steps forward; he asked her to move in with him—and then to take an even bigger leap.

Zeke asked Jillian to join him as he tried to start a new company overseas. "He just called me one day and said, 'Want to go with me?'" she says. The three-month trip became an indefinite stay, and Zeke finally popped the question as they transitioned into a new stage of life abroad. "I swore I was never doing marriage again," she says. "I was so disappointed in the concept after my first one." But to Zeke, her *best friend*, she said yes.

What changed her mind? A grown woman's perspective, and trusting what she felt instead of how things *should be*. She said the early feelings of safety, feeling wanted, with her ex had been misleading indicators of commitment; this time, she was gauging her connection with Zeke, checking their long-term compatibility and watching him reveal his character. "I had to let go of this idea of total security, and *trust* this person," the now-35-year-old says of her husband, Zeke. "I was patient and self-aware as our relationship developed; I didn't want to date other people. We are honest with each other, to a fault. He knows me; he can look at me and know something is up. I respect him, and we have so much fun together."

She and Zeke chose each other, in their own way and in their own time. "I finally have a relationship I'm proud of," she explains. (Oh, and in 2017, they became parents. Don't you just love a *real* happy ending?)

---

### WHAT YOU SHOULD LEARN FROM JILLIAN

o Zeke and Jillian had a deep friendship first, and she trusted him. She believed what they had was the foundation of a great relationship, and he would come to that conclusion in his own time—despite a (perhaps misguided) tenacious belief that he'd need to focus on business over relationships for a good long while.

- o Zeke did not need to sow his wild oats or see other women; Jillian knew he was only seeing her. So while he hadn't verbally committed to a relationship, he was committed to Jillian in action; his pattern was one of reliability, trust, and putting her best interests first.
- o Zeke had qualities of character that Jillian respected, like leadership skills, the ability to inspire, and a supportive nature.
- o Jillian ignored others who said Zeke wasn't worth the lack of label. She was prepared to stand up to the majority opinion—one key sign of a self-actualizer.
- o Jillian chose "who" (Zeke) versus "what" (a relationship). The power of their specific bond was stronger than any label.

## When to Wait: You're Confident in the Connection—and Yourself

Devon, now in her 40s, learned some hard lessons through her own failed first marriage. She admits she was less than supportive of her ex, taking ownership of her faults, but she also chose the wrong guy—one who cheated on her throughout their relationship. So when she began dating again several years ago, she knew she had to make wiser decisions about the next man to come into her life. She had to look harder for quality instead of relying simply on chemistry.

Already on top in the business world—colleagues say Devon "rules with an iron fist in a velvet glove"—this EG wanted the best out of a relationship. And one fine day, her boss told her that she'd need to get in contact with some guy named Aaron for a work project, slapping a magazine on her desk and pointing to this doctor from Boston. "One look and I just *knew*," she says. "I was so freaked out I threw the magazine away."

Her boss wasn't about to let her off the hook, though, telling her to get in contact. Aaron immediately and completely defied her attraction to "overconfident types." He blew her away, in fact. This laid-back, silly-yet-sensitive guy was serving as a physician for patients in underprivileged neighborhoods. He was brilliant, with a huge heart. Something new, something mutual; she immediately connected with him.

However, Aaron was a Mr. All That But. He was emotionally unavailable when he met Devon, in that oh-so-common state of confusion—surprise!—after a very recent divorce. Frankly, he wasn't going to pursue Devon at all, despite their many shared passions. Her EG exterior was too tough a nut for Aaron to contemplate cracking at that point in his life, which left Devon with a tough decision in a vulnerable position. Could she *really* be in a relationship where she had to give a bit more at the start?

Devon is known for her discernment, and she deployed it and determined that Aaron's character warranted the risk. She believed in their connection—even if he wasn't "ready"—and used the wisdom of her prior failed relationship to guide her decision-making with this new guy. She also used her EG confidence to slow her roll and not place lofty demands on Aaron from the get-go. "A lot of smart, strong women will try to *force* what they want while dating," she says. "In reality, you need to use your executive-functioning skills and encourage some open two-way communication." (Yes. This EG said "executive-functioning"!)

Devon was honest and direct about her feelings for Aaron as they developed over time. She did not beat around the bush, nor was she passive-aggressive about Aaron's pacing. She put herself out there, but she did not push him. "I learned that 'settling' was not going to make me happy, and because I believed I could help guide Aaron to the place he ultimately wanted to be and just be there for him, I invested in him and cared for him early on," she says. "He had to see he could trust me, before he could be vulnerable with me."

Aaron and Devon shared lots of phone calls about hopes for the future, unmet dreams, *and* what went wrong with Aaron's ex specifically— baggage he was still sorting out emotionally. Rather than press him to get over it before he was ready, Devon just let him vent it out. At the same time, she attempted to figure out what Aaron needed in a new relationship, to see if they were even compatible long-term. She reinforced his decisions to pursue activities that made *him* happy, and attended every event in a show of support—from his speeches to his more creative hobbies. Devon simply went *all in* first. "He still needed 'selfish time' to grow and heal, which I never would have tolerated from someone in the past," Devon says. "But it was as if I knew that I was laying the foundation of a house, and if I laid it on unsteady sand, it wouldn't last forever."

This was not an inherently easy process for Devon, who says that postdivorce, Aaron's crawl toward full commitment and investment was pretty slow. "There were definitely times when I asked myself, 'What the f\*ck am I doing with this man?'" she says. "And I did walk away at one point." That point? When she felt disrespected. "I was *always* there for him. If he called, I'd drop everything," she says. "But if I'd call, he would never pick up." So she started dating again—a fact she shared with Aaron. "I told him I was too valuable to chase him, and I was getting my life under way."

One night while she was on a date with another guy, she left her phone in the car—and she came back to 57 missed calls from Aaron (not one of his prouder moments, she says). Devon had put in enough time with Aaron that he seemed to suddenly realize he had something to lose: this amazing woman, who genuinely valued his strength of character and who had supported him during a tough time. From that day forward, Aaron finally went *all in* himself and fell madly in love with a supportive full-package partner, whom he now admires daily—they married in 2015. "Aaron always says that's why he fell so hard for me— my strength," she says. "It makes me incredibly powerful in my career, but I have also learned to be soft in matters of the heart...You can't be a bulldozer all the time and maintain a relationship. I realized part of having a successful relationship is becoming vulnerable yourself."

Let's be honest—vulnerability is always "frightening," as Devon puts it. "I am tough, but sensitive deep down," she insists. "Girls I know, like me—we try to hide it at all costs, then we analyze the crap out of the relationship...But I realized that, on an emotional level, I'd never felt in my life how I felt about him. I knew he had baggage, but he was worth it."

We've talked a ton about the male timeline and guys' need for esteem before they can pursue the woman of their dreams. But remember, *women* need enough self-esteem, too, to hang in there for men they deem worthy of their time and efforts. "I didn't need my confidence to come from Aaron," Devon says. "I knew I'd be fine either way, so I followed my gut. Honestly, I think sometimes you just have to put yourself out there—having your own self-esteem, independent of the relationship. You just cannot negate the importance of that."

Self-esteem is the ability to be vulnerable while dating. If you don't act like you're an impenetrable wall that lacks an emotional response, it'll give you more options. You get to decide where to invest your precious energy, knowing you *will* bounce back from any disappointment.

## WHAT YOU SHOULD LEARN FROM DEVON

○ From an emotional connection standpoint, Devon knew that Aaron triggered something in her that she'd never experienced. She didn't try to rationalize her feelings.

○ Devon could see Aaron was different from other men she'd fallen for—who were mostly hot, cocky jerks. Aaron was off-type, in a good way. If a guy is not your type, but you're still interested, that must mean you really like his qualities of character.

○ Speaking of…Devon *did* admire Aaron's character. He had dedicated his life to helping less fortunate others, and his kindness and compassion were worth the investment.

○ Devon stuck it out for Aaron, knowing she would be okay if things didn't work out in the end. She derived her self-esteem from other sources—like strong family ties, her smarts, and her career—and not solely from a romantic relationship.

○ Devon swears she had times where she thought, *WTF am I doing with this man?* But she listened to her gut about his character, their compatibility, and the connection, even when he wasn't behaving exactly the way she wanted at the moment.

## When to Wait: He's Reciprocating, Even Slowly

Remember kindergarten besties Carli and Walker (her Almost Boyfriend)? There's more to their story.

To recap, these two popped in and out of each other's lives for many years—including a brief round of dating smack-dab in the middle of college, which Carli waves off as insignificant. "We were still so young," she says. "It just wasn't that serious."

However, when the two had graduated from college and both wound up in similar areas of New York City, their relationship finally took a turn in the romantic(ish) direction. Carli had explored plenty of dating options through the years, and it was no longer something she could deny: The chemistry and connection she felt with Walker was something else.

So, the girl kept dropping hints that she was interested in dating for real, but this shy guy was still carrying wounds from a past relationship, and not ready for THAT. He liked Carli—perhaps even *more* than liked her—but he wasn't sure he was ready to jump in with this EG. Not yet, anyway. "If I date you," he told her, "we'd have to stay together."

This is the point where some women might break and issue an ultimatum. Carli could have told Walker that his time was up. It had been two decades, with months of romantic tension sprinkled throughout! Either he needed to pour in some more effort now, or leave her alone for good . . . But Carli didn't do that. She simply let Walker have a week to himself. No contact. "I did *really* like him at that point, but I was able to go with it," she says. "I knew he wasn't dating anyone else—I knew he respected me way too much for that."

She was vulnerable, but honest, too. She let Walker know that she had feelings for him, but also that she'd be okay no matter what. "I remember telling him, at one point, that if I didn't end up with him, I might not be as happy, but I'd *still* be happy," she recalls. Carli, a newly minted attorney, was basking in a sea of self-confidence—and she had read the signs. She was not delusional.

Not only did these two share history and a connection, Walker was also invested. He would tell her that he missed her sometimes when she wasn't around. He'd always text to ask if she got home okay after the two parted ways. Walker's actions said he cared, even if he was reluctant to pull the trigger—which he ultimately did after that week of no contact.

Not that Carli instantly got a superstar boyfriend. Walker wasn't completely accustomed to a real relationship. Each had two serious relationships on their record, but Carli had done more "emotional work" in hers. She put him through the paces. "I wanted to know after three to four months if he loved me," she says. "I explained what being 'in love' was like, as opposed to simply loving someone—how you feel when that person is around, when they're not around." This slowly sunk in.

Carli had always seen Walker as a long-term investment. She showed him what an authentic relationship was like—and he loved her that much more for it. The two are now married. "We made sense," she says. "We were better together—and our families were on board. Both of us are Jewish. It's so nice to be from the same area."

Had they gotten together before they were close to 30, the relationship may not have gone the distance. Walker, quiet but sure, claims that he always knew Carli was a different kind of girl—but that he wasn't ready to pursue her when he was still so young and not-figured-out. "He felt like after college, it would have been too soon to settle down, and he would have been trapped," she says with a laugh. "So I just kept showing interest."

---

### WHAT YOU SHOULD LEARN FROM CARLI

○ When Walker wasn't in the picture, Carli played the field. She always felt she had other options, and knew that if the guy she *really* liked didn't pan out, she could move on.

○ Carli knew who she was and what she had to offer—her esteem was high and not dependent on Walker's ability to commit. She recalls telling Walker, "If we don't end up together, I'd still be happy." That's confidence *and* vulnerability right there.

o Walker is a humble guy, so Carli made moves. A guy who really likes you won't *always* have the confidence to put himself out there, but he'll respond positively to your initiatives if he's worth the investment.

o With that in mind, as they grew closer in their 20s, Walker never missed a chance to hang out with Carli. He was consistently available, despite the fact that their relationship status was ambiguous.

o Timing is important, and it must be mutual. If it doesn't work out right away with someone, it's okay to keep tabs. Even if you're not seeing someone every day, those years of contact build up. You are creating a history with the person, and getting to know them on a deeper level.

## Meet the Getaway Girl

Lynne is a 26-year-old engineer. Living in Michigan and raised in Alabama, she radiates warmth and Southern charm and loves cars, motorcycles, camping, and yoga. She is a carefree spirit, and men fall for her. Hard. All guys. All the time. I've analyzed the secret to her allure, and it's this: She is genuinely interested in *people*, and when she talks to guys, she makes each feel special.

She asks them about their dreams and hobbies, and what their work lives are like. She remembers small details that she'll ask about on another occasion, and picks up on the topics each man likes to discuss most. She talks enough about herself to keep guys interested, but always redirects attention back outward. She's enthusiastic and lighthearted, and down for just about anything—a road trip, skiing, dancing.

Lynne told me she always *tries* to be single...until she meets a new guy with an interesting story. "I don't know what happens! I'm determined to be more independent, and then suddenly I'm in a relationship," she says.

If the End Goal woman is the happily-ever-after at the end of the journey, the Getaway Girl is the vacation in the middle of it all. Bubbly, curious, spontaneous, warm, and open, the Getaway Girl always does well with the guys. She has specific qualities that men fall for, *especially* as they're climbing the corporate ladder (or Maslow's hierarchy, building that well-rounded *life*) and they're not where they want to be just yet.

She cannot escape male interest, even when she's trying to do so. Why is a Getaway Girl so appealing to so many modern men?

- She makes every guy feel special and interesting.
- She listens attentively in conversation and asks engaging, open-ended questions.
- She takes initiative in getting to know a person who catches her eye, reaching out by text and making plans.
- She takes up activities and subjects that the other person likes; she is constantly open to trying new things and finding mutual interests.
- She is warm, friendly, and social.
- She uses touch in conversation, and laughs often.
- She doesn't rely on social media. She is present, engaged, and in the moment.
- She is nurturing and supportive of dreams, goals, and plans.
- She is a team player. She meets each guy halfway and never expects him to do all the work.

And here's the big one. Are you ready?

- She makes relationships seem easy instead of hard.

Lynne is catnip to guys who aren't ready. She's smart, sweet, and seems attainable—in the best possible way. Sometimes, men convince themselves they'll pursue that kick-ass End Goal woman as soon as they're set in their careers, but along the way, they meet a Getaway Girl like Lynne—who might even be an in-development EG. They build history, grow with her, and (if it's right) eventually marry her.

Unlike End Goal women, Lynne meets dating prospects where they're at in life *right then*. She isn't asking what their five-year plans are, and she's not banking on their "potential." In a career world where there's nothing but pressure, Lynne takes the pressure off. She admits she's "affectionate, and loves to be nurturing." When she likes a guy, she likes him for the man he is, again, *right then*. She lives in the moment, carefree and supportive. For your average EG, this is damn aspirational.

Ethan, a superdriven 26-year-old Ivy League grad and now PhD candidate in California, tells me: "There are people out there who might score lower on an IQ test—whatever *that* shows—who could help me become a better person. She could help shape the way I approach people and problems and life. The thing that's most important is that I really enjoy curious people." The Getaway Girl is just that.

Lynne doesn't have everything as figured out as your typical EG. She is not exactly sure where her life is going; she wants to travel, explore her career options—and, yes, have time to herself! (Which she is doing within the confines of a relationship, at present. She is 100 percent independent.) She'll get married someday, if it makes sense and she's in forever-love. But she's living for today, not ten years down the road.

I know, I know. For most EGs, Lynne is probably hitting every annoying nerve right now. She seems like everything you are not. She seems to have this whole dating thing in the bag and she's not even trying! But let's learn by breaking down her appeal.

The Getaway Girl's vibe is so seductive for men who are still figuring out what direction they want their lives to take, and not ready right now for the seriousness of an End Goal prospect. You have the tendency to think ahead; you live in untapped potential. You often see a guy for the man he wants to be, and that's an awesome quality. Because lots of men tell me they want a woman who makes them better.

So love his dreams—but don't forget that you also need to love him for the man he is *now*. Your interest can't ride entirely on who he wants to be. You have to be his little escape from the rigors of personal achievement. While growing in a relationship is vital, so too is taking a time-out to just enjoy each other. That's the beauty of sex, spontaneous weekend vacations, and theoretical discussions.

When a guy is trying to piece his life into proper order, the appeal of the Getaway Girl is that she's *carefree*. She's a safe space. She gets him *out* of his head. She is willing to take exhilarating risks and live in the moment, follow her gut into the intrigue of a new relationship, and appreciate her feelings for what they are. And the good news is, there's a little bit of Getaway Girl in all of us.

## The Spectrum

You can think of all women as lying along a spectrum, from Getaway Girl to End Goal. Some are a little more EG; others, slightly more GG. No one has it *all* figured out, and no one is entirely carefree. There are days when your life is in secret shambles, EG, when the dishes are in the sink and you're eating peanut butter from the jar for dinner. And Lynne certainly has her EG moments—you should hear the way she talks about her long-term goals, the exciting plans beyond her PhD program.

Likewise, different connections might cause you to cling to your EG ways or act as cool as a cucumber, like a GG. How many times have you met a guy you weren't immediately superinto, and were chill as an iceberg? How many other times have you met a guy you immediately felt the potential with, and wanted him to move at your carefully plotted pace? Every relationship is different, and you get to control your behavior and attitude toward it—so you can be a dominant EG who employs GG tactics sparingly, sliding back and forth along the spectrum. The key is to know when men need a pressure release valve.

Creative director Harper is about as firmly planted in the EG camp as one can be, and yet the newly minted West Coaster threw caution to the wind (in some ways) when she met Brody. "I'd done the self-discovery thing," she says. "I'd been to therapy. I hadn't dated in nine months, and I was open to trying new things I might have otherwise said no to." Harper describes her vibe then as "relaxed" for the first time in her life, so much so that she was willing to fall for her first-ever Tinder date—who looked like a player (she was projecting) but had written a pretty killer profile.

Brody sums up his now-wife's multifaceted appeal so well. While he was a Real Deal, confident in who he was and where he was going when he met Harper, he'd also dipped into some unstable territory; he says he was "financially in a little bit of a transition." He claims this was kind of a plus when he reflects on it. "When I asked Harper to marry me, it was a risk for her," he says. "And *that* sealed it. She could see past my financial situation and was willing to be a team player." Harper wanted a strong partner, but she was willing to accept the situation as it was. She was just chill enough, just a *little* bit Getaway Girl, without losing her EG superpowers. She felt strongly connected to Brody and was willing to trust her feelings instead of worrying too much about a future there was no way to be certain of.

This was so appealing to Brody, who never doubted his trajectory. "I always knew I'd be successful," Brody says. "And before Harper, I thought, 'When I do succeed, if I don't meet someone beforehand, I'll never really know if she loves *me*.'" Brody knows with complete confidence that Harper fell for him as a person, right where he was at, not simply what he might be someday. As such, the two have built a beautiful, *successful* married partnership.

Someday *will* come for you, too. But there is beauty, and there are strong bonding opportunities, in the messy moments that come with the wait; just tap into your GG side.

## Stop Panicking: The Implications of the Short-Term Lane

Does channeling your inner Getaway Girl mean you're in the short-term lane? *No one wants to be in the short-term lane!* you think. *I am long-term material! I have so much to offer!* I know that, so don't go into panic mode quite yet.

Entering the short-term lane alongside the Lynnes of the world doesn't mean that your relationship will come with an expiration date. We talked back in Chapter 9 about the inherent problems of livin' in the future. Many men simply need the space to see where the relationship goes—especially those guys who are still unsure what shape their life will take. David, a 25-year-old marine biology student living in Hawaii, has never been superintentional in dating. "I've always been more of a relationship guy," he explains. "I've had a decent amount of hookups, but nowhere near a lot."

His strategy for relationship formation is more "no strategy" at all: He meets a girl, gets to know her, and sees where it goes. This includes his current girlfriend. "I'm a combination of lazy and shy," he says with a laugh. "I don't like approaching girls I don't know! All my girlfriends were friends before we started dating... The friend zone is my happy place."

Note that David has always started as an Almost Boyfriend—a guy there's attraction with, but who needs a slow-growing bond to get comfortable. He's young, not a player, and a little bit reluctant to put himself out there. So if you're into someone like him, realize it's a slower, longer prospect.

David is laid-back, but commitment-oriented. It's not that he is a playboy who doesn't seek out real connections over casual sex—it's that he's not thinking about marriage tomorrow. The fact that he has always formed relationships in this manner can be attributed to one of two factors: personality and age. Sometimes, it's one or the other for guys.

In fact, an EG who seems like she's looking for a big commitment right away—like moving in together or marriage—may signal she's more short-term, according to James, the resident physician who wasn't ready to settle down with Lindsay. "I know a girl is short-term if she's an emotional wreck, but also if she's a bit older, starts telling me that all her friends are married, or talks about past relationships."

See, single James is glued to his timeline—that past serious relationship that ended dramatically taught him that he needs to put his career goals first. Marriage is not on his mind as a short-term goal; if he feels the pressure of heavy commitment looming, especially before he's emotionally attached, he'll cut the cord. Doing well in his residency program and settling into a new city are his top priorities. However, it's not that he isn't *open*.

Most guys, in theory, are open to the right person, James insists. (After all, he seriously considered marriage at age 25!) But, he says, relationships have to come without the deep-seated pressure of long-term commitment so early, a.k.a. the Getaway Girl's sweet spot. If not, there will be infinitely higher odds that a "not ready" guy will shut it down. "Certain serious things are dealbreakers right now," James explains. "A girlfriend with a great career could be a roadblock. A girl who wants to get married creates a roadblock. All these things paint a girl in a certain light." If you can see he's "not ready" early, and embrace the ambiguity, you give yourself more options. Letting him stay in a short-term, easygoing headspace can actually create a long-term bond. Other women have done so, and they've scored a great catch. You just need to channel your inner Getaway Girl.

If you are glued to a timeline of your own, he will put his first; if you're not, if it truly is about the guy, then you'll need to learn to go with the flow a little bit more. If you want more options in your dating pool, you'll need to reveal yourself more slowly and more methodically. Look for signs that he is ready or not ready, early and often. Don't show your hand until you have this data. And trust me: He will tell you.

James, who admits he is "guarded" about his freedom since his relationship with Lindsay, makes sure to tell every girl he goes out with that he's just arrived for residency, he's really busy with his career, or some version of the "I need casual" speech—an immediate sign to filter him into the "not ready" camp.

If your guy is more like David, the perpetual Almost Boyfriend, there will likely be a lack of true movement; he's going to take his time, he cannot be crowded while he's in the decision-making process, and he may need liquid courage (!).

So let's say you really like him and you can feel the potential of the connection. You have three options when it comes to waiting it out (or not).

**Drop him.** Not worth the time, energy, and risk at this stage of your life? Not a problem. Next!

**Friend-zone him.** If you want to get to know him slowly without risking your heart and emotions in the process, let the romance cool a teensy bit and create friendship vibes. This works especially well if there is a physical distance barrier, the guy is moving, or he's a David-like shy type.

If there's truly a connection of some kind worth exploring—especially the all-important emotional and intellectual connections—he will likely still be happy to engage with you on these lighter terms. You might need to initiate more contact to keep the ball rolling, as men often operate on the "outta sight, outta mind" philosophy, but he should still be receptive to you.

A man worth any kind of investment should respond positively to your gestures of friendship every time. This is a lower-risk, lower-reward strategy—perfect if you want to explore potential and figure out more about what you want in a man but don't want to get burned. In fact, you can do this with as many guys as you want. That's the beauty of friends: You can have as many as you want.

**Date him, revealing yourself slowly.** I don't want you to be anything but yourself—but the rate you reveal yourself at is entirely within your control. If you want to be *efficient* in the dating market, the slow reveal isn't going to produce results very quickly—and remember that holding back isn't in your best interest with Real Deals, who you want in your dating pool. Revealing yourself naturally, as the situation demands, is wise.

I'd recommend this tactic if you want a *wider* pool of options—more specifically, if you'd like to explore connections when you know a guy's not ready but there's a click. Let's call this "manageable authenticity."

## How EGs Can Employ Manageable Authenticity

Let's think of manageable authenticity as "EG lite." It's the slow burn to commitment. You are going to be yourself. You're just going to *live in the present* until your prospect recognizes the undeniable connection that you identified from the get-go. Let's talk about when to deploy.

## Who

This strategy is generally reserved for men who are in no rush—men who feel they have options. These guys think they are not ready, and they're committed to their timelines. They *will* talk about wanting long-term love. They just think it's like 18,000 light-years away, and they're comfortable with that.

## What

Keep it light. If you enjoy witty banter, people-watching, and commentary on social issues, here's your moment! Talk about the White Sox. Talk about that great TED Talk you watched. Talk about how overrated *Hamilton* is. Whatever. Let your enthusiasm shine—because you *are* excited to spend time with him! No need to play it cool while you are on each date. Seek to live in the moment, fully engaged in the present.

*Stop talking about the future. If you can't do that, you can't date a guy who isn't really ready.*

## How

You're going to let him take the lead. In fact, with a guy who is "not ready," my best advice is this: In the beginning, let him do most of the work. If he is interested in pursuing you, he'll do it. If he's feeling insecure around your sparkle, he won't. A fairly confident "not ready" guy will want to feel *his* agency at every step of the relationship-formation process; your job will be not dwelling on him, living your single life, and responding to his initiatives only for however long you still feel a relationship with him is worth pursuing.

Blowing him off when you really like him? Not a good idea. Making it known you had a good time and want to see him again? Perfect. Respond positively when he asks for a date, but keep your life full and busy otherwise—moving forward at all times. If anything, this trajectory is appealing to a guy who isn't ready. Delays won't be the issue they'd be with a Real Deal, who is more obviously in search of a compatible partner and won't want to fool around.

## When

The moment will come—in fact, it'll probably happen a lot—when he starts to bring up all his personal barriers to a serious commitment. You're going to be supportive of his dreams early on, and emphasize that you don't ever want to stand in the way of his goals. And you're going to mean it. "A girl who doesn't try to change you or rope you in is very attractive," says James. This guy will need to fall in love accidentally, even if you quietly and intentionally fall on purpose.

Remember, he still needs to rise to your level, and you're not going to change yourself to fit his needs. You will gauge the connection the whole time and decide if this one guy is worth it. But you are not going to bombard him with attention or demand intimacy too quickly. And once intimacy has been established, you will trust the connection.

This is a risk. He could walk away. He has predecided he isn't ready for something serious. He is going to give you every indicator that he isn't ready for the future right now. You are going to listen to his words and respect that. You can't force him to change his mind, but you can allow him the time and space to do so on his own. By showing off your value, living your life, and allowing him to come to you of his own accord, you set the table for *maybe*.

## You Don't Always Win

What makes a Getaway Girl so irresistible, to "not ready" men especially? She taps into her nurturing side (guy feels supported) while remaining curious (guy feels admired), she's open to advice and encouragement (guy feels respected), and she's willing to show her flaws and problems so a guy can help (guy feels valued). I think those traits exist within every woman, yet lots of EGs have learned to repress or downplay them to establish a sense of equality in competitive career and academic environments.

Again, think of these women like two extremes on a spectrum: Getaway Girls are the ladies who exhibit the fun, approachable, playful side of what it means to be a modern-day woman, and End Goals embody the independent, fierce, conqueror side. Both are amazing in their own way, and no woman is strictly one or the other. For instance, Samantha (you met her in chapter 6) seems like the quintessential Getaway Girl on the surface. She's bubbly and always down for a good time, friendly to everyone she meets, and upbeat in virtually every situation. She *is* the Getaway Girl. Except she's also not.

See, Samantha is really into politics and learning about different religions. She has deep philosophical beliefs about the world and human nature. She is looking for the best in relationships, but she's also one of the most authentic, independent girls I've ever met. And when she met Jamal, her last boyfriend (Mr. All That But), in college, they hit it off immediately—so much so that he wanted to pursue the relationship long-distance for a year while Samantha traveled abroad to work in Spain and he began med school. They dated for two years before the stress of his med school program became too much for him to sustain a relationship. He saw a future with Samantha, but he couldn't make that future just happen.

And do you remember what he told her in their last conversation? "I wish I could just press pause on you." Yes, seriously.

Samantha, the surface Getaway Girl, is absolutely an End Goal woman. Jamal wanted to be "that guy" for her. He just couldn't.

Samantha was devastated. But as I will continue to advocate in this book, like any End Goal woman should do, she licked her wounds and got back on track with her life. She leaned into her friends, put her head down at work, moved across the city to a great little apartment with three hilarious roommates, and started dating someone new.

Sometimes, that happens. Life's a pickle. But she did *everything* right. Relationship prospects are always a gamble, and some are higher-risk than others.

You need to ask yourself this question: *Am I looking for someone who's ready and relationship-centered right now, or is* this one guy *and* this one connection *most important?*

The choice is yours.

# CHAPTER 14

· · · · · · · · · · · ·

# the case for seeking the real deal

The best and worst part about the Real Deal is that he's "ready." He has ventured all the way up Maslow's hierarchy of needs. He has built his sense of esteem and feels confident about who he is and what he has to offer in a relationship—and he wants a woman who is headed in the same direction.

I know what you're thinking: *He sounds like a unicorn. This guy is not real.* Thankfully, I can assure you that guys like this are real, but there are some reasons you probably see less of them in the dating pool:

- Most men like to ease into relationships when they're not 100 percent sure of who they are and where they're headed in life, as they build that all-important esteem.
- A Real Deal is actively open to a great relationship, so he's not *trying* to screw around with endless dates for long periods of time.
- A Real Deal knows what he's looking for, so he's a more selective dater than a guy who's trying to figure out what works for him or is simply swiping right for variety.
- If there's no chemistry up front, you'll dismiss him and not think of him as a Real Deal.

The flip side of the Real Deal is that, because he's "ready," he's going to move a lot faster or feel a lot more serious than your average guy. Instead of a guy endeavoring to rise to your level…you might have to rise to his. *Gulp.*

You can tell a Real Deal from a "not ready" guy when you start to talk to him. He has this self-assured manner. He's confident yet humble. Real Deals are a wealth of information, because they've done a lot of self-reflection on their wants and needs. They've had girlfriends before, which required a learning curve. They finally know what they're looking for, how to make a relationship work, and what kind of time and effort they're willing to put in when that special girl comes along.

Ultimately, guys with these qualities are the ones you want to end up with. All men who become "ready" will move into Real Deal territory before they settle down. Or at least they should.

## Signs He Might Be a Real Deal

You want the visible markers, right? Of course you do! You're basically trying to figure out what the needles look like in a complicated dating haystack. No guy is going to perfectly fit a box with a preset 18 behaviors, but there are some markers showing you that a guy is a keeper who will require minimal work, confusion, or waiting time.

**Real Deals are confident.** They know who they are, where they're going, and what they're looking for—finally. They are usually on a somewhat steady trajectory, or on one that has stabilized. Remember, confidence is quiet; cockiness is obnoxious. Guys who pursue too strongly up front and then drop off the map, making you wonder, are not Real Deals.

**Real Deals are not in the middle of a major life change.** They're usually not about to move cross-country for work (or haven't just moved), they're not contemplating grad school or a new career field, they're not fresh off a breakup where it suddenly…died. They're more than likely coming off a period of personal growth and development, ending up in a more stable place.

**Real Deals have usually had a major relationship in the past.** More often than not, these guys have held down a long-term relationship for multiple years, have evaluated how things went south, and now understand the effort it takes to make it work with a woman. Guys who are not Real Deals do not have the same experiences; you're more likely to see a string of flings, each under a year long.

**Real Deals have been "grown-ups" for a good long while.** A guy who has just exited campus hookup culture is less likely to know how to date like an adult. A man who's a late bloomer may not have the relationship experience to sustain something serious—or may still want to play the field before he settles down.

**Real Deals are self-aware.** They know the role they need to play in a successful relationship, and the behaviors to bring that about. They do not shy away from taking initiative, putting in effort, or going "all in." They're cool with vulnerability, and can acknowledge their own faults.

**Real Deals are aware of your needs.** If you seem hesitant, they notice and act to make you feel more secure. If you have questions, they answer them honestly and directly. If you're behaving badly or sending mixed signals, they call you out. They are patient. They are forthcoming. They are real.

What's interesting is how many Real Deal guys clearly understand women, or even people in general, on a level non-RD men simply do not. It's not uncommon for a Real Deal guy to be introspective, have thought deeply about relationships, have embraced therapy, know a lot about psychology, or have grown up with sisters.

## The Magic Formula of a Real Deal

Forward thinking + specific goals
+ experience = Real Deal

Let's apply this to dating—where the ability to analyze and theorize how the here and now will translate into future results is a very valuable skill. Per chapter 9, most women start thinking about the future much faster than men; they are assessing whether or not to keep seeing a guy based on whether he might potentially make a good boyfriend—how qualities might evolve over time in a positive or negative way, to match the women's goals and desires (or not). On the other hand, "not ready" guys especially seem to live in the here and now for longer; they often assess how they should view you right off the bat, based on your present looks, qualities, speech, behaviors, etc., as well as how much feeling you inspire in them. They are trying to figure out your lane, track, box, what have you, to determine how they relate to you.

Problem is, building a life with someone is not about putting your prospects in boxes and generating *initial* chemistry (just one part of the Connection Trifecta anyway). If a man is avoiding thoughts of the future, if he can't (or won't) be real with himself about what works for long-term, *often because he just doesn't know*, he will struggle to build real relationships.

My personal theory is until men (or women!) have the capacity to effectively predict how certain characteristics will evolve and grow over time, and gauge how this meshes up with their long-term wants and needs, they're going to be really poor judges of compatibility—and this ability is gained only through experiences, introspection, and growth.

When I ask men what they are (or were) looking for, Real Deals are very specific. Every Real Deal's compatibility list will be different. However, they are able to tell me what they want when asked—or they were able to recognize that their EG wives would make incredible partners soon after they met them. One told me he was so impressed with his now-wife's perseverance, and the fact that they couldn't even sit through a movie together without chatting because they had so much to talk about, that he knew within two weeks that he loved her. Another told me that he "had a pretty good idea" his wife was "something special" on the first date, when she shared "thrifty" stories about growing up in poverty. "She had this depth that I was looking for," he recalls. Another said he was looking for someone forthcoming, because he had an ex who would never tell him what was wrong when she was upset, thinking she was biting her tongue to prevent a fight; that "passive" nature felt artificial to him, and he wanted someone who was strong enough to be real.

The guys who aren't fully ready, on the other hand, are more vague in their assessments of what they want in a long-term partner—someone nice, someone caring, someone who is family-oriented. Safe answers. Level-three Maslow answers. But they haven't gotten beyond that, which of course is no surprise. They don't really know what they're looking for yet; they haven't amassed the experiences or they're not totally ready to think about the future.

Consider what constitutes a "catch." If you're operating in the game-like atmosphere of dating, someone elusive and mysterious is a catch. If you're operating in the world of relationship-building, a catch is someone who has qualities that are rare and valued in your eyes—qualities that sync up with your long-term goals. That's what predicts the sustainability of any couple: You're attracted, you value what the person brings to the table, and you want the same things in life—not just now, but out into the evolving future. Real Deals have the insight to fully appreciate you, EG. To the right guy, you're the gift that keeps on giving.

Most superhappy couples tell me that they are always learning new things about their significant other—even 5, 10, 20 years into a relationship. We all like some mystery. It's like unwrapping a present. But perhaps a shift in thinking is in order: A catch in the dating game is someone *he* can't have; a catch in the relationship market is someone *other men* can't have, because an EG chose him (*and* he chose her, of course).

An honest-to-goodness catch is someone who provides you with a sense of mystery that never really ends. It's the difference between a present you have to wait to unwrap for a few weeks and a present you have to wait to unwrap for a few weeks, followed by another present once you've unwrapped the first.

## Real Deals 101

Unfortunately, Real Deals don't wear a blinking sign. You could be standing next to a Real Deal at the bank, sitting next to one at the office, passing one on the subway platform, and *never know*. Sigh. The best thing you can do is be on the lookout.

Real Deals lead, take the high road, and are generally looking for a life partner—so watch how men behave, express themselves, and react to you.

### Real Deals like maturity.

The same behaviors and traits that will turn off a guy who's "in progress"—whether that's your career, your smarts, your poise, or your early weekend nights—will turn a Real Deal on.

Consider this: Your maturity might signal to a developing guy that you're not a great dating candidate for him now. James, 27 and just starting his surgical residency, likes to date girls who are a few years his junior. "I feel like I have more in common with younger girls," he says. "They're a little more flaky, more relaxing and fun. The maturity kind of evens out." He confesses to discounting women who are a couple of years older, have lots of married friends, and are set in their careers. Based on experience, he assumes they'll want to settle down quicker and "that's a roadblock," he explains.

Samuel, the banker from NC, on the other hand, is 26 and fully ready. He's been dating since middle school, so he wants…well, a woman, not a girl. He claims to gravitate toward and "feel most comfortable with older women." For instance, he noticed when someone he was seeing got a little sloppy on the second date. "She drank more than me," he says, "and I don't want to sound sexist for judging how much you're drinking. But more and more recently, I've been thinking about finding the right person to settle down with—and it's good to be present when you're getting to know someone."

Quality doesn't need to be faked, and communication doesn't need to be delayed, says 30-year-old lawyer Marcus. "I don't like the game," he insists. "I want all cards on the table. Yes, I like a sense of adventure. I love girls who simply say what they want, and know what they want. Someone who is more mature, who can have a conversation about anything—where there's no guessing."

## Real Deals are consistent.

When Brody first met Harper, they hit it off immediately—but he sensed she was pushing him away with "bad behaviors," from years of carrying around an "independent woman" facade, years spent acting like she cared less with guys. Remember when he told her, "I have the special skills necessary to handle you"? He practiced consistency and follow-through.

"I had a gut feeling about him," Harper says, "and the number one reason was that Brody always did what he said he was going to do. He never made me wonder or gave me a reason to worry."

Brody was a psychology student in college, and had needed to pull out his psych knowledge many times over the course of his life. "I think the sort of maturity you need in relationships comes with experience and age," he says. "I've worked with kids with autism and misbehaving teenagers—acting out and rebelling. In Harper, I recognized what were the bad behaviors versus her true self. She was kind of bratty at times—but she'd never been given the tools and habits to change."

Instead of playing it cool, Brody called Harper every night at the same time. He kept reiterating how he wanted her in his life. After four dates, he brought up exclusivity. After a few weeks, he said he'd cleared out a drawer in his place for her. "He set a rhythm," Harper says. "Then you develop this natural cycle, where you realize you're not setting the pace. It was the small reminders over and over and over that he wasn't going anywhere. You realize he really is thinking of you when he's not with you."

According to Brody, behavior breakthroughs happen "all of a sudden." But when did Harper realize Brody was *for real* and let her walls down? "When he proposed," she says.

Brody kind of chuckles in protest. "I actually don't think she took me seriously until a few months after we were married, which is when she actually opened up and let me lead," he insists.

"Oh, *gosh*!" Harper says with an amused laugh. Ah, love.

### Real Deals know what they're looking for.

When guys aren't necessarily ready, you'll notice it in their language. Lots of times, what they want is contradictory—because what they're looking for today is not what they're looking for down the road. Or they'll be quite vague—because they're not thinking of the future, and lots of girls *could* fit the role of kind, easygoing, and unlikely to apply pressure.

A Real Deal is specific. He knows exactly what he wants. Brody, for instance, had started dating women with immigrant backgrounds, because he felt they knew the value of teamwork and combining efforts for the greater goal of the relationship. "Not someone who made me feel like they were shopping on Amazon for a husband," he says.

Samuel starts to bristle when he feels like women he's dating try to get too involved in managing day-to-day tasks—cooking, cleaning, even checking his phone. "They want to control all aspects of your life," he says. "I like a more open, free-flowing type of relationship. I'm also looking for that personality chemistry. Can we talk for hours? Will we agree most of the time? Does she increase my understanding? I am trying to get a sense of the intangibles."

When Elijah ended his dormant marriage and then proceeded to make a beeline for Lily to ask her out...well, Lily was very, very reticent about that idea. "I said, 'Take six months, and then call me,'" she recalls. Little did Lily know, her colleague and friend had already had this realization: "I need to be with someone like Lily, who is intelligent and beautiful, softly challenging and powerfully insightful." Not: "I should go sleep around, hit the beaches of Bora-Bora, grow a beard, and sell coconuts on the boardwalk."

Really, he wanted the *actual* Lily, if she would give him a shot. So, his reply to her suggestion? "If I take six months and then I call you, I might miss this once-in-a-lifetime opportunity to ask you out."

Lily says that Elijah was able to make her see that the "rules" she once clung to for dear life were unlikely to find her love.

"We live in a world divorced from humanism," Elijah says. "We check lists to decide what the right move is for us. I cared about Lily's reaction, but I did not care about the social norms."

Elijah had thought it through: He knew what he wanted, and that was Lily. And if not Lily, then someone much like her. He'd lived a life absent of real connection for long enough.

## Real Deals promote a dynamic of emotional safety.

With Lily's hesitation, Elijah realized he might need to have some serious talks with her right away. See, he'd had lots of revelations while his marriage was on the rocks—and he was also in therapy to heal and grow. "We were friends, so we had some in-depth conversations," he says. "We decided that we get to make the rules...I wanted to take charge without being overbearing. I remember having my heart in my throat."

Lily says Elijah wanted to go about dating her "in the most ethical way possible," and with those open conversations came a sense of security. "We can talk about anything," she says. "Someone once told me, 'Pick someone who will never punish you for bad information.' It's so true. I know Elijah is on my side."

But Elijah and Lily had some history. Let's say you don't. Even so, early on in dating, a Real Deal will still make you feel emotionally safe. He will not try to play power dynamics or gain the upper hand. He'll want to hear from you, and he won't pull away if you grow closer—because he wants to feel emotionally safe, too. "I want to feel like a girl is interested in me," says Marcus. "It's great when I don't have to do all the work—I want to see her, too, so I like when she takes a leap. A strong woman can give signals that she wants to move forward."

Tip: Every once in a while, try reaching out to him—call him on the phone, ask him to join you for happy hour after work. A player will lose interest, and an insecure guy will distance himself, which is 100 percent fine. But a Real Deal will be *so* pleased.

Consider it a filtering mechanism.

### Real Deals can be as happy for your successes as you are for theirs.

Remember, a lot of men tie their egos up in their careers and their general success in their fields. However, an emotionally mature Real Deal with high levels of self-esteem will never begrudge you your success. Take it from Samuel, who tells his sisters they need to find a man who's on board with "their mission"—and to separate their career from their relationship. It's not a competition. "Most men recognize having an ambitious wife is good for the guy, too," he says.

Take happily married entrepreneurs Andrew and Emma, for instance. Andrew couldn't be happier for Emma's successes, and vice versa; you must find someone who supports you, as one member of a team. "When there's something one of us wants to accomplish, we help each other achieve it," Emma says.

When Emma wanted to go to grad school and then build her own company, Andrew supported her. She was afraid to quit her job, but he urged her to, saying, "Do it!" She did, in fact, start the company she'd always wanted to run.

When Andrew wanted to leave his stable job for a more entrepreneurial role, Emma returned the favor—even though it meant she was suddenly the more successful partner. "Emma pushes me to be a better version of myself," he explains. "She is always encouraging me to pursue things. The reality is that without her encouragement, I wouldn't be reaching for my dreams."

Emma won't take all the credit, though. "Previously, he gave me the stepping stone to pursue *my* dream—which elevated my career, so that I could give him that springboard. I am always so wowed to have a husband who is so secure."

Men emphasize over and over again: Their egos can be easily

bruised. But if a guy's secure in himself, his ego will not be dented by your successes. He will be able to celebrate them with you.

## Approaching with Confidence

We need better *dating* advice for the modern age. (Meaning: *Dating, v.*—legitimately building a relationship with a potential long-term partner.)

We need to counter years and years of "If he likes you, he'll pursue you."

Women have more agency in sustaining a relationship than ever before, if they choose the right guy who actually wants one. Meeting a guy step for step while dating is a good strategy—in fact, I just talked to a guy friend who is currently in a relationship, and he has one piece of advice for single girls. He says, "If you don't meet him halfway in this day and age, he's going to think you're not interested." (So much for the relentless pursuer you were promised in *He's Just Not That Into You* and *The Rules*, right?)

An End Goal woman may need to work on tossing out her defensiveness in dating. I know you feel you've been wronged by guys, confused by research, and completely misunderstood in your dating dilemmas. (I know you want to scream, "I am not picky, dammit!" from the rooftops. I feel you.) But starting today, you are cleaning your dating slate. And you are going to meet every Real Deal prospect by "mirroring" him from a place of confidence.

If he's passed through your filter into this category, and he's exhibiting signs that he's ready to date you now, you are going to assume he *is indeed ready*. You are *not* going to assume that texting first will send him running for the hills, or that he's going to PANIC if you ask for his Saturday night (because that's a couples night, right?! Cue the horror music). You can feel free to approach him expecting a positive response. That doesn't mean you quadruple text him all the time, because that would raise some red flags in just about any rational dater. But you can totally establish a one-to-one ratio in your communications, ask-outs, and investments.

If he texts you first one day, you can text him first the next. If you want! (Sort of like with healthy eating and calories, you want to be aware of the counts, not controlled by them.) If he suggests catching a movie one weekday, you can suggest dinner and karaoke on Friday night. If he gives you a compliment, try to give him one as well. Don't play coy. Don't play it cool. He is going to need a reminder that the woman of his dreams is feeling him, too. Mirroring his efforts builds a sense of rapport, belonging, and engagement as you both invest in the relationship. Soon, you'll fall into sync and it'll feel extremely natural.

## Maslow Has Some Advice

Of course, this section would not be complete without some Maslow. Our favorite humanistic psychologist identified characteristics of self-actualizers[1]—so you can always watch for them as you get to know a potential Real Deal.

Now, this list is not an ironclad checklist that you should run down on every first date. No! Some of these behaviors will take time to gauge. Some of these behaviors he may not have yet.

And a man doesn't need to exhibit every single one of these characteristics to be self-actualizing; this is not a practice in perfection. However, the more of these characteristics you witness, the more you realize you're considering a guy who knows himself well. He knows what he believes and what he's looking for in life. And those are wonderful things to know, things that will help him have a growth-oriented relationship instead of one that's solely focused on his personal journey (*cough* not ready *cough*).

Understand what I'm saying? Good.

### Maslow's Characteristics of Self-Actualizers

**He sees reality clearly and can deal with uncertainty.** Does he seem to understand the world *as it is*? Does he see your relationship accurately? Is he okay with putting himself out there when he may not know your feelings, allowing you to respond at your own pace?

**He accepts himself and others, just as they are.** Does he seem comfortable with himself? Or does he exhibit shame, guilt, or preoccupation about certain facets of himself? Does he try to change you, or accept you as you are?

**He is spontaneous in his thoughts and actions.** Are conversations and ideas natural, not contrived? Can he adapt on the fly, or does he seem overly rehearsed?

**He is problem-centered...not self-centered.** Does he seem to want to fix and question problems that are happening in the world? In your relationship? Or does he want to change only himself and focus on his own development, unconcerned with problems that exist outside his personal bubble?

**He has a well-developed, unique sense of humor.** Does he seem to have his own humor, with its own quirks and randomness? Or does he allow friends and society to dictate what he finds funny? Does he poke fun at interesting facets of reality, but not at the expense of others?

**He is able to look at life from an objective standpoint.** Is he able to take a step back and view situations and problems from an place of open-mindedness, considering others' perspectives, or is he always defensive and adamant about his beliefs?

**He is highly creative, innovative, and goal-oriented.** Is he constantly growing, able to learn and spawn new thoughts and behaviors? Is he an innovator, generating *his own* ideas? Does he enjoy creative experiences for the sake of personal expansion?

**He knows what he believes, independent of popular opinions— but doesn't take the opposing view just to be controversial.** Does he follow the status quo because that's what others do, or does he carve his own path? Can he state his own beliefs diplomatically, even if they're not held by the vast majority? Does he say things simply for shock value, or because he actually believes them?

**He shows concern for others, and for humanity as a whole.** Does he want to do right by others—whether his mom, or someone he doesn't even know? Is he interested in social issues, politics, global affairs, humanitarianism? Does he genuinely care about his friends and family?

**He can appreciate the common, everyday pieces of life.** Does he always need to be doing grand, exciting things? Or can he appreciate the beauty of a Netflix-and-chill, go-to-the-farmer's-market, cook-at-home-together kind of day?

**He has deep, meaningful relationships with a few people.** Is he selective about those he spends his time with? Does he talk about his close friendships? Or does he seem to have trouble making friendships stick?

**He has had "peak experiences."** Does he discuss moments of impact? Moments in life that changed him? Humbling experiences that were revelatory in nature, where he came away with a new, deeper understanding of the world?

**He values his privacy.** Being alone is a skill. Does he seem to understand this and have developed the ability to hang out by himself? Does he take time for personal development? Does he keep some thoughts to himself, or blurt out way too much to almost-strangers?

**He respects others and shows compassion.** Is he kind and respectful toward every single person he encounters, despite their race, religion, sexual orientation, political beliefs, socioeconomic status, and the like? Does he promote harmony and community?

**He has a strong moral and ethical compass—and actually lives by it.** Does he do the right thing, even when it would be easier not to? Does he adhere to a specific value system or set of beliefs, and know why he follows them?

## You Need to Do the Emotional Work

Self-actualizing Real Deals are decidedly less concerned about the pacing of the relationship. They're not going to hold you at arm's length as they freak out about whether or not you're more serious than what they're looking for at that very moment. They're not going to try to hold the upper hand in the relationship and create a power dynamic, so you know who's BOSS. There are men like that. They take work. You've probably dated at least one or two and been burned. In the process, your mental and emotional world has taken a hit.

A lot of women have developed bad habits while dating men who are less than ready. You have learned that an air of independence ensures that you will not look needy, so you talk about how busy you are at work right now. If he doesn't reply to a text for nine hours, you decide you won't reply until the next day at an arbitrary time like 5:00 p.m. You have created an internal set of rules to keep yourself at just the right distance, to make sure you're never really vulnerable to hurt and disappointment (or so you tell yourself).

Instead of dating as a means to an end, a means to a relationship, dating becomes that *game*—which is not conducive to the authenticity required for a genuine partnership.

So when a Real Deal is evaluating you, it's not uncommon for him to see mixed signals, especially if you're distancing yourself and acting like you aren't really looking for a relationship right now. Depending on his level of experience, confidence, and ability to see through all that, he may or may not be able to understand where those behaviors are coming from. But there's a good chance you'll miss out on a great guy by sending out red flags like they're smiles. Therefore, in case he's not 100 percent in tune with your random, negative hurt-girl behaviors: *You need to actively stop yourself from self-sabotaging.*

When you're pretty sure you've got a Real Deal on your hands, I want you to do everything in your power to fight your protective instincts and exhibit authentic, vulnerable self-actualizing behaviors. I know you know what "overboard" looks like, and you're not going to go there. You're not going to shower him with attention that's not warranted for the current depth of intimacy in the relationship. Let him take some initiative. But also listen to yourself. Here's what I want you to do:

- Stop worrying about when to send him texts or emails, and do what feels right.

- Stop thinking about him all the time. No, I'm serious. For now, live your awesome life. You have a lot going on, you're too awesome to stop it all for any one guy—and your Real Deal will still be there when you get back.

- Look for consistency. Does he do what he says he's going to do? If he misses the mark, does he apologize with a reason instead of blowing it off or making excuses? Believe in him when he isn't giving you reasons to doubt.

- Be receptive to his initiatives, whether they are spontaneous and last-minute, or planned and thoughtful. (No, that's not a 1:00 a.m. *Come over* text. But a 4:00 p.m. *I'm getting off work early, do you have plans tonight?* text is A-OK.)

- Show interest when you want to. Thank him for dinner, tell him you had a good time, treat him with kindness, take his hand, bake some cookies. Whatever feels right to you. Express appreciation and reciprocate positive actions in ways that feel natural and authentic to your personality.

- Stop stressing about the timeline. Let your relationship unfold naturally, and ignore the peanut gallery around you telling you he should do this or that. "Should" is often a toxic word.

- Believe his positive signals, when they are *far outweighing* the negative—just like you would believe a "not ready" guy's negative signals when they are far outweighing the positive. If he makes one mistake, chill out and trust the connection and the favorable trajectory you feel.

- Throw away your rules and listen to your gut. Do you feel he is honest and moving the relationship forward? Or do you feel there are barriers?

- Keep your standards high, but lose the expectations. "Expectations" is just a fancier word for "rules." They are ruining your love life and creating an artificial dynamic of demands, instead of authentic action.

- Pay attention to the way he is vulnerable toward his flaws and any need for improvement. Does he tell you why you should not date him (he's not ready)? Or does he tell you how he's grown or is growing, indicating reasons why you should (he's ready)?

- Ask yourself if you feel respected, if your emotions are being taken into account, every step of the way. Ask yourself if this *feels* right and his relationship-supporting actions *feel* authentic to you. When that answer is yes, I want you to stop questioning his motives.
- Let him do nice things for you. Let him embarrass you with kindness and thoughtfulness. You deserve it.
- Fight the temptation to distance yourself the moment you get triggered from a bad past experience. Try not to blame the sins of an old flame on this new guy.
- Be kind. Be forthcoming. Share your feelings. Act excited. Be vulnerable.
- Fall in love.

## CHAPTER 15

# the case for moving on

You will date some men who are just okay. You will give it a chance. You will be fairly happy while you're with them, enjoy each date, maybe even enter into a relationship for a short time. But sooner or later, you will also become fairly certain that it's not a long-term fit.

This relationship does not have the "it" factor. The end will feel sad, but it will also feel right. You will be able to move on—to make a clean break. You will want him to meet someone new. Maybe you'll randomly see him in a coffee shop and say hi, or you'll smile when he gets a new girlfriend and changes his relationship status on Facebook.

This is the best-case breakup. The worst-case breakup is a different beast.

Maybe you met him in some magical 21st-century way—maybe he added you on Facebook after you talked all night at a party, or you had the weirdest gut feeling when you both swiped right on Tinder. Or maybe you had a throwback meet-cute—you met at a bar as your group tag-teamed with his on trivia night, or he introduced himself on the street while you were waiting at a stoplight. There are a million ways a man can enter your life, and yet almost all exit through the same door labeled DONE.

I truly believe in *feeling* "it." In your gut. A deep cut that hits your soul and keeps sinking deeper as you get to know him more. It could be almost instant. Maybe it grows over a period of weeks or months. But it keeps propelling you both forward toward the maybe-forever you've always sought.

How do we define "it" exactly? Positive momentum. Favorable trajectory. *Potential.* A collision of intellectual, emotional, and physical chemistry that creates a complementary pairing that feels uniquely full. I want you to know you are whole on your own, EG, but you are *full* with those certain special partners, with whom you sense *growth*.

I believe in that intrinsic feel for potential; it's an alarm deep in your core that goes off only when you encounter "it." Trust that.

Also, realize that connection, chemistry, perfect fits, and "it" do not necessarily a long-term relationship make. Sometimes, "it" doesn't work. Often, it's timing. Sometimes, he can't see the future you see. The worst-case breakup is when you feel "it"—and yet he walks away. Or possibly worse yet, he perpetually injures you with immaturity and indecision until you are forced to cut the cord. From "it." From rare, deep, could-be-forever "it."

In these moments, I want you to be brave. Never beg for someone to stay; never let someone emotionally drain you until you believe "it" is synonymous with pain.

I want you to walk on and refuse to look back. Let me tell you why.

## Being Single: What the Data Says

Look around a small town and you're likely to see lots of men and women in their 20s who are married with children. I came from a small town just like this. Most of my high school peers have set up house and started families, and they seem fine.

Meanwhile, career folks are dating but putting off the settling-down process. I'm now a city girl with a downtown apartment, enjoying my freedom while single and writing this book. I know only one couple, in my very large social circle, with a child. Most of my friends, single or in relationships, are in no rush to marry or procreate. We are decidedly on delay.

If you take a look at the wedding announcements and Vows stories in the *New York Times*, you will get a modern-day look at well-educated couples marrying (many for the first time) in their late 20s, 30s, and 40s. Oh, the role timing plays in so many of these relationships.

While writing this book, my good friend and I began tossing emails back and forth whenever we'd find a new couple in a wedding announcement, Vows write-up, or Modern Love column that fit today's trajectory. Vina Zhu Pulido and Anthony Tuan Nguyen met through mutual friends at a Harvard-Yale football game in 2010, then fell out of touch for three years while going to med school and living in different cities—but they claim they never stopped thinking about each other.[1] They started a long-distance love that eventually got closer when they both wound up in Boston. Six years after meeting, they tied the knot.

Then there was Vows' Ben Gliklich and Jessie Della Femina, who met as high schoolers.[2] They were in for a bumpy courtship. The groom had wanderlust, and the bride wanted to stick to her New York City roots, but the pair always seemed to gravitate back to each other. And when Ben was ready, he knew exactly with whom he wanted to settle down; the duo married at ages 31 and 32.

They're among the many couples who split, live some life, and then find each other in the future, when they can commit to something as monumental as "it." The dating timeline of the future is peppered with breakup-and-makeups, for couples who meet a great match too young and need to travel down side streets of independence before they get on the road to commitment.

There's no downside to waiting for men to be "ready" while developing yourself as a person and a relationship partner, which is an awesomely 21st-century thing to do (see: "The Case for Waiting," chapter 13). Recent economic studies show marriage trends that have emerged in the last 30 years or so, as women have begun to rise in status on their own—and here's what they find.

According to a study published in the journal *Social Science Research*, more years in the labor market are indicative of higher rates of marriage for men, but *not* for women.[3] But women who marry later in life tend to earn more money, especially those who wed in their 30s.[4] So…smart, successful, modern women, exploring all life has to offer them, aren't settling down quickly. For all you twenty- and thirtysomething EGs out there, I've been saying this, but it's worth repeating: *You're not alone.*

Researcher and economist Na'ama Shenhav, PhD, now a professor at Dartmouth College, calls the decline of marriage "one of the most striking social trends in the United States." In a 2016 paper, she set out to show how an increase in women's wages, relative to men's, was completely changing the relationship game.[5] From her economist's lens, she found that "greater social and financial independence" led to more female decision-making power, causing EG-like women to hold out or distance themselves from men who they might have wound up tied to in another era.

She explains her findings like this: "A 10 percent increase in relative wage options leads to a 7% decline in marriage [among women]. I show that the reduction in marriage is explained by a lower propensity to enter into a first marriage, with little impact on the likelihood of divorce. I also provide suggestive evidence that the reduction in marriage is among women that would have married lower quality spouses. These findings imply that the convergence in wages can explain 20% of the decline in marriage among women over the last three decades."

This is huge, and it plays right into assortative mating. Men and women are delaying marriage to their equals, although perhaps for different reasons. Women are financially independent, and no longer need to marry; they aren't settling for someone dissimilar to them in important ways like education, earnings, career, and goals. Men are gaining more years in the workforce (and likely setting their course) before taking themselves off the market. Although degreed adults are delaying serious love on the whole, research indicates you *will* settle down eventually—perhaps more commonly in the traditional way. According to 2017 Pew Research Center data, men and women age 25 and older with a four-year college degree are more likely to marry than their counterparts with only some or no college.[6] So take heart.

The implications here are important: A woman's male equal must rise through the ranks of success and self-knowledge, and then he must find the woman who is his best match in an absolute sea of potential options and combinations. Fitting *pretty well* or feeling sorta sure isn't good enough—for idealistic modern men *or* women. Support and love won't do, either. Deep soul mate connections that will help us become better human beings—that's what today's singles seek out. That's also big, *scary* stuff.

I've talked to men about "it" (a self-actualizing, Maslow's-need-#5-type bond), which is a different entity than, entirely separate from, a relationship (Maslow's need #3). It is The Relationship and The Connection that makes you feel the need to step it up. You will force some guy to grow, simply by being amazing, incredible, self-actualizing *you*—and he'll do the same for you.

Inherently, you feel that. But that's a lot of personal development for your future spouse, a lot of dating, a lot of learning to gauge connection *and* long-term potential, and a lot of sorting through the masses to find *you*—the EG girl who contains "it." (Or find you again, perhaps, in some cases.)

Shenhav found that a 10 percent increase in the relative wage (compared to men) led to a 5.3 percent decline in the probability that a woman *is married*, and her research also discovered that same 10 percent increase in the relative wage eventually leads to a 4.4 percent decline in the likelihood of a woman *being never married*. This suggests that women are holding out, waiting for "it"—and that strategy works. In addition, that 10 percent wage bump also increases the odds of a woman marrying a man who is more educated than herself, and about the same age—not substantially older.

That's a great match, prepared to last a lifetime, and that's the match I want for you. It's not hopeless; remaining single now is only increasing your odds of encountering "it" down the line, which is why many EG women are marrying later in life. They are holding out for a higher-quality partner—to discover that uniquely perfect fit, a compatible guy who has had time to mature into his role as a modern man and develop himself along the way. In the current dating landscape, it's important to recognize that meeting your match could be a long game—but not an unexciting one; there's plenty of room for adventure along the way.

In fact, I want you to *like* being single. If you do one thing for yourself and your future match on this long journey to love, it's this: Learn how to be okay on your own.

## It Is Better to Be Single Than in the Wrong Relationship

You need to meet new people to eventually find The One. So as much as solo chillin' with Netflix may sound like a perfect Saturday night after a long week at work, sometimes you need to set up dates and get out there. Still, in the middle of the hustle of dating today, I also want you to listen to yourself. It's okay to stop looking for a while, to reset. But how do you know when you've reached the precipice and need time alone?

- When you feel emotionally dry or weak
- When you are healing from the wounds of an epic breakup
- When you feel external pressure to date around but not personal desire
- When you don't know *why* you're dating anymore or *what* you want

It's easy to date mindlessly. It's sort of like binge eating; it feels kind of exhilarating while you're doing it—you're indulging some deep-seated need for a dopamine hit—but you're never satisfied in the end. Sometimes, you actually feel worse about yourself, especially if you're a goal-oriented person who has lost sight of her vision.

Bella DePaulo, PhD, a project scientist and former psychology professor at the University of California, Santa Barbara, has spent her whole life "single at heart." And for over two decades, she's also worked to dismiss myths about singleness as a sad, bummer lifestyle. It might be hard to refrain from dating. It might even be hard to stand up to your friends and say, "I am happy this way"—for however long you just need to do you. DePaulo gets this.

She also doesn't want you to be tricked into believing that marriage and relationships are the only way to be happy. "It is part of a world-view, a way of thinking, that people are invested in," she tells me. "They want to believe that people who get married become happier and healthier and that they are worthier and more valuable people than single people are, but the ideology of marriage is even appealing to some single people. It promises something seductive: Get married and all the pieces of your life will fall into place. You will have your life partner, and you will have a clear path through the rest of your life (get married, have kids, stay married, have grandkids). And, by getting married, you will also become happier and healthier and a more valued member of society."

That's a cool idea. It's so cool that it's been touted in magazines, on websites, and in numerous studies for years and years. But the data does not *really* support this, according to DePaulo. "Researchers have focused overwhelmingly on the supposed benefits of getting married—which they have greatly exaggerated or just plain misrepresented—but even with a relative neglect of single life, there is evidence for its benefits," she explains.

DePaulo has scrutinized the data from studies on singleness and married life.[7] She has found that there is plenty of research to show that single men and women spend more time bonding with friends, siblings, and parents, whereas coupled-up men and women tend to become a bit insular. On top of that, singles are more likely to step up and help a parent or other person in extreme need—for three months or more.

Studies often focus only on those who are currently married, without taking into account those who wind up divorced, DePaulo says. And that, she explains, is sort of like studying the business practices and culture of start-ups without tracking which go out of business. She even makes the case that marrieds usually do better than single people in their health and happiness only within the first four years or so. One 2012 study even showed that hitched men and women were not happier, healthier, less depressed, or carrying around higher self-esteem than singles.[8]

Here's the deal: I wouldn't be writing this book about relationship-building if I didn't think relationships were fulfilling and worthwhile. You probably wouldn't be reading this book if you didn't hold that belief. I also want to be completely clear: There are perfectly valid reasons to stay single, for a time at least. And while *the right* relationship is worthwhile, it is better to be single than in the wrong relationship.

DePaulo has lived singleness, and she's studied it. She's seen the benefits firsthand. "Single life offers you the opportunity to get deeply acquainted with *you*, to think about who you really are and who you want to be, apart from any pressures from a partner—which you may or may not recognize—to be a certain way or to like certain things or to have particular goals," she says. Single seasons are great times to rebuild or reinforce self-esteem, foster new friendships, devote time to your family, and just generally focus inward.

It's important to create a life where you can stand on your own two feet—one of deeply personal esteem, where you have the foundation to self-actualize. You are proud of who you are as an individual, and that satisfaction exists apart from relationships. Build your life up; build it strong. Fill it with friendships, career goals, travel plans, education for the sake of learning, passions, causes, spirituality, *human* love. That way, no matter what happens in dating, you get to choose to stay or leave, attach or detach—from a place of power.

You will never be someone's dependent. No guy will ever own you. You can find happiness, and greater meaning, while single *or* in a relationship. A relationship will only enhance the life you're envisioning for yourself, not make it worthwhile.

That's why I'm teaching you *how* to move on. Sometimes, heartbreak, losing "it," can be the best teacher.

## Learning from Mr. Wrong

You've probably said, "I should have seen it coming." Maybe you did. Maybe you needed that roller-coaster relationship experience.

They say life is a cruel teacher; you get the test first, and then the lesson. Love is no different. You need to teach yourself, through a series of trials and errors. Sometimes, that means staying, even when it makes no sense to anyone else. No one is born with the answers to what and who will make you happy in a relationship, or how you're going to get there.

Sometimes, you need to ask yourself what the most important thing is at that very moment. Is it amassing experiences, points on the map that you can compare to other men? Is it making mistakes so you can figure out exactly what "love," "connection," and "partner" really mean to you? If there is a lesson to be learned and you feel you can't move on until you understand what it is, then stay.

Sometimes, you need to stick it out. You need to take that risk and fully pursue it if you feel unsure about the outcome—like the relationship could go either way and you won't be able to live with the what-ifs of a plug pulled too soon. Sometimes, you need to stay until you can clearly see the outcome in your mind's eye.

Sometimes, you need to teach yourself what love is and what it isn't. Either way, you will learn—when he responds positively (the Real Deal), when you can't put up with his behavior anymore (the Almost Boyfriend), when you've played the relationship out until the finish and he slams the door in your face (the Disappearing Act), or when he continues to wound you with negative behavior (Mr. All That But).

That final sting of closure isn't actually him hurting you; it's him setting you free. It's always jarring to be rocked into a new portion of your life. But stick it out. Because closure is something you pursue on your own terms, for yourself.

Even if you don't see right away, trust me. Every guy means something, even if he isn't your someone. Leave it all on the floor. Don't just put him behind you. Heal. Grow. Move forward. Be free of the questions.

## Moving On 101

Research shows that when we break up, we undergo an identity crisis of sorts. According to Jennifer Jill Harman, PhD, a professor of psychology at Colorado State University, who studies intimate relationships, splits force us to detach and find new meaning alone.⁹ "As we become more intimate with a romantic partner, we start to integrate them and the relationship into our social identity," Harman says. "We go from 'me' to 'we,' and there is considerable research showing how this happens mentally. For example, we confuse adjectives that describe our partners with adjectives that describe ourselves—even when they don't—the more intimate we are with a person."

The best thing you can do after a breakup is find yourself again.

Remember Maddy? She was devastated when Karl pulled his Disappearing Act after that bittersweet summer road trip—but she was able to refocus her mind on schoolwork in the latter half of her college career. She even started dating again, albeit not quite as seriously. She says she was dating "in reaction to Karl," but not out of need. The emotional energy spent in that realm of her life was more minimal. At the end of one year, Karl actually wanted to get back together. Maddy said no. "I'm always creating narratives," she says of her relationships and life events. "That one was wrapped up for me."

Wrapping up each narrative is 100 percent what you need to do. You see, now Maddy was building a life that did not live and die by Karl's desire to be with her. "I was throwing myself into my female friendships," she says. "I thought, 'I owe it to myself to have this circle of support' "— which had disintegrated while she was with Karl. She finished her final two years of university, moved to New York, started her career, lived alone, and discovered just how capable she was as her own person.

It can be the hardest thing in the world to build a life of your own, while single, after finding "it." But Maddy did. Sometimes, finding and losing "it" can be a reminder to check in with yourself. When you are too young, or too absorbed in a relationship, you *do* become a *dependent*. Especially as a woman, especially if you lean toward a traditional gender dynamic (consciously or subconsciously). You can easily morph so deeply into coupledom that you lose yourself in the process. If you are no longer choosing a partner from a place of power. If you live and die by the health of your relationship you're not in the best position to be in one.

## Should I Stay, or Should I Go?

Sometimes, you won't be forced to move on, but rather you'll have to choose. If your partner is questioning things after months or years together (like in cases of Mr. All That Buts, or close Almost Boyfriends), how do you decide to stay in the picture or leave? Men today may not make the decision for you. They may take as much from you as you are willing to give, as they attempt to work through whatever is making them "not ready." So when you sense he's not ready or he tells you he's not ready, you'll have to read the situation and make some tough choices. Here are some questions to ask yourself:

### Where do I derive my esteem right now?

Remember Maslow: Esteem is internally decided, externally guided. If you find that your esteem is intricately linked to your relationship, then maybe you're not truly ready to be in one—or in *that* one, or in that one *right now*. The moment you feel like you wouldn't be okay if you were to lose your other half is the moment you need to question if the bond is worth hanging on to.

In looking back, Maddy thinks she was too young and inexperienced at age 19 to ever make a long-term relationship work—as was Karl, a couple of years her senior. Even if they did have that special something. Their self-esteem wasn't fully developed. And it needed to be.

Take Bella DePaulo's advice and use that time. "If you live by yourself, you can create a home that makes you feel at home, that reflects who you are," she says. "You have more flexibility to have both time alone and time with other people, in the proportions that suit you best. When you live single, you can nurture those friendships which may last a lifetime."

She thinks single life may be even more important for women who want to pursue their dreams in the workforce. "I do think career investments are great for single people, maybe especially single women," DePaulo says. "Work can be deeply fulfilling if you find something you love, and if you can support yourself, you have a certain strength and independence that gives you power and protects you from making bad decisions to be with someone because it seems safer financially."

DePaulo echoes a sentiment I have proposed to many single women in my life: Your career, the skills you develop on the job, the degrees you earn, and the experiences you have while pursuing your education and dreams *can never be taken away from you.* "A marriage, in contrast, is fragile," she explains. "It can end at any moment." Even the very best ones.

Remember, *settling is a way of life.* I want you to come to love from a place of power and strength, which you have the opportunity to do today in a way no generation of women ever has. That's also why I want you to remember what you are embodying: an end goal.

### ⚡ Do we have enough history that he will feel the potential of our connection?

If you feel "it," but not a lot of time has passed, you may want to stick it out and invest in him slowly. If he's obviously dating other people, then just mirror him; don't go all in. He makes a move; you reciprocate. You make a move; he reciprocates. As long as that cycle is on repeat, you are okay to stick it out for a while. Months, even.

Let him see what having you in his life is like. You should be investing your time elsewhere, too—even if you'd rather tear your hair out than go on dates with other guys. Be open. Allow someone else to sweep you off your feet. If he doesn't commit, he is taking the chance to lose you.

If he's not dating others and he is being emotionally and physically faithful to you, then you can let him slowly wade into Official Relationship Territory.

This is not always the case, though. If you have history, ask yourself:

Is he faithfully committed to me in his actions?

Sometimes, a guy meets a girl who has potential "it" way before he was planning on it. He was just having fun dating, and then bam! He recognizes he has stumbled into self-actualizing connection. But he panics. He wasn't necessarily done playing the field. He's not sure he can keep you long-term; you make him feel infantile for wanting a different, unsettled lifestyle. He may like the freedom of singleness—to go out, drink with the boys, and not be accountable for his actions to anyone.

That's the thing about some men: They can compartmentalize. So he can feel a deep soul mate connection with you and still feel the need to date (or sleep around) if he hasn't really done that. If he's dating other people, or feels he needs to, *and your connection is well established*—you've been longtime friends with sparks, or you've been in a relationship and he has doubts about his readiness—that's when you let him go.

Walk away.

🌹 **He's not faithfully committed to me, but why can't I just pull back a bit? Can I stick it out? Just for a while? Be friends?**

Tempting, but no. The reason you need to leave is simple: contrast. He needs to feel what the absence of you is really like. He must come to understand that *you* and *your connection* is the bar he will compare all others to. He needs to see that you are better than "options" and "variety" and "freedom." Coming home to his best friend and talking about his day, the latest theory he has about science/life/humanity/religion/politics, or random internet memes/witty humor is a million times better than coming home to an empty bachelor pad or a woman he's not afraid to lose.

If it's meant to be, it will be. But you need to show him that there's no other connection like yours, and he won't have the history or bond with another girl like he has with you—and he needs to *believe* that. I have talked to a lot of men. I've witnessed how they act. I truly believe that men often fall in love given distance and perspective. They often create space, assess how the relationship functions from afar, and then make their way back if it's really what they want.

If your boyfriend or fiancé says he's not ready, that he wants to date around or maintain a certain single lifestyle, let him. Withdraw your support and presence immediately. If you hold his hand through a time when he is not really faithful to you and committed to building a future, agree to an open relationship you're not okay with deep down, or agree to stay friends while he sorts his life out, he will not feel the power of your absence. You won't be happy with half a partner, even if he has that magic "it" factor. *Settling is a way of life*, remember! Settling for part-time commitment, part-time investment, and part-time "it" is still settling.

I want you to approach every relationship with a giving attitude. I want you to authentically connect, and even in your hurt, have the bravery to teach a man what he's lost when you walk away. If you leave nothing else behind, and you shouldn't, I want you to leave him that lasting lesson in rare connection. Allow yourself to become the bar to which he compares all others—not just a woman who's willing to be toyed with. Besides, you never know what the future will hold.

## We All Have to Grow Up

How often couples break up and get back together is a very hard phenomenon to track—but some researchers have tried. According to a recent study published in the *Journal of Adolescent Research*, of the 792 people between the ages of 17 and 24 tracked, 44 percent had reunited with an ex within the previous two years.[10]

There are certainly reasons for this. According to University of Texas psychologist Art Markman, PhD, modern-day commitment is equal parts *right person* and *right time*. Millennials especially are "willing to play the field" when it comes to dating, career, traveling, and trying different jobs in different cities.

This is an example of psychologist Jeffrey Arnett's "emerging adulthood" phenomenon, where many young people lean on their parents for support, wander into the right jobs, date casually, and don't aim for financial independence until later in their 20s.

"Boomers had more social pressure to find a career and to settle into a relationship," Markman told me during a 2016 interview for *Elle*. "Gen Xers did tend to marry a bit later and have children a bit later than boomers—but still followed a relatively straightforward trajectory from college to career. Millennials are taking longer to settle into careers and are more likely to switch career paths. [This affects the decision] to settle down into a long-term relationship and to commit to marriage."[11] It's a long road to growing up—and sometimes a romantically bumpy one.

Other research shows that perhaps 60 percent of people will have a breakup-and-makeup.[12] It's not uncommon. It's not necessarily healthy either; most reported more negatives than positives with those relationships compared to partners who haven't had a breakup (or two). This research also looked into the reasons couples come back together. Lingering feelings, companionship, or familiarity with that partner topped the list. Less specifically, "having no better alternatives" was also cited. Most breakups were not mutual, the study found. Most renewals, however, were initiated by both parties' desire to get back together, even though dating alternative partners actually reduced the likelihood that a couple would renew their bond.

Researchers note how such *makeups* tend to reflect themes like believing deeply that this partner is the one for you. Couples who have "on-off relationships...tend to have high levels of love and involvement in their relationships despite greater fluctuations in commitment, lower satisfaction, and greater conflict."[13]

I want to be clear about that last point: High levels of love and involvement but lower levels of commitment and satisfaction are not what I desire for you. With those high levels of love and involvement, you are often the more invested party.

Remember, breakups occur for a reason—to answer questions about happiness with alternative partners, to change jobs or coasts, to grow independently and explore life alone. And when couples start dating around, like the research says, the odds of ever reconciling go down.

So when your ex calls you up after two and a half years and says you were always The One, it's a shocker. Right? It was for Maddy, when Karl called her to say she'd always been just that—but he still wasn't even sure he could do real commitment (yes, those words were exchanged). "I was living out West, dating someone I felt was great," she recalls of that surprising moment. "Karl was still out East. He did not feel like a real option. On the phone, when I got this call, he seemed insane. It's a crazy thing to do."

While Maddy told Karl no, she did start to have recurring thoughts about her previous relationship. These cloudy, murky, was-that-relationship-as-good-as-I-remember thoughts. But she kept him out of sight, out of mind, to the best of her ability . . . even though Karl would check in every few months or so to see how she was doing.

But she didn't give in after that out-of-the-blue phone call, and still refused to see him. "It was not a low moment for me," Maddy says. "I was liking city living. I had lost a lot of female friends with Karl, so I was nurturing those friendships and spending time with the girls. I was making a concerted effort in the relationship I was in. I was living alone in an apartment, I was independent, I was killing cockroaches! It was fun and freeing."

Maddy was doing everything right in the Handbook of Moving On: dating new people, living alone, investing in friendships, creating a career, building a life. But Karl was her bar, just like she was his. And he did not give up. Karl kept casual tabs on Maddy—a text here, an email there—every few months or so.

Never before have couples had more avenues for getting back together. Today, it's easier than ever to remain connected to an ex—for better or worse. You are probably entwined on all social media plat-forms, from Facebook to Snapchat, Instagram to Twitter. You are likely seeing photos of him looking happy and fabulous all the time. Such are social media's charms. And you're always just a call, text, or email away from potential reconciliation. Karl used those mechanisms to stay on Maddy's radar.

Having not yet found another guy with real, true "it," she could not help but wonder if all the amazing qualities that brought them together the first time still remained. That similar dark sense of humor, their shared backgrounds and history. "He was so smart and funny, intensely confident," she says. "I felt so fortunate with him, and I kept coming back to that. So many people can be cynical. Karl was always so positive, appreciative, and grateful."

Maddy couldn't shake him—even though she spent two and a half more years after that fateful phone call trying to do just that. "I felt like he had always pushed me in positive ways," she explains. "His positivity and optimism forced me out of my worldview. He was driven, independent, and motivated. Being with someone like that attuned me to growth." Eventually, she agreed to meet him.

Five years after their split, Maddy and Karl came back together over coffee in New York City. He quickly proposed—but before she could say yes, they had demons to deal with. Their new policy? Transparency. "The way we did trust was by laying all cards on the table," she says. "We had all the conversations we didn't want to have, about who you'd dated and how it went. We eliminated all elements of surprise that might have popped up later on."

Eventually, they felt they'd shared just about everything they'd missed in those five years—and the connection they'd felt since they were 19 and 21 still remained. "A lot of trust is feeling ready and really *wanting* to trust a person," Maddy says. She made the choice to loop back to Karl as a grown, independent woman—who wanted the very best in a partner or nothing at all.

Maddy and Karl married in 2015. "As much as it hurt in the moment, I feel intensely grateful for how our story played out; I am very appreciative for the time we had apart," she says. "Although a lot of elements look romantic in retrospect, there are some unique to our generation. People really struggle with what else is out there."

She also can't discount the role of technology. "Had Facebook not been in existence, or Instagram, would I have been so present in his mind?" she says. She lives by the maxim, hokey as it is, "If it's meant to be, it will be."

"It really does seem like Karl and I were meant to be," she says. "Some relationships never really die."

## This Is Not a Permission Slip

Why am I telling you about Maddy and Karl? Not so you will start flipping through your little black book, but so you can see that anything is possible in life. People grow and change.

That said, even if a guy does mature into partner material, sometimes (more often than not) he will never meet you again on the pathway to commitment. He will grow in a divergent way, meet someone new. You will become the bar, but not a forever love.

So always walk away with the mentality that it is over. That's it. I promise that if you wait and hope, you will never find "it" again—with *that* ex, or with anyone else. Build your life around yourself. In the words of the great writer Jorge Luis Borges, "Plant your own gardens and decorate your own soul, instead of waiting for someone to bring you flowers." *Go.* Move on. In a perfect world, there is something greater out there. At the very least, there is someone out there with great potential who has not cast a toxic wake of hurt over your relationship.

Men do sometimes realize their mistake in letting you walk away—from time to time. But breakups, more often than not, signal a major flaw and the end of an era. Even if they realize they've made a huge mistake in letting you go, they may never act to fix it. Or they may never realize what they've truly lost. Some will remain too selfish and undeserving of you *forever. People* can be this way, not just men.

"It" doesn't mean forever; it only means connection. That's the cruel, honest truth, and I need you to live with that.

So, EG, hear me. The case for moving on is not about leaving and expecting him to boomerang back to you. It's not about hoping he figures out his great loss. *It's about moving on with the knowledge of what exists in terms of connection.*

That first cut, or second, or third, becomes the bar to which you compare all others. It is a data point of the best sort. Every new relationship falls in alongside the others, and pretty soon you discover where each type of connection ranks. You will develop a better idea of what you need and yearn for in a long-term partner.

Collect this data; it is a vital part of your growth. Your lifelong "it" is out there. You've probably encountered something close before. Never, ever give up on that feeling—that connection. You never have to settle for less...but never try to convince someone to stay who doesn't fully see your value and clearly is not ready. Happiness won't follow.

# wisdom for the (modern) ages

One of the best parts of writing is the process of discovery. You're always armed with an idea and some research when you start, but you find this rich narrative, so much bigger than you ever imagined, by the time you finish. For me, this book was certainly that. I, a lifelong student of love, rediscovered why relationships matter so much.

I was single when I started writing *The Love Gap*, and I was single when I finished. That was intentional; I didn't want my own dating and relationship experiences to color the pages of this book. I knew it was *your* story, as much as it was mine. When I turned in the first draft, I needed about two months to recover fully from the emotions I'd stirred up. Then I started to reenter the dating universe, armed with everything I'd learned over the past two years—knowledge that I've now handed over to you.

As I began to date again, Disappearing Acts and Almost Boyfriends were still outside my door . . . of course! I just knew how to handle them better, live in ambiguity, and gauge what was worth it to me. I probably now have five guys in my wider circle who might become something more, someday, and I'm continuing to keep an eye out for a Real Deal. (As you know, they're not easy to find.)

The greatest gift of my newfound knowledge is the ability to let go and enjoy the ride. I'm not struggling for control anymore. Instead, I'm watching as doors open (and close) around me, loving every second of the journey. I feel very light, perhaps for the first time ever. Understanding the romantic landscape, and having a plan to operate within it, has reduced the anxiety and confusion I used to feel about dating. And I know I am not alone.

I inadvertently end up discussing my work almost everywhere. So many people are at their wits' end trying to understand themselves, their prospects, their needs, and how to build relationships in this modern age. It's been amazing to see how interested people are. In this project. In love. In learning. In finding The Relationship—someday, if not today.

Men and women alike have *so many questions*. Believe it or not, I even spent a first date talking some 28-year-old guy through the intricacies of his "I can't have a girlfriend right now" spiral. (He proceeded to tell me our talk was "better than therapy!"...Yay? I think yay.) In any case, I finally feel like I have *so many answers*. I hope you do, too.

Before I leave you for good and send you out into the world to find that great and magical "it," I want to give you some final, more personal, pearls of wisdom to consider. After letting the contents of this book marinate in the back of my mind for around six months, I came up with five essential maxims for keeping your cool while navigating the Love Gap. And it's in listicle format. Because would I really be a magazine writer if I didn't go there?

## 1. Never make yourself less to make a man more comfortable.

Just after I submitted the first draft of this book, a study published by Harvard researchers caught my attention.[1] Students admitted to an elite MBA program were asked questions related to ambition and their future job desires. The researchers wanted to know how single women's answers might fluctuate if they thought it would affect their relationship prospects.

When the unattached female students thought only the program's career office would be privy to their answers, they requested only slightly smaller salaries than their male counterparts and said they'd be willing to work just as many hours and travel just as much. However, when single women were told their peers would see their answers—eligible men included—they said they'd take $18,000 less per year in income, want to travel seven fewer days per month, and need to work four fewer hours per week. They also rated themselves as less ambitious and less leadership-oriented overall. The men and married ladies, on the other hand? There was no change in their answers, whether public knowledge or privately relayed to career counselors.

The researchers hypothesized that single women downplayed their ambition because they thought it would hurt their odds on the marriage market, evidence that the Love Gap is often felt, if not fully acknowledged. I said this at the beginning of the book, and I'll say it again: I never want you to be less to find a guy. Never.

Being less to "score" a man who doesn't fully accept your authentic self, whether you're a badass boss lady or any other incarnation of goal-reaching EG, is a recipe for long-term unhappiness. When you are willing to accept less simply to have a relationship, you are signaling that you're willing to give up the lion's share of the "bargaining power" in the relationship, according to economist Marina Adshade, PhD, a lecturer at the Vancouver School of Economics. "This determines how big decisions are made, and who has the most say," she explains. That includes who will work and how much, when to have kids and how many, what to spend money on and how much, and more.

You have worked too hard for your financial independence and for the power it gives you to *choose* a relationship—from a place of desire, not need—to give it up. Adshade strongly advises against this strategy for landing an SO, too. "Even if this was sustainable, and you were able to take less bargaining power to get a relationship...research shows us *equal* partnerships are the happier relationships today," she says. Once you are ready for real love, filter relentlessly for your guy—and invest wisely in men who could also be ready. Don't become smaller.

Speaking of ready...

## 2. Just like the guys you encounter, it's okay if *you* aren't always ready for love.

Unreadiness is a long-term state for many men, who are still building themselves into the guys they'll one day be. It's also a short-term state for men who are going through transitory periods of life, like divorce, a big move, or a career change. And it's a period you may pass through, too.

Honestly, the perfect guy for me could have jogged past with a blinking neon sign while I was writing this book, and I would not have noticed him. You, too, will go through periods of your life when you have tunnel vision. Perhaps men are more fixed on their timelines and less flexible in their ability to juggle love and career and life—but that doesn't mean you're never going to be that way.

Do not beat yourself up over the men who enter your life during these seasons, who will perhaps *feel* like missed connections when you reemerge from hibernation. Just like you are willing to give men time so frequently—Almost Boyfriends, Mr. All That Buts, etc.—you deserve that same time to yourself. You deserve space for perspective. You deserve periods to focus only on you, to heal, to build up your esteem.

You also deserve patience. If you meet someone special—a Real Deal, heaven forbid!—during a time when you're totally *not* ready to fall in love, don't be afraid to get in touch when you make your way out of the tunnel. He might still be open to you when your search has relaunched. If he's the right guy, and ready, he may just have the understanding and self-esteem to hear you out. If he's the wrong guy, he'll likely be unreceptive—but then you won't have any regrets, and you can stop wondering. Nothing lost there.

## 3. Write *your own* love story.

Your life is a giant narrative. The choices you make and the beliefs you hold will shape the pages' contents. No story is the same. No *love* story is the same. You get to decide yours.

Love stories can be messy, or they can be almost seamless. They can take years to come to fruition, or they can shoot off like a rocket and never slow down. But you get to decide what you believe about love, and choose the trajectory of your relationships. To do that, you will have to ask yourself what you want and what you believe, over and over again, as you adopt Almost Boyfriends, deal with Disappearing Acts, wait, date around, and decide who is worth your time and energy. You must think:

- Do I believe it's more important to find the *right person* and build a relationship with him, despite any bumps in the road? Or do I believe it's more important to create the *right relationship* with a compatible partner, steadfast in all ways?
- Do I believe love is rare, and you invest when you find it? Or do I believe love is an everyday choice to build a relationship with someone who's in the same headspace I am?
- Do I believe "love" is a singular noun, and I have to find The One, or is it a mass noun, uncountable, found and nurtured in numerous places? How much of "love" is a verb, something you *do*? Can choosing to love someone every day create the kind of relationship you want? Or can "loving" the right person change your life?

You might not even know what you believe about love right now, at this very moment, but I want you to remember that it can take many forms. It can be a long road, or a short one. It can be more about investing in a specific person, or it can be more about building a specific kind of relationship. Neither choice or trajectory is less worthy or fulfilling—and ideally, they all end with the same healthy, lasting bond. And as the writer of your own story, you can also change your mind at any time.

Only *you* get to write the ending of your own story. Sometimes, you wait for that deep connection to come around, against all odds, because you know it's worth it; sometimes, you date until you encounter that partner who meets you halfway, who chooses you every day.

I can't tell you what to believe; I can't even tell you what I believe for myself just yet. That's an exhilarating example of the agency we have. That's modern-day romance.

## 4. Throw out the old wisdom—or at least take a hard look at it under the microscope.

Growing up, we were told a lot of potentially harmful things about love and relationships. For instance, one of my personal favorites was always "If it's the right person, timing doesn't matter." Ohhhh, *really*? I guess our parents didn't know what course our futures would take, but I've already gone into great detail here about why timing is critical.

"Relationships are hard work" is another maxim with limited validity. Are they work? Absolutely. If you want to keep it fresh, you want to keep growing, you want your partner to feel supported, then you need to be consistent, you need to communicate—even when you don't feel like it. But how *hard*, exactly, do relationships have to be? You have the power, unlike past generations, to choose the right person. You are not constrained by proximity, and you can maintain a relationship long-distance if you must. You don't need to tie yourself to a provider to survive; you are your own, and you have the power. You can find someone you're deeply compatible with, who's committed to the same goals, who views love the same way you do. You can marry later in life, wait until you're sure you've found a healthy "it." You have more options than ever. It doesn't have to be hard. In fact, I think the choice to be with your partner should be easy.

Also, on a slightly lighter, but important, note...sex matters! Physical chemistry matters. Somewhere along the way, I feel like women were told, "Sex is a chore, and men are going to want to have sex until they die." Um. Yes? So should you! I have met women who think they are not sexual creatures, who don't think they ever really have physical urges. Most of them are not with the right person, or have consistently dismissed sexual chemistry as unimportant in the whole scheme of things. I can promise you, it's important—in fact, it's the one element that separates a romantic relationship from a friendship. It's that primal connection that can pull you back together in the middle of a heated argument, or a pile of chores, or a moment when you're feeling out of sync and disconnected. Never forget the Connection Trifecta, which is like a three-legged stool. If that sucker has a busted leg, it's not going to be very sturdy, is it?

While I love the generations who have been doing life and creating love for a long while, and their wisdom is sometimes sage, we need to evaluate the messages we've internalized that might be holding us back from our best loves today. Not everything Mom or Grandma told you is right—or right *for you.*

Can we just agree to pass all the old wisdom under a microscope going forward? Remember, there are no rules, and there are no givens.

## 5. Make sure commitment excites you.

One of the big questions today is: *How do I know if I'm settling?* In the weeks and months since writing this book, I've been asked another question over and over again—which is almost a trickier version of the first: *How do I know if I've met the right person?*

Eventually, over time, you can usually determine if someone is wrong for you. But it might be trickier to know if the person is *right* for you. How do you know if you have long-ranging compatibility? How do you know if this person is the best possible choice for you? If he could be The One? Well, "right" is somewhat of a black hole.

I stumbled across the answer when I was talking to a friend of mine over drinks at this cool upstairs bar in Ann Arbor, Michigan. She was angsty—and she really didn't know why. She was thinking about taking herself off the market for a guy she'd been dating for a few months. But she told me, "I can't shake the feeling that I'll be missing out on something if I commit to him."

Therein lies the answer: A relationship, the "right" connection, should excite you with its potential for growth. A "right" commitment should feel like it expands your possibilities in life, instead of shrinking them. Spending time with the "right" guy will seem to open more doors than it closes as you consider no longer actively investing in other prospects.

My greatest hope is that when you enter into a deeper stage of commitment, you'll do it because you genuinely want to—not because you think you're destined to be a little bit miserable in all relationships or you "can't have it all." I want you to feel excited about the prospect of commitment, not scared or worried or resigned to some "meh" fate.

I honestly believe that when you're with the *right* person, you will feel comfortable committing. But why is that? Because you know who you are, you know what you want, you've tested the market long enough to know what's out there, and you're building history with someone who loves and "gets" you. (Feeling understood by your partner is important; so says research.)[2] The right person knows you better than anyone, and helps you become your best self—constantly growing and becoming more *together*.[3] Wait for *that* love, that feeling of certainty.

That's "right." And that's what you deserve.

# Glossary

**Almost Boyfriend, n.** a guy who looks like a boyfriend, acts like a boyfriend, and treats you like a girlfriend, but, for whatever reason, is failing to fully commit to an exclusive relationship.

**assortative mating, n.** the tendency for people to pair off with those similar to themselves in qualities like attractiveness, education, earning potential, and social factors; even more common in the age of app and online dating, where you may gravitate toward these similar prospects.

**Back-Burner Prospect, n.** (1) a potential partner you maintain casual contact with, often via technology and social media, leaving the door open for romantic developments later on; (2) an EG who an Almost Boyfriend keeps tabs on, who he may just pursue when he's "ready."

**bar, n.** the best connection you've ever encountered in your life, and the person you compare all others to; the one it might have worked out with had things been a little different; anything less than the sum total of this connection feels like settling.

**Commitment Trifecta, n.** a sense of connection, compatibility, and belief in the character of a guy; you want to experience all three before committing; (also known as the three *C*s of commitment).

**Connection Trifecta, n.** emotional, intellectual, and physical chemistry with a guy you're seeing; the ingredients that embody "it."

**Disappearing Act, n.** a guy with whom you have an incredible, been-waiting-forever-for-this connection, who suddenly exits stage left with little to no explanation and no closure.

**End Goal (EG), n.** (1) a smart, successful, "full package" woman; (2) the type of woman with the sort of allure, substance, and connection that a man wants—someday, when he's "ready"; (3) the type of woman everyone thinks is great but who is usually single.

**esteem, n.** (1) one of Maslow's basic needs, coming before self-actualization; (2) knowing who you are and what your role is, as well as feeling mastery of skills and respect from peers; much more malleable, unique, and interdependent for modern women, much more established, concrete, and independent for modern men; (3) in relationships, knowing who you are, what you're looking for, and what you can bring to a partnership.

**filter, v.** to sort through the mass chaos of prospects and options; to get rid of men who aren't the right fit or aren't treating you how you want to be treated, while getting to know guys you're interested in and want to invest energy in.

**Getaway Girl (GG), n.** (1) a carefree, curious, awesome-in-her-own-right woman who embraces the moment and helps men detach from their day-to-day stressful lives; may be a little less figured out than an EG; (2) the woman who men feel best dating when they're not ready; (3) to various degrees, a side existing within *every* woman.

**hard to get** (1) **adj.** elusive, mysterious, and perpetually just out of reach in the dating "game"; rare, desired, and worth pursuing in the realm of relationship-building; (2) **n.** a game intended to establish a woman as "high value" and maintain the upper hand with men, popularized by the dating self-help book *The Rules* back in the '90s.

**hierarchy of needs, n.** a theory first proposed in 1943 by psychologist Abraham Maslow, explaining the basic needs that drive and motivate people; this includes physiological, safety, love and belongingness, and esteem needs, as well as self-actualization.

**"it," n.** (1) the magical connection contained within the potential right guy; what you're waiting to *feel* while dating, before you pair off; (2) derivative of "it" factor.

**Love Gap, n.** the reason men don't always pursue the women they claim to want—frequently, women just like you.

**manageable authenticity, n.** the strategy of being completely true to yourself, but controlling the rate at which you reveal yourself to someone you're dating; best utilized when dating a guy who is not ready.

**mitigate expectations, v.** to prematurely tell a partner what you cannot handle or what your relationship cannot be, either right now or long-term; employed by men who aren't ready and are trying to communicate that in an attempt at preserving their independence.

**Mr. All That But the Bag of Chips, n.** a man you're seeing who is absolutely everything you want in a partner, with that sparkling "it" factor of connection...but who is not ready to offer that full-fledged commitment.

**not ready, adj.** (1) a state of being where you're still working on yourself or figuring your life out; (2) in a mind-set of making choices or changes, like finding the right job, settling into the right place, finishing a degree, recovering from a breakup or divorce, etc.; can be a short-term phase or long-term state.

**paradox of choice, n.** a concept pulled from psychologist Barry Schwartz's 2004 book of the same name; the idea that humans like *some* choice, but too much choice often cripples decision-making and leads to anxiety; recently popularized by Aziz Ansari in his book *Modern Romance*, to explain an inherent problem with dating in the era of app and online options.

**ready, adj.** (1) state of being where you're genuinely open to a potential long-term relationship; (2) knowing who you are, what you can offer a partner, and what you're looking for in a long-term connection; (3) a prerequisite for actively pursuing an EG.

**Real Deal, n.** the holy grail of men, the manna from heaven, the diamond *not* in the rough—a guy who's steady, sure, open, and *ready* for a real relationship.

**self-actualization, n.** (1) the apex of Maslow's common hierarchy of needs, where basic needs have been mostly fulfilled; (2) a mind-set in which you're continually growing and striving to reach your fullest potential; in doing so, you can also begin to extend outside yourself and help others fill their needs and reach their goals.

**self-actualizing partnership, n.** a growth-oriented relationship for the modern age, where you're learning, expanding, and becoming *more* with a partner who makes you better; #relationshipgoals for tons of modern daters, who have so many options available.

**settling, v.** feeling like there is likely a better match out there for you, a higher-quality connection, but choosing to commit to someone for reasons of comfort, history, fear, pressure, or loneliness.

# Resources and Further Reading

*A shortlist of the books and papers I consulted while writing, as well as a selection of inspirations, influences, and helpful resources I discovered while learning about modern relationships over the past several years.*

## Websites and Blogs

Hooking Up Smart (http://www.hookingupsmart.com)
Dr. NerdLove (http://www.doctornerdlove.com)
*New York* magazine's Science of Us (http://nymag.com/scienceofus/)
*Psychology Today* blogs (https://www.psychologytoday.com)
Science of Relationships (http://www.scienceofrelationships.com)
*New York Times* Vows (https://www.nytimes.com/column/vows)
*New York Times* Modern Love (https://www.nytimes.com/column
   /modern-love)

## Books and Academic Papers

*The Social Animal* by Eliott Aronson
*The First Sex: The Natural Talents of Women and How They Are Chang-
   ing the World* by Helen Fisher
*Why Him? Why Her? How to Find and Keep Lasting Love* by Helen
   Fisher
*American Hookup: The New Culture of Sex on Campus* by Lisa Wade
*The Evolution of Desire: Strategies of Human Mating* by David Buss
*Modern Romance* by Aziz Ansari and Eric Klinenberg

*The Science of Happily Ever After: What Really Matters in the Quest for Enduring Love* by Ty Tashiro

*Dollars and Sex: How Economics Influences Sex and Love* by Marina Adshade

*From First Kiss to Forever: A Scientific Approach to Love* by Marisa T. Cohen

*Attached: The New Science of Adult Attachment and How It Can Help You Find—and Keep—Love* by Amir Levine and Rachel S. F. Heller

*The Seven Principles for Making Marriage Work* by John Gottman

*The Five Love Languages: The Secret To Love That Lasts* by Gary Chapman

*A Theory of Human Motivation* by Abraham Maslow

*Motivation and Personality* by Abraham Maslow

"Rediscovering the Later Version of Maslow's Hierarchy of Needs: Self-Transcendence and Opportunities for Theory, Research, and Unification" by Mark E. Koltko-Rivera

# Acknowledgments

The decision to write this book was one of the most terrifying, overwhelming, and exciting of my life. Looking back, I'm not sure how I got it all together—but I know that I could not have done it without a legion of support and encouragement along the way.

Major thanks to my agent, Melissa Flashman. You were the first to recognize a need for this book in such a game-changing time in the world *and* relationships. Having your guidance from day one has made the journey infinitely easier. Thank you for your wisdom, support, and fascinating dating stories (of course).

Brittany McInerney—I could not have asked for a better editor; your energy and excitement powered me through the writing and editing process. You let my voice shine through, while also helping me elevate every argument and piece of advice. This book became so much more with you on board. Thank you also to everyone else at Grand Central who worked on *The Love Gap*, particularly Kallie Shimek and Andy Dodds. You guys were *so helpful* in completing this book!

I have to acknowledge all the experts who donated their time and insight to this project, including Karla Ivankovich, Art Markman, Marisa T. Cohen, Art Aron, David Buss, Lisa Wade, Marina Adshade, Lora Park, Bella DePaulo, Paul Eastwick, and Ty Tashiro, as well as Susan Walsh and Harris O'Malley. Your work informs my work, and makes what I do possible—and I relish every chance I get to pick your brains.

To the more than 100 men and women who I interviewed for this book: I wish I could have included every detail of every fascinating story! Thank you for allowing me into your personal lives. This book is the product of your continuous support and unrelenting honesty. I still feel so humbled by your openness and your belief that this book's contents are worthwhile. My gratitude is beyond words.

I also have to thank my writing mentors over the past decade. Luann Haskins, my high school journalism adviser: You were the first to insist I was a good writer; thank you for that early encouragement. To Lolita Hernandez, my creating writing instructor at the University of Michigan: You've read more of my writing than any other human being, and you've pushed me every step of the way. Thank you for telling me to finally write this book.

I'd be remiss not to thank my entire group of friends. You asked me questions about the draft (when I desperately needed to vocalize my internal dialogue), came to my idea roundtables, connected me with people who you thought would have great stories, and encouraged me to believe in my work. I am one of the lucky ones, with a huge "squad" of adult friends who choose to hang out and support each other. You continue to amaze me.

A few friends deserve special mention. Stephanie, you read every word of countless proposal drafts, and all your feedback was incredibly helpful in the early phases of this book. Katie, thank you for allowing me to bounce theories and new research off you, and for responding with a ridiculous amount of enthusiasm. Elizabeth, my writing buddy on this book, I can't tell you how amazing it was to have the encouragement and kind words of another author as we both awaited publication! Carrie, thanks for letting me vocalize my worries and discuss relationships ad nauseam; you're one of a kind.

Quick shout-out to my editors and colleagues in the magazine and web world, who have been both helpful and kind over the past two years: Thanks for your time, connections, and support of this book, and for putting up with my time away from the freelance world and my frequently erratic schedule.

Thank you to my parents. To my mom, Martha, my best friend and greatest supporter: I would not be me without you. To my dad, David, undoubtedly my biggest fan: Your character and work ethic has always been the standard for which I reach. My writing career really began the day you guys let me pass up that retail job at 18 so I could "figure out how to write on the internet." (I appreciate your *belief in me*, even though I know you weren't sure writing on the internet was a thing.) You have both set such incredible examples for me in life and in love. It's a tough act to follow; I hope to make you proud.

To my grandmother, Doris, who passed away when I was a teenager and popped into my mind countless times while I was writing this book. I'd like to think tiny flickers of her individualism, curiosity, and courage exist inside me today; I only wish I could thank her personally.

My faith has always been my guiding light—glory to God for providing me an opportunity to tell these stories. My *Love Gap* journey was a profound blessing; I have this newfound appreciation for life's perfect imperfections, the way we *all* struggle, and the power of understanding. That, in itself, has made all the energy poured into this book worthwhile.

Lastly, a huge thanks to you, dear reader. I hope this book's contents inform your journey toward love—and help you see the myriad of potential ways your story might unfold.

# Notes

### Introduction

1. Kimberly Cutter, "Susan Downey: Iron Woman," *Harper's Bazaar*, Dec. 9, 2009, www.harpersbazaar.com/culture/features/a458/susan-downey-interview-0110/.

### Chapter 1

1. U.S. Census Bureau, "Facts for Features: Unmarried and Single Americans Week: Sept. 18–24, 2016," news release, Aug. 26, 2016, https://www.census.gov/newsroom/facts-for -features/2016/cb16-ff18.html.

2. Match.com, "Singles in America: Match Releases Its Fifth Annual Comprehensive Study on the Single Population," news release, Feb. 4, 2016, http://www.multivu.com /players/English/7433451-match-singles-in-america/.

3. Zahra Barnes, "Why 'The Clooney Effect' Is Amazing for Your Love Life," *Glamour*, Jan. 13, 2016, https://www.glamour.com/story/why-the-clooney-effect-is-amaz; Tanya Basu, "The Clooney Effect," *Atlantic*, Feb. 26, 2015, https://www.theatlantic.com/business /archive/2015/02/the-clooney-effect/386018/.

4. Lora E. Park, Ariana F. Young, and Paul W. Eastwick, "(Psychological) Distance Makes the Heart Grow Fonder: Effects of Psychological Distance and Relative Intelligence on Men's Attraction to Women," *Personality and Social Psychology Bulletin* 41, no. 11 (Nov. 1, 2015): 1459–73, https://doi.org/10.1177/0146167215599749.

### Chapter 2

1. Daniele Marzoli et al., "Environmental Influences on Mate Preferences as Assessed by a Scenario Manipulation Experiment," *PLoS ONE* 8, no. 9 (2013), https://doi .org/10.1371/journal.pone.0074282.

2. Peter M. Buston and Stephen T. Emlen, "Cognitive Processes Underlying Human Mate Choice: The Relationship Between Self-Perception and Mate Preference in Western Society," *Proceedings of the National Academy of Sciences* 100, no. 15 (2003): 8805–10, https://doi.org/10.1073/pnas.1533220100.

3. Marisa T. Cohen and Karen Wilson, *The Relationship Between Mate Selection Preferences and Academic Motivation*, Mar. 2015, Annual Meeting of the Eastern Psychological Association.

4. Raymond Fisman et al., "Gender Differences in Mate Selection: Evidence from a Speed Dating Experiment," *Quarterly Journal of Economics* 121, no. 2 (May 2006): 673–97, https://doi.org/10.1162/qjec.2006.121.2.673.

5. Adam Karbowski, Dominik Deja, and Mateusz Zawisza, "Perceived Female Intelligence as Economic Bad in Partner Choice," *Personality and Individual Differences* 102 (Nov. 2016): 217–22, https://doi.org/10.1016/j.paid.2016.07.006.

6. Dan Cassino, "Thought of a Woman President Rattles Male Voters in New Jersey," PublicMind Poll, Fairleigh Dickinson University, Mar. 23, 2016, http://view2.fdu.edu /publicmind/2016/160323/; Dan Cassino, "Even the Thought of Earning Less Than Their Wives Changes How Men Behave," *Harvard Business Review*, Apr. 19, 2016, https://hbr .org/2016/04/even-the-thought-of-earning-less-than-their-wives-changes-how-men-behave.

7. David M. Buss, "The Mating Crisis Among Educated Women," Edge.org, 2016, https://www.edge.org/response-detail/26747.

8. Y. Joel Wong et al., "Meta-Analyses of the Relationship Between Conformity to Masculine Norms and Mental Health–Related Outcomes," *Journal of Counseling Psychology* 64, no. 1 (Jan. 2017): 80–93, https://doi.org/10.1037/cou0000176.

9. John M. Gottman and Nan Silver, *The Seven Principles for Making Marriage Work: A Practical Guide from the Country's Foremost Relationship Expert* (New York: Harmony Books, 1999).

10. Jennifer S. Mascaro et al., "Child Gender Influences Paternal Behavior, Language, and Brain Function," *Behavioral Neuroscience* 131, no. 3 (June 2017): 262–73, https://doi .org/10.1037/bne0000199.

11. David Cotter and Joanna Pepin, "Trending Towards Traditionalism? Changes in Youths' Gender Ideology," Online Symposia, Council on Contemporary Families, Mar. 30, 2017, https://contemporaryfamilies.org/2-pepin-cotter-traditionalism/.

12. Nika Fate-Dixon, "Are Some Millennials Rethinking the Gender Revolution? Long-Range Trends in Views of Non-Traditional Roles for Women," Online Symposia, Council on Contemporary Families, Mar. 30, 2017, https://contemporaryfamilies .org/7-fate-dixon-millennials-rethinking-gender-revolution/.

13. Stephanie Coontz, "Do Millennial Men Want Stay-at-Home Wives?" *New York Times*, Mar. 31, 2017, https://www.nytimes.com/2017/03/31/opinion/sunday/do-millennial -men-want-stay-at-home-wives.html.

## Chapter 4

1. Robert B. Zajonc, "The Attitudinal Effects of Mere Exposure," *Journal of Personality and Social Psychology Monograph Supplement*, 2nd ser., 9, no. 2 (June 1968): 1–27, http:// www.morilab.net/gakushuin/Zajonc_1968.pdf.

2. Susan Walsh, "How to Use Familiarity to Create Attraction," Hooking Up Smart, Sept. 22, 2012, http://www.hookingupsmart.com/2011/03/15/relationshipstrategies/how -to-use-familiarity-to-create-attraction/.

3. Lucy Hunt, Paul Eastwick, and Eli Finkel, "Leveling the Playing Field: Longer Acquaintance Predicts Reduced Assortative Mating on Attractiveness," *Psychological Science* 26, no. 7 (July 2015), https://doi.org/10.1177/0956797615579273.

4. Dylan Selterman, "Who's Hot, Who's Not? Time Will Tell," Science of Relationships, July 27, 2015, http://www.scienceofrelationships.com/home/2015/7/27/whos-hot-whos-not-time-will-tell.html.

5. Jayson L. Dibble and Michelle Drouin, "Using Modern Technology to Keep in Touch with Back Burners: An Investment Model Analysis," *Computers in Human Behavior* 34 (2014): 96–100, https://doi.org/10.1016/j.chb.2014.01.042.

6. Julie Beck, "The Psychology of 'Backburner' Relationships," *Atlantic*, Oct. 24, 2014, https://www.theatlantic.com/health/archive/2014/10/the-psychology-of-backburner-relationships/381848/.

## Chapter 5

1. Kate Ratliff and Shigehiro Oishi, "Gender Differences in Implicit Self-Esteem Following a Romantic Partner's Success or Failure," *Journal of Personality and Social Psychology* 105, no. 4 (2013): 688–702, https://doi.org/10.1037/e527772014-679.

2. Nir Halevy, "Preemptive Strikes: Fear, Hope, and Defensive Aggression," *Journal of Personality and Social Psychology* 112, no. 2 (2017): 224–37, https://doi.org/10.1037/pspi0000077.

## Chapter 8

1. Arthur Aron et al., "The Self-Expansion Model of Motivation and Cognition in Close Relationships," in *The Oxford Handbook of Close Relationships*, Jeffry Simpson and Lorne Campbell, eds. Apr. 2013, https://doi.org/10.1093/oxfordhb/9780195398694.013.0005.

2. Helen Fisher, "Why We Love, Why We Cheat," TED Talks, TED2006, Feb. 2006, https://www.ted.com/talks/helen_fisher_tells_us_why_we_love_cheat; Helen Fisher, "Web Thinking: Women's Contextual View," in *The First Sex: The Natural Talents of Women and How They Are Changing the World*, 3–28, (New York: Ballantine Books, 1999).

3. Jesse Singal, "Here's the Biggest Study Yet on the Differences Between Male and Female Brains," Science of Us, Apr. 6, 2017, http://nymag.com/scienceofus/2017/04/heres-the-biggest-study-yet-on-sex-based-brain-differences.html.

4. Madhura Ingalhalikar et al., "Sex Differences in the Structural Connectome of the Human Brain," *Proceedings of the National Academy of Sciences* 111, no. 2 (Jan. 14, 2014), https://doi.org/10.1073/pnas.1316909110; Olga Khazan, "Male and Female Brains Really Are Built Differently," *Atlantic*, Dec. 2, 2013, https://www.theatlantic.com/health/archive/2013/12/male-and-female-brains-really-are-built-differently/281962/.

5. Muping Gan and Serena Chen, "Being Your Actual or Ideal Self? What It Means to Feel Authentic in a Relationship," *Personality and Social Psychology Bulletin* 43, no. 4 (2017): 465–78, https://doi.org/10.1177/0146167216688211.

6. Stephen M. Drigotas et al., "Close Partner as Sculptor of the Ideal Self: Behavioral Affirmation and the Michelangelo Phenomenon," *Journal of Personality and Social Psychology* 77, no. 2 (Aug. 1999): 293–323, https://doi.org/10.1037//0022-3514.77.2.293.

7. Abraham Tesser, "Toward a Self-Evaluation Maintenance Model of Social Behavior," *Advances in Experimental Social Psychology* 21 (1988): 181–227, https://doi.org/10.1016/s0065-2601(08)60227-0.

8. Kurt Bauman and Camille Ryan, "Women Now at the Head of the Class, Lead Men in College Attainment," U.S. Census Bureau, Oct. 7, 2015, https://www.census.gov /newsroom/blogs/random-samplings/2015/10/women-now-at-the-head-of-the-class-lead -men-in-college-attainment.html.

9. Wendy Wang and Kim Parker, "Chapter 1: Public Views on Marriage," Pew Research Center's Social & Demographic Trends Project, Sept. 23, 2014, http://www.pewsocial trends.org/2014/09/24/chapter-1-public-views-on-marriage/.

10. Muriel Niederle and Lise Vesterlund, "Do Women Shy Away from Competition? Do Men Compete Too Much?" *Quarterly Journal of Economics*, Aug. 2007, 1067–101, https://doi.org/10.3386/w11474; Jeff Guo, "Why Do Some Studies Show That Women Are Less Competitive Than Men?" *Washington Post*, Jan. 2, 2015, https://www.washing tonpost.com/news/storyline/wp/2015/01/02/why-do-some-studies-show-that-women -are-less-competitive-then-men; William Harms, "Women Less Interested Than Men in Jobs Where Individual Competition Determines Wages," *UChicago News*, Jan. 21, 2011, https://news.uchicago.edu/article/2011/01/14/women-less-interested-men-jobs-where -individual-competition-determines-wages.

11. Jeffrey Kluger, "Ambition: Why Some People Are Most Likely to Succeed," *Time*, Nov. 6, 2005, http://content.time.com/time/magazine/article/0,9171,1126746-4,00.html.

12. Robin J. Ely, Pamela Stone, and Colleen Ammerman, "Rethink What You 'Know' About High-Achieving Women," *Harvard Business Review*, Jan. 16, 2015, https://hbr .org/2014/12/rethink-what-you-know-about-high-achieving-women.

13. Derek Thompson, "Too Many Elite American Men Are Obsessed with Work and Wealth," *Atlantic*, Apr. 27, 2016, https://www.theatlantic.com/business/archive/2016/04 /too-many-elite-american-men-are-obsessed-with-work/479940/.

## Chapter 9

1. Karen S. Cook and Eric Rice, "Social Exchange Theory" in *Handbook of Social Psychology*, ed. John DeLamater (Madison, WI: Springer, 2003), 53–76.

2. Lora E. Park et al., "Desirable but Not Smart: Preference for Smarter Romantic Partners Impairs Women's STEM Outcomes," *Journal of Applied Social Psychology* 46, no. 3 (2016): 158–79, https://doi.org/10.1111/jasp.12354.

## Chapter 10

1. Lori Gottlieb, "Marry Him! The Case for Settling for Mr. Good Enough," *Atlantic*, Mar. 14, 2008, https://www.theatlantic.com/magazine/archive/2008/03/marry-him/306651/.

2. Jessica Knoll, "Why He Should Love You This Much More Than You Love Him," *Cosmopolitan*, July 2012, 108–09.

3. Claire Cain Miller and Quoctrung Bui, "Equality in Marriages Grows, and So Does Class Divide," *New York Times*, Feb. 27, 2016, https://www.nytimes.com/2016/02/23 /upshot/rise-in-marriages-of-equals-and-in-division-by-class.html.

4. Carmen DeNavas-Walt and Bernadette D. Proctor, "Income and Poverty in the United States: 2014," U.S. Census Bureau, Sept. 2015, https://www.census.gov/content /dam/Census/library/publications/2015/demo/p60-252.pdf.

5. U.S. Census Bureau, "Earnings Gap Within Couples," news release, Nov. 23, 2015, https://www.census.gov/newsroom/press-releases/2015/cb15-199.html.

6. Rebecca Johnson, "MacKenzie Bezos: Writer, Mother of Four, and High-Profile Wife," *Vogue*, Feb. 1, 2017, http://www.vogue.com/article/a-novel-perspective-mackenzie-bezos.

7. Chip Bayers, "The Inner Bezos," *Wired*, Mar. 1, 1999, https://www.wired.com/1999/03/bezos-3/.

8. Carey K. Morewedge and Colleen E. Giblin, "Explanations of the Endowment Effect: An Integrative Review," *Trends in Cognitive Sciences* 19, no. 6 (2015): 339–48, https://doi.org/10.1016/j.tics.2015.04.004.

9. Daniel Kahneman, Jack L. Knetsch, and Richard H. Thaler, "Experimental Tests of the Endowment Effect and the Coase Theorem," *Journal of Political Economy* 98, no. 6 (Dec. 1990): 1325–48, https://doi.org/10.1086/261737.

10. Frank Newport and Joy Wilke, "Most in U.S. Want Marriage, but Its Importance Has Dropped," Gallup, Aug. 2, 2013, http://www.gallup.com/poll/163802/marriage-importance-dropped.aspx.

## Chapter 11

1. Christopher Munsey, "Emerging Adults: The In-Between Age," *Monitor on Psychology* 37, no. 6 (June 2006): 68, http://www.apa.org/monitor/jun06/emerging.aspx.

2. Antoine Bechara et al., "Deciding Advantageously Before Knowing the Advantageous Strategy," *Science* 275, no. 5304 (Feb. 1997): 1293–95, https://doi.org/10.1126/science.275.5304.1293.

3. Justin Sonnenburg and Erica Sonnenburg, "Gut Feelings—the 'Second Brain' in Our Gastrointestinal Systems [Excerpt]," *Scientific American*, May 1, 2015, https://www.scientificamerican.com/article/gut-feelings-the-second-brain-in-our-gastrointestinal-systems-excerpt/.

4. Varun Warrier et al., "Genome-Wide Meta-analysis of Cognitive Empathy: Heritability, and Correlates with Sex, Neuropsychiatric Conditions and Brain Anatomy," *Molecular Psychiatry*, June 6, 2017, https://doi.org/10.1038/mp.2017.122.

5. Abraham Maslow, *Motivation and Personality* (New York: Harper & Row, 1954); Saul McLeod, "Maslow's Hierarchy of Needs," Simply Psychology, Sept. 16, 2016, https://www.simplypsychology.org/maslow.html.

6. Ladder Theory, http://www.laddertheory.com/.

7. "Madonna-Whore Complex," Penn State Psych Blog, 2015, https://sites.psu.edu/aspsy/2015/10/03/madonna-whore-complex/.

## Chapter 12

1. Jean M. Twenge, Ryne A. Sherman, and Brooke E. Wells, "Declines in Sexual Frequency Among American Adults, 1989–2014," *Archives of Sexual Behavior*, 2017, https://doi.org/10.1007/s10508-017-0953-1.

2. Elaine G. Walster et al., "'Playing Hard to Get': Understanding an Elusive Phenomenon," *Journal of Personality and Social Psychology* 26, no. 1 (1973): 113–21, https://doi.org/10.1037/h0034234.

## Chapter 13

1. Laurie Sandell, "Chrissy Teigen Is a Member of the Mile-High Club," *Cosmopolitan*, Apr. 28, 2014, http://www.cosmopolitan.com/entertainment/news/a24251/chrissy-teigen-on -june-2014-cosmo/.

2. Katie Connor, "Chrissy Teigen Doesn't Care Who John Legend Dated Before Her," *Cosmopolitan*, Nov. 18, 2016, http://www.cosmopolitan.com/entertainment/celebs/a8101668/ chrissy-teigen-december-2016/.

## Chapter 14

1. Saul McLeod, "Maslow's Hierarchy of Needs," Simply Psychology, Sept. 16, 2016, https://www.simplypsychology.org/maslow.html; B. R. Hergenhan, *An Introduction to the History of Psychology*, Sixth ed. (Belmont, CA: Wadsworth, 2009).

## Chapter 15

1. Vincent M. Mallozzi, "Vina Pulido and Anthony Nguyen: Putting Aside a Harvard-Yale Rivalry," *New York Times*, Dec. 23, 2016, https://www.nytimes.com/2016/12/23 /fashion/weddings/vina-pulido-and-anthony-nguyen-putting-aside-a-harvard-yale-rivalry .html.

2. Jane Gordon Julien, "Of All the Taco Bells in All the Towns...," *New York Times*, Dec. 16, 2016, https://www.nytimes.com/2016/12/16/fashion/weddings/of-all-the-taco-bells -in-all-the-towns.html.

3. Michael T. French et al., "Personal Traits, Cohabitation, and Marriage," *Social Science Research* 45 (2014): 184–99, https://doi.org/10.1016/j.ssresearch.2014.01.002.

4. Kay Hymowitz, Jason S. Carroll, W. Bradford Wilcox, and Kelleen Kaye, "The Knot Yet Report," http://twentysomethingmarriage.org.

5. Na'ama Shenhav, "What Women Want: Family Formation and Labor Market Responses to Marriage Incentives," Jan. 12, 2016, https://economics.ucr.edu/seminars _colloquia/2015-16/applied_economics/Shenhav%20paper%20for%202%204%20 16%20job%20talk%20seminar.pdf.

6. Kim Parker and Renee Stepler, "As U.S. Marriage Rate Hovers at 50%, Education Gap in Marital Status Widens," Pew Research Center, Sept. 14, 2017, http://www .pewresearch.org/fact-tank/2017/09/14/as-u-s-marriage-rate-hovers-at-50-education -gap-in-marital-status-widens/; Claire Cain Miller, "How Did Marriage Become a Mark of Privilege?" *New York Times*, Sept. 25, 2017, https://www.nytimes.com/2017/09/25 /upshot/how-did-marriage-become-a-mark-of-privilege.html.

7. Bella DePaulo, "Everything You Think You Know About Single People Is Wrong," *Washington Post*, Feb. 8, 2016, https://www.washingtonpost.com/news/in-theory/wp /2016/02/08/everything-you-think-you-know-about-single-people-is-wrong/.

8. Kelly Musick and Larry Bumpass, "Reexamining the Case for Marriage: Union Formation and Changes in Well-Being," *Journal of Marriage and Family* 74, no. 1 (2012): 1–18, https://doi.org/10.1111/j.1741-3737.2011.00873.x.

9. Jenna Birch, "Why Breaking Up Is So Hard to Do," Yahoo Beauty, Jan. 20, 2015, https://www.yahoo.com/beauty/why-breaking-up-is-so-hard-to-do-108290192247.html.

10. Sarah Halpern-Meekin et al., "Relationship Churning in Emerging Adulthood," *Journal of Adolescent Research* 28, no. 2 (2012): 166–88, https://doi.org/10.1177/0743558412464524.

11. Jenna Birch, "Generation Break Up Then Make Up," *Elle*, June 14, 2016, http://www.elle.com/life-love/sex-relationships/a37074/generation-breakup-then-makeup/.

12. René M. Dailey et al., "On-Again/Off-Again Dating Relationships: What Keeps Partners Coming Back?" *Journal of Social Psychology* 151, no. 4 (2011): 417–40, https://doi.org/10.1080/00224545.2010.503249.

13. Catherine A. Surra and Debra K. Hughes, "Commitment Processes in Accounts of the Development of Premarital Relationships," *Journal of Marriage and the Family* 59, no. 1 (1997): 5, https://doi.org/10.2307/353658.

## Conclusion

1. Leonardo Bursztyn, Thomas Fujiwara, and Amanda Pallais, "Acting Wife: Marriage Market Incentives and Labor Market Investments," *American Economic Review*, May 2017, https://doi.org/10.3386/w23043.

2. Amie M. Gordon and Serena Chen, "Do You Get Where I'm Coming From?: Perceived Understanding Buffers Against the Negative Impact of Conflict on Relationship Satisfaction," *Journal of Personality and Social Psychology* 110, no. 2 (2016): 239–60, https://doi.org/10.1037/pspi0000039.

3. Muping Gan and Serena Chen, "Being Your Actual or Ideal Self? What It Means to Feel Authentic in a Relationship," *Personality and Social Psychology Bulletin* 43, no. 4 (2017): 465–78, https://doi.org/10.1177/0146167216688211.

# About the Author

**JENNA BIRCH** is a journalist who writes about relationships, health, and wellness. Her work appears frequently in print and online in publications and on sites including *Cosmopolitan, Glamour, Elle, Self, Woman's Day, Marie Claire, Psychology Today,* Yahoo.com, *Women's Health,* and many others. She lives in Ann Arbor, Michigan, and this is her first book.